16 March 2006

To Joe,

With admiration for your dedicated wartime service with the 4th Armored Division

I feel honored to be a comrade of yours during our war.

Sincerest best,

Al Szymor

GASOLINE TO PATTON

ALSO BY BRIGADIER GENERAL ALBIN F. IRZYK

HE RODE UP FRONT FOR PATTON

GASOLINE TO PATTON

A DIFFERENT WAR

ALBIN F. IRZYK

BRIGADIER GENERAL (RET.)

Elderberry Press, INC

OAKLAND

Elderberry Press, INC

1393 Old Homestead Drive, Second floor
Oakland, Oregon 97462—9506.
TEL/FAX: 541.459.6043
www.elderberrypress.com

Elderberry Press books are available from your favorite bookstore, amazon.com, or from our 24 hour order line: 1.800.431.1579

 Library of Congress Control Number: 2004112633
Publisher's Catalog-in-Publication Data
Gasoline To Patton /Albin F. Irzyk
ISBN 193276206X
1. Memoir.
2. Military History.
3. George S. Patton, Jr.
4. U.S. History.
5. WWII.
6. Europe.
7. War in Europe.
8. Tank
I. Title
This book was written, printed and bound in the United States of America.

DEDICATION

To: "The Team"

For their love and constant, loyal support
Evelyn

Jane/Dave Al/Teri Laura/Pete

Bryan Stacey/Mike Abby Jeff Julia

Riley

ACKNOWLEDGEMENTS

I am deeply indebted to three close friends, Linda Womack, Paul Meyer, and Don Fox, for their careful examination of the draft manuscript, and for their suggested changes and corrections, which helped greatly to improve this book. Many thanks, also, to my granddaughter, Stacey Pickett, for assisting this less-than-expert computer user to better produce, organize, and retain his printed pages.

CONTENTS

WAR AS I KNEW IT
By
George S. Patton, Jr.

"By the end of August, the Germans were on the run. At this point Gen. Patton presented his case for a rapid advance to the east for the purpose of cutting the Siegfried Line before it could be manned. Bradley was very sympathetic, but SHAEF, Supreme Headquarters, Allied Expeditionary Force, did not concur."

"All supplies – both gasoline and ammunition – were to be thrown into First Army's move north so Patton's Third Army had no gas with which to move; he was heart-broken."

"It was my opinion then that this was the momentous error of the war."

General George S. Patton

BRAVE MEN, GENTLE HEROES

Paul Walmsley as a Staff Sergeant served under General Patton during WW 11 in the 77th Antiaircraft Artillery Automatic Weapons Battalion. In "BRAVE MEN, GENTLE HEROES" by Michael Takiff published by William Morrow in 2003 he wrote as follows:

After the breakout from the Normandy hedgerows in late July 1944, Allied Ground Forces advanced so swiftly across France and Belgium that they soon were outrunning their supply lines. Materiel of all kinds grew scarce, but no commodity was more coveted than gasoline. At the end of August, George Patton's Third Army, the fastest of all the Allied outfits, had to pull up and wait five days after a requisition for four hundred thousand gallons was answered with a shipment of 31,975. "My men can eat their belts, " Patton complained, " but my tanks gotta have gas."

"There was plenty of gas in liberated France, but Allied supplies were still being unloaded way back where the campaign had begun, in Normandy, three hundred miles behind Third Army's spearhead. In between the French railway system lay in shambles, just as Allied bombing Commanders had intended. Some gasoline was flown to Patton by pilots like Bill Perkins-but most of it had to be moved by truck. One convoy after another plied French roads, but the truckers could deliver to Third Army and the rest of the Allied forces only a small fraction of the million gallons a day they needed to keep moving.

"Patton wasn't the only Allied Commander clamoring for more gasoline. At the direction of Supreme Allied Commander Dwight Eisenhower, the attacking Armies were arrayed along a broad front. To the north and west were the British and Canadian forces of the Twenty-first Army Group, led by Bernard Montgomery. To the south and east was the American Twelfth Army Group, led by Omar Bradley and made up of First Army, commanded by Courtney Hodges, on its left flank and Patton's force on its right. Ike's strategy had as much to do with holding together an alliance as with seizing territory, but the Anglo-American partnership was put to the test by Montgomery and Patton, both of whom repeatedly petitioned Eisenhower to be the anointed leader of a concentrated, fatal stab to Germany's heart, and to be granted the resources to deliver it. Gasoline may have been hard to come by as Eisenhower sought to manage the war, but he faced no shortage of ego among his talented but vexing subordinates.

"Ike held firm until September, when Montgomery presented him with his imaginative Market-Garden Plan, designed to put British tanks in Berlin within weeks. Eager to establish a bridgehead over the Rhine, Eisenhower finally agreed to put Allied supplies at Monty's disposal. As the fiasco unfolded in Arnhem, Patton, his men, and his thirsty tanks were forced to take up defensive positions. They would not go back on the offensive for a month and a half."

"The cutoff of Patton's gasoline underlies one of the lasting "what-if's " of the Second World War. Lines of supply behind Third Army were overextended in September 1944, to be sure, but in front of it German forces were crumbling. By November, however, when Third Army's gasoline spigot was opened once again, the Germans had had time to regroup. They mounted a fierce defense of their homeland and even managed a counterattack in the Battle of the Bulge, that nearly proved catastrophic to the Allies cause.

"But was it the time to regroup that differentiated the faltering German soldiers of the summer from the staunch fighters of the late fall, winter, and early spring? Or was it the territory at issue? In the summer, the Germans were fighting to hold territory they had occupied; once the Allies had crossed France, the Germans were fighting to keep the invaders from their home. Had the battle been taken to the Fatherland in September would its defenders have closed ranks, as they did later? Or would summer's disarray have persisted, leaving Third Army an open road to the Fuhrer's bunker?

"No one can know what would have happened had Patton, instead of Montgomery, been armed with the knife to stab Germany's heart But it is known that Montgomery was given the opportunity to end the war in 1944, that he squandered it, and that the war lasted another seven grueling months."

PREFACE

"It was my opinion then that this was the momentous error of the war."

General George S. Patton, Jr..

Military history over the centuries has been replete with fateful decisions made by leaders occupying critical positions. Fateful decisions are momentous – they have tremendous significance and, almost without fail, lasting consequences. Fateful decisions can lead to great and even euphoric successes. Conversely, fateful decisions can be disastrous.

General Robert E. Lee made a fateful decision at Gettysburg. Pickett's charge across open fields into the teeth of well-dug-in defenders occupying dominant terrain was a disaster. The Southern cause never recovered. After that fateful afternoon, it was down-hill all the way.

Nearly a century later, General Dwight D. Eisenhower made a fateful decision. In the face of uncertain and threatening weather and conflicting advice, he said, "Okay, let's go!" The Normandy invasion was, "On!" He set in motion the most massive operation in all of military history, and it was successful. Needless to say, it had lasting consequences.

Some weeks later, Gen. Eisenhower would make another fateful decision. Its consequences would be immense. Whereas his Normandy decision was epochal – known now and forever by the entire world – his second fateful decision, surprisingly, is comparatively little known. Historians have alluded to it, but amazingly, they have neglected or chosen not to challenge it, or explore it in depth. I am not only puzzled, but totally and completely dismayed and distressed that over the years they have, apparently, chosen not to speculate about it, and to "just leave it alone." Perhaps they believe that, under the circumstances prevailing, the decision was a sound one, and, thus, there is no reason to debate it.

The decision was anything but a sound one, and there is every reason to debate it. My purpose at this late date, therefore, is to examine that decision, because it appears that no one else has, and because I had first-hand knowledge of the battlefield at that time, to debate its wisdom and merits, and determine if there was, indeed, a better way.

Thus, I write not as an historian, but as a *participant*. The polemic which I offer and voice is that of an individual who "rode" a tank of the Eighth Tank Battalion, Fourth Armored Division, in Gen. Patton's Third Army.

My Fourth Armored Division was a major player in many of the events which will be discussed. Of the 281 combat days which the Third Army had, the Fourth Armored was in Third Army 280 of them. The Division had many nicknames. Among the best known were, "Patton's Spearhead" and "Patton's Best," and it was certainly both of those. Patton, himself, would later state, "The accomplishments of this division have never been equaled. And by that statement, I do not mean in this war, I mean in the history of warfare. There has never been such a superb fighting organization as the Fourth Armored Division."

I was the Operations Officer of the Eighth Tank Battalion, and during the early weeks of combat in France, I was constantly its advance guard Commander at the point of the action. Later, I assumed command of that battalion, and its one third of the tanks of the division. My role positioned me so that I was able to observe close up and at first hand the actions and events that led up to the necessity for that critical decision by Gen. Eisenhower. Once it was made, I was shocked and stunned by it. To me, it was so illogical that it was beyond comprehension. I also observed at close hand the consequences of that decision. From that moment on until this day, a period of 60 years, I have been greatly and deeply troubled by what I have always been convinced was the wrong decision. It has never stopped gnawing at me. Now that I am in the twilight years of my life, I feel compelled at last to air my opinions, to give vent to my feelings, and to get it "off my chest." I will never stop wondering about what might have been.

Gen. Eisenhower, before making that decision, had merely two courses of action open to him. Surely he must have examined, compared, and solicited advice about them.

Had he chosen the other course of action open to him, I firmly believe that the resulting and lasting consequences would have been radically different. The face of history would have a different profile.

What about those lasting consequences? It is my opinion that had General Eisenhower chosen that other course of action *the war in Europe would have been over before the end of 1944.* There would have been no "Market Garden," no "Battle of the Bulge." The Russian advance would have stopped outside East Germany, perhaps significantly changing the

face of post-war international relations and politics. Much more importantly, there would have been far less suffering, and many thousands of
casualties would have been spared.

In this drama, Eisenhower had two principals, only two main charac-
ters: one was British GENERAL BERNARD LAW MONTGOMERY
and the other was American GENERAL GEORGE S. PATTON, Jr.

In order to be able to understand and evaluate Gen. Eisenhower's
decision, a considerable amount of background information is required.
*This will, of necessity, include a detailed examination of the competence and
achievements of the two principals,* as well as the series of events which
brought "decision time" to the Meuse River as the month of August
ebbed.

THE "MONTH OF THE BIG BUST:"

HOPE OF FINISHING THE WAR BEFORE THE END OF THE YEAR VANISHED

September
1.   Eisenhower assumes Allied Ground Command.
     Bernard Law Montgomery promoted to Field
     Marshal.
     Eisenhower moves his Headquarters from London to
     Granville on the western coast of the Cherbourg
     Peninsula.
     4th Armored Division has two Combat Commands on
     the east side of the Meuse River.
     4th Armored Division's tanks are topped off ready to
     continue moving to the east.
1./4. While Patton's forces sit alongside the Meuse, the
     British make a spectacular advance and close some of
     the gap that had existed.
2.   Eisenhower at Bradley's tactical Headquarters at
     Chartres begins his efforts to create appropriate
     contact with the front by meeting with his 12th Army
     Group Commander and the leaders of his Armies and
     the Ninth Air Force.
2./10. 4th Armored Division remains out of action, makes no
     advance.
3.   XII Corps uncovers 100,000 gallons of German
     gasoline.
4.   Antwerp reached. The predicted extensive damage to
     the port has not occurred. The quays were in good
     condition, warehouses and sheds were mostly intact,
     even the port's cranes and other unloading machinery

were practically untouched, and almost all were in working order. So it was almost immediately a usable port for the Allies. However, one difficulty stood in the way. It could not be used until the Scheldt estuary was cleared of German resistance. Despite Eisenhower's announcements in late August and early September that Antwerp was vital as a port, and was desperately needed – it was not until November 9th that the 21st Army Group reported that the Scheldt had been opened and seventeen days later on November 26th that the first Allied convoy unloaded in Antwerp.

5. 240,265 gallons of gasoline are allocated to Third Army.
Infusion of gasoline enables Third Army to resume some action. XXth Corps, to the north and opposite the fortified city of Metz, attempts to secure a Moselle bridgehead. North of Nancy the 80th Infantry Division of XII Corps also attempts to secure a Moselle bridgehead.
The 4th Armored Division continues to remain halted.

6,7,8. Eisenhower provides Patton with 1,393,710 additional gallons of gasoline, despite protests from Montgomery. This will at best last for ten days, but will be enough for Patton to get to the Moselle and beyond.

10. Eisenhower gives approval for operation "Market Garden."
4th Armored Division finally moves in the late afternoon and closes in on the Moselle.

11. Tanks of the Eighth Tank Battalion of the 4th Armored Division *ford* the major Moselle River south of Nancy, and are the first elements of Third Army to secure a toe-hold on the east bank. The remainder of Combat Command B and the rest of the Division cross the next day.
The invasion of Southern France ends on this day, when soldiers of the Third Army link up with the invasion troops in the town of Saulieu, forty miles west of Dijon.
German General Hasso von Manteuffel takes command of the Fifth Panzer Army.

13. Combat Command A of the 4th Armored Division

crosses the Moselle north of Nancy, and attacks to the east.

XV Corps rejoins Third Army.

16. Combat Command A of the 4th Armored Division from the north and Combat Command B from the south link up and complete the encirclement from the east of Nancy, which, due to their efforts, was seized the previous day with relative ease by the 35th Infantry Division.

17. Operation "Market Garden" is launched.

19. Combat Command A, 4th Armored Division, receives heavy German tank counter-attack at Arracourt. Major elements of the 4th Armored Division will be engaged in vicious tank battles with the Germans for the next ten days. These tank battles will be known as the Arracourt (Lorraine) Tank Battles, and would be the most intense of the war in the west. Elements of the 6th Armored Division (from Brest) move into position near Nancy.

19. Savage battles in Western Arnhem proved decisive to the British defeat. The effort to capture the critical objective of operation Market Garden failed.

20. SHAEF moves to Trianon Palace Hotel, Versailles.

21. During the early evening, the 1st British Airborne Division pulls back from their positions at Arnhem. For all intents and purposes the "Market Garden" operation is finished, resulting in a disaster.

24. Market Garden's failure to seize and hold Arnhem dooms Allied hopes for an early end to the war.

26. Elements of Third Army, including the 4th Armored Division, move into defensive positions.

28. The Arracourt Tank Battles end with the loss to the Germans of 281 tanks.

CHAPTER 1

GENERAL BERNARD LAW MONTGOMERY:

EARLY ON

British General Bernard Law Montgomery was a puzzle, an enigma. He had an abrasive personality, and his air of personal omnipotence and haughty grandeur was hard for his associates to take, even for those who occupied the most lofty positions in British government and society. Prime Minister Winston Churchill once said of him, "In defeat, unbeatable; in victory, unbearable." Yet, he was a hero to the British people, and virtually deified by the British soldier.

He was a 26-year-old lieutenant early in World War I. He entered combat during the first stages of what would be a very long war. It was in October 1914, during the devastating First Battle of Ypres, that a German sniper sent a bullet through his lungs. The wound came extremely close to being fatal. For his actions in that battle he was awarded the Distinguished Service Cross, a high and prestigious decoration for such a junior officer. Fate intervened for him in a very positive way, as it would often in the future. He was taken out of combat and spent the rest of the war on the General Staff. Had he not been removed from combat, by the law of averages and the high mortality rate for lieutenants, he would almost certainly have been killed, and the world would never have known a General Montgomery. He ended the war as a Lt. Col., having carried out his duties as a *staff officer* in an impressive manner.

He first became a "name" during the British debacle at Dunkirk in May of 1940. As would happen so often during his long career, he landed on his feet, even during the trying and desperate hours when elements of the British Expeditionary Force suffered a devastating defeat, and were saved by the tremendous armada of small boats which ferried them across the English Channel from France to Britain.

It was reported that he had acquitted himself well as the Command-ing General of the British Third Infantry Division. His actions gained for him prominence in the British military, and the British public first "learned" about him.

As he would more than once during the months to come, he lucked out. Had Hitler not issued his famous "stop" order, Montgomery's Third Infantry Division, together with many other units, would have been overrun and certainly destroyed by tanks of Rommel's 7th Panzer Division. Yet, amazingly, Montgomery, apparently not recognizing or appreciating his close call, brazenly declared that although he had not confronted a single enemy tank, he believed that a well-trained and mobile Infantry Division could handle the finest Panzers.

After the severe British loss at Dunkirk, Gen. Montgomery next emerged as Southeastern Commander of Home Forces. While he held that position, a daring raid was planned to take place at the French coastal city of Dieppe, northwest of Paris, on August 19, 1942. The fundamental purpose of the raid was to test the practicability of a cross-channel invasion. Tanks, vehicles, and men reached the beaches, but the operation was badly bungled, and turned out to be a disaster. Because of its failure, the question of the practicability of such an operation was not fully answered.

Although many words have been written about the raid, few of them record the role that Montgomery is reputed to have played. That he participated in the planning for that raid is not generally known. He would blunder here as he would again in the future. His views on the operation clearly revealed his ignorance of modern mobile warfare.

The plan for the Dieppe Raid was originally called "Operation Rutter," but later changed to "Operation Jubilee." The plan called for armored flanking attacks north and south of Dieppe. If this maneuver were successful, it would have isolated German forces in the city from their reinforcements, and the infantry would have launched a simulta-neous frontal assault.

Montgomery, again exhibiting his abysmal lack of knowledge and appreciation of the role, capabilities, and mobility of tanks, favored the elimination of the flanking attacks. This changed the operation to a frontal infantry assault with *supporting* tanks coming in *behind* the infantry. "Operation Jubilee" was a total disaster. The devastation on the Dieppe beaches by the afternoon after the raid was absolutely hor-rible. The beaches were littered with burning landing craft, knocked-out Churchill tanks, and dead soldiers everywhere.

Had the raid been carried out as originally planned, with armor and infantry understanding the roles and capabilities of each other and working as a team, the operation might well have succeeded. Since that did not happen, many hundreds, mainly Canadians, were lost, and the Germans crowed about and gloried in their great victory.

As for Montgomery, he escaped criticism and was untainted by the operation, as he would be again and again in the future. Two weeks before the raid took place he was ordered to El Alamein in Egypt, and, apparently, it was out of sight, out of mind, insofar as the Dieppe raid was concerned.

El Alamein was a dirty little Arab town, and it was there that Gen. Montgomery, some days before the Dieppe Raid, was given command of the British Eighth Army. Despite his military qualifications, he was not a natural choice for Army Command.

Before Montgomery arrived and assumed command, Gen. Sir Claude Auchinleck, Commander in Chief, Middle East, known as the "Auk," had shown great leadership by stopping a year-long retreat with his battered, worn, and beaten Eighth Army.

With great tactical sense he formed a defensive line from the Mediterranean Sea to the impassable Qattara Depression. His great foresight worked, for he stopped cold and tripped up an aggressive, determined, charging German General Rommel, who had his sights set squarely on Cairo and the Suez Canal. After the battle ended, a very frustrated Afrika Korps had fallen back to regroup and await supplies and fresh troops.

The "Auk" did not stop to rest on his laurels, but took full advantage of the situation by immediately starting to reform his Army to go on the attack, to move from defense to offense. He abandoned the traditional format of infantry forward with tanks in support, to one of armor and lorried infantry attacking in tandem, operating as a team. Essentially, Auchinleck was borrowing a page from his opponent, Rommel, who employed those techniques with his highly successful Panzers. The "Auk" was again demonstrating great leadership. But unfortunately, and perhaps tragically, he, as had happened to Rommel – but in a completely different sense – would abruptly be stopped cold in his tracks.

Prime Minister Churchill, apparently, not convinced that he had the proper and inspirational Commanders in place for the actions that were about to occur, decided that he needed to make a first-hand inspection. He arrived in Cairo on August 4. Apparently gnawing inside Churchill was the strong belief that it was psychologically necessary for his Army and his nation to have a taste of success, of victory, which was long overdue. He apparently had grown increasingly impatient with Auchinleck, and was displeased with what he believed to be Auk's failure to capitalize on his recent success against the attempt of Rommel to push on to Egypt. He also was of the opinion that it was taking too long for the "Auk" to launch an offensive.

At the Cairo GHQ, Churchill discovered that Headquarters in favor of waiting at least until September to attack Rommel's positions, so as to allow enough time to receive reinforcements, regroup, and plan its offensive. Churchill was anything but pleased, and that did it! The "Auk" would not be able to finish making his greatly needed recasting of forces, and the somewhat revolutionary change-over. Despite his recent accomplishments and great leadership, he was abruptly relieved of his command, and ignominiously sacked by Winston Churchill.

General Sir Harold Alexander was released from his responsibilities to "Operation Torch," which was upcoming, so as to be able to take over his new post in the Western Desert. Churchill was looking for a winner, and did not believe that the "Auk" was it. There are some who consider Churchill's decision to have been a characteristically impetuous one, and believe that he committed a serious mistake. Others believe it to have been a selfish, political one, because he was being pressured for a military victory that would help keep him in office.

Auchinleck was a highly respected soldier with an already impressive record in the desert. However, in Churchill's eyes he apparently lacked the charisma, the "flash and dash" that Churchill must have believed he needed to flaunt a military victory. He took a chance, gambled, and fate brought on the scene a Gen. Montgomery, who knew absolutely nothing about desert warfare. Did Churchill in the months ahead perhaps wonder, if he had gotten more than he had bargained for?

Churchill and Alexander selected Lt. Gen. W. H. E. Goff to replace the "Auk" as the Commander of the British Eighth Army. Astonishingly and tragically, Goff was killed in an air crash just days after his selection. Almost by default, the job fell to General Bernard Law Montgomery, who had been positioned to be Gen. Alexander's replacement as Commander of the British First Army for the "Torch" operation, the invasion of French North Africa. Once again, as it would continue to do in the future, fate worked on behalf of Montgomery. Many would later believe that the arrival of Montgomery in Cairo was not only a positive but an historic stroke. This man, who was arrogant and not one to be loved, would nevertheless become an inspiration to all who served with and under him.

As soon as he was in command, he recognized that there was much for him to do. Montgomery quickly notified a very frustrated Churchill that it would take him two months to train what he termed a totally demoralized Army into a capable fighting force able to grapple with "a very tricky Rommel," thus needing more time than the "Auk" originally wanted. Churchill must have wondered what he had gotten himself into.

Montgomery launched himself upon his first priority of tasks, which was to improve and strengthen the defensive positions which he had inherited. Those positions were admirably suited for defense. He had three prime, important advantages. The Qattara Depression on his left flank was virtually impassable – a forbidding and most formidable anchor. On the right was the proximate Sea. The third important element was the height of the Alam el Haifa ridge.

Montgomery was well aware that Rommel had been heavily reinforced and was now out there in some strength. But because of his own virtually impregnable positions, Montgomery was supremely confident that Rommel could not execute one of the outflanking maneuvers that had become his trademark. The British expected Rommel to attack at full moon on August 26, but that did not happen.

Montgomery used the unexpected time afforded to him to great advantage. He and his senior Commanders put their heads together, and came up with some plans of deception which would be effective in misleading the Germans. Additionally, they had a surprise for the German Commander in the form of a clever and unexpected placement of mines.

The German attack, which would be known as the Battle of Alam el Haifa, came during the early hours of August 31. From the very beginning for Rommel, events quickly went from bad to worse. The Germans were hit hard by British air power and splendid defensive use of artillery. The attack was hampered, as well, by the minefields, which they had not expected. Then, very early in the engagement, two of the most senior German Commanders were put out of action by British fire. No matter what they tried, the Germans and their Italian allies were repulsed, and lost men and tanks. The battle lasted but four days. On September 3, Rommel recognized that it was futile to continue, and broke off the attack.

Despite the great success of the operation, Alexander and Montgomery decided to remain on the defensive until they received reinforcements in men and equipment, which they believed were essential in order to be able to move on to the offensive and defeat the enemy. The United States stepped right in to help re-equip the Eighth Army. President Roosevelt and General Marshall had arranged, almost without asking Churchill, to deliver 300 new 35-ton Sherman tanks, which were a vast improvement over the M3 Grant. To help Eighth Army to reassert itself in the desert, it was not only modern tanks that the US supplied, but over a hundred self-propelled guns, as well. On top of that, a large number of 155 mm US howitzers were shipped to the Eighth Army.

Allied airpower had been built up impressively. That, and the improvement in sea power, ensured that an ever-greater volume of supplies was reaching the Allies. However, that was exactly the opposite of what was happening to the Axis forces. Rommel had an extremely long supply line which stretched all the way back to Benghazi. The Germans and Italians now experienced a considerable reduction in supplies of fuel and arms necessary to reinforce the Panzerarmee Africa. At this point for the British the arrow definitely pointed up, while for the Germans/Italians it was definitely pointing down. However, the Axis forces had used the available time to lay thousands of mines.

By mid-October Montgomery was ready. But what of Rommel? He had left the front, it was reported, because of poor health. He had turned his command over to General George Stumme with instructions to follow the agreed-upon plan for the operation.

Earlier, Churchill had not looked with favor upon an intimation by Auchinleck that it would take him until September to go on the offensive. It was now late in October. Finally, Montgomery launched a surprise attack at 9:40 in the evening of October 23. It worked, for the Axis forces were unprepared and completely surprised; they had had no idea when it would come, and were not ready when it *did* come. The best evidence of that: Rommel was still away from his command, and the two senior Italian Commanders were away on leave in Italy. If ever there was an example of Goliath attacking David, this was it.

The kick-off was absolutely thunderous – the greatest thus far, and for a long time after. 592 Allied guns opened up simultaneously, and for 15 minutes (a long time for such a barrage) this enormous collection of firepower hammered at the Axis positions. Allied air power had been built up impressively. The Desert Air Force was now a most formidable element with which to reckon. It had reached a total of 1,200 aircraft. During this battle, the Royal Air Force would use many of them with telling results, killing large numbers of German troops and tanks. The results were devastating to the Germans. Communications were cut, mines detonated, troops disoriented. On the ground, mines were detonated by British forces utilizing sappers with mine detectors and tanks with flails.

The British divisions moved out and made considerable progress, but after three days of action, they, by the 26th, had failed to punch their way through to the Axis rear, which Montgomery's plan had demanded. There were other radical and unexpected developments. One concerned Rommel's Deputy, General Stumme, who, astonishingly, died in the field of a heart attack. Two days later Rommel was back in command.

Because the objectives of Montgomery's plan had not been achieved, his tanks were held up and remained ineffectual. The Axis forces, however, had been taking heavy losses.

When Rommel returned, he had relatively few tanks available, and these were widely dispersed. Characteristically, he immediately concentrated what tanks he had, and, leading from the front as always, he took his composite task force and hit Montgomery's forward infantry positions. It was an action like this that later led professionals to claim that he was one of the most able Field Commanders of WW II.

But despite his best efforts, by the 31st Rommel was in desperate straits. He would, however, not give up, and continued holding his line by bringing up his last reserves. At this point one would have expected Montgomery to go for the jugular, move in for the kill. But, amazingly, it was clearly apparent that, instead, there was a decrease in the intensity and ferocity of Montgomery's drive. Instead of pushing forces forward, he was, of all things, withdrawing troops into reserve. As was to be expected, Churchill was greatly upset by this tactic, and had to be calmed by his senior military Commanders.

After just over 11 days of vicious combat Rommel had been severely punished. He was down to 30 tanks. Almost without fuel, he was still able to out-maneuver his predictable, slogging, timid opponent, and to dance around him so as to be able to escape to fight another day.

The victor? Not David this time, but the mighty Goliath! Praise was heaped high upon Montgomery. He had soundly trashed, punished, and trounced Rommel; he had roundly defeated the "Desert Fox;" he was the one who proved that Rommel was not invincible; he showed that Rommel had met his match, for at the hands of Montgomery, the Axis forces lost 25,000 killed or wounded and gave up 30,000 prisoners, of whom nine were generals; he was the one who forced Rommel to retreat as fast as he could all the way to Tunisia; he was the one who gave the British Army and nation the great victory for which they had thirsted and hungered for so very long; he was the one who had virtually eliminated the Afrika Korps as a viable fighting force; he would always be known as the great victor and hero of the Battle of El Alamein; he was the savior of Britain, and from that day forward would become an icon to the British people and its soldiers.

BUT!

After the first three days of action, the British forces failed to push their way through to the Axis rear, which Montgomery's plan had demanded. Consequently, Montgomery's tanks were held up, making them ineffectual.

When he had Rommel on the ropes, he did not go in for the "kill." Instead, there was a decrease in the intensity and ferocity of Montgomery's drive, and instead of pushing forces forward, he withdrew troops into reserve.

Montgomery failed to follow up more swiftly and to trap Rommel completely. The Africa Korps was so depleted that it was hardly a viable force, yet it continued to out-maneuver and evade Montgomery's unimaginative and ponderous advance.

He had backing him up elements of an Air Force of 1,200 planes, and at the start of his attack he had that thunderous kick-off with the 592 Allied guns.

Also at the start of the battle, in addition to superior air power and powerful artillery supporting him, he had 1,200 tanks available to him, as opposed to Rommel's 200 beaten, bruised, scarred, war-weary tanks – a 6/1 advantage.

Yet, in the combat which followed, British troops suffered 13,500 casualties. Men were needlessly slaughtered advancing through mine-fields in the face of murderous machine-gun fire. Tanks did not advance until the infantry had cleared the minefields, and even then the tanks moved cautiously and reluctantly. Six hundred, or half, of the 1,200 British tanks were destroyed or immobilized. It appeared that Monty was still a WW I Commander.

As a result of the battle of El Alamein, what was learned about Montgomery as a leader, tactician, *Field Commander*? What could be expected of him during the many difficult battles and engagements that lay ahead, during the remaining months and years of WW II?

He made a name as a cautious Commander. That conservatism would turn out to be a great virtue, for the British people and soldiers would admire that caution as an unmistakable sign that he was eager to save soldiers' lives.

Montgomery had been a traditional staff officer during most of WW I. He became an advocate of, and would practice, the set-piece battle and attrition warfare so characteristic of that war. The "set-piece battle" was a careful, meticulous, detailed, well-planned offensive. These plans were rigid. Nothing was left to chance. There was no flexibility. When an unexpected opportunity suddenly appeared, there was no agility available ready to exploit it.

Monty knew virtually nothing about tank capabilities and tactics. Unfortunately, he did not seem to want to learn about them. He believed, simply, that tanks were to be used only as mobile support artillery for the infantry. Thus, during the battle, tanks not only played a supporting role, but one that was inefficient and unimaginative, as well.

He believed in balance. That, basically, called for a careful disposi-tion of all arms and reserves, so that the forces would never be caught on the "wrong foot."

He also believed in a "tidy front." In the months ahead that would turn out to be a great disadvantage. Tidying up the battlefield slows down a Commander – costs him his momentum. Such a practice takes from a Commander the chance to be aggressive and opportunistic.

This is the picture of Montgomery that emerges, as we leave him rid-ing on an exceptional high during the early days of November 1942.

CHAPTER 2

GENERAL GEORGE S. PATTON, JR.:

EARLY ON

General Montgomery, as has been pointed out, was a traditional staff officer during most of the First World War. Conversely, Gen. Patton during that war was anything but a staff officer. He was "combat" through and through. He sought combat during that war, experienced it, and would so do throughout his career.

Montgomery was an infantry officer who knew little of tanks, and did not seem interested in learning about their employment and broad and extensive capabilities. Patton, on the other hand, was a kind of mid-wife, for he was on hand for the "birthing" of the American Tank Corps.

On November 10, 1917, he was the first US Army officer to be assigned in France to that newly created Tank Corps. Right after that occurred, he was ordered to proceed to Langres, France for the purpose of establishing the first Army tank school.

He performed those duties so well that he was soon to have the necessary trained personnel to man two tank battalions, which he was instrumental in having organized. At the beginning of April, 1918, and already a Lt. Col., Patton, as was certainly his due, was appointed to command the first US light tank battalion, appropriately designated the 1st Light Tank Battalion.

Patton had taken issue with both the British and French use of tanks. He did not agree with tanks being a supporting arm, as the British had used them at Cambrai.

He did not accept the French method of placing tanks behind the infantry reserve battalions, in which position they followed placidly, until their intervention was required.

Patton created and taught a new doctrine, which was that two of the three companies of his battalion were placed in the assault echelon, with the remaining company held back ready to be thrust into action at the appropriate place.

He would have his first taste of combat during the battle of the Saint-Mihiel salient. Although the battle – the AEF's first – lasted barely thirty-six hours, it was a triumphant experience, for the Americans demonstrated that they could fight with the best of them. Patton shared the pride and satisfaction. For him it was a most rewarding combat debut and successful baptism of fire. The results of his training methods were immediately evident in the teamwork and heroics of his men. Patton enthused that in the final tank action of the Saint-Mihiel offensive, he was leader of the only (known) successful operation of tanks absolutely unaided by other troops in attacking and routing an enemy.

But as his daughter, Ruth Ellen Totten, would later say, "His date with destiny, so long anticipated and dreaded, came on September 26, 1918."

Patton had exulted. He was promoted to full Colonel before his 33rd birthday. Then followed the Meuse-Argonne Offensive, with Patton in command of the 1st Tank Brigade. And on the 26th, with all hell breaking loose, cowardice evident, and confusion galore the Patton legend was born – as he described it, "I saw that we must go forward or back, and I could not go back, so I yelled, 'who comes with me?' There was considerable yelling, but only six of us started— my striker, me, and four doughs. I had hoped that the rest would follow, but they would not, and soon there were only the three of us, but we could see the machine-guns right ahead so we yelled to keep up our courage and went on. Then the third went down......"

Shortly after, one of the machine-guns severely wounded Patton, and only the striker escaped unscathed. In that action southeast of Cheppy four of the six were killed, Patton seriously wounded, and one unharmed.

Sometime later, during his long recuperation, Patton would receive an award which he passionately coveted, the DSC – Distinguished Service Cross, awarded for extraordinary heroism. He would later say of his award, "I would rather be a 2d. Lieutenant with the DSC than a general without one." When he received it he said, "I shall always prize it more than anything I could have gotten in the war."

So it was on September 26, 1918 that the legend of General George S. Patton, Jr., was born.

The war was soon over. And as always happens during the aftermath of a war and a return to peacetime, the military suffered greatly. Demobilization came on a massive scale. The Nation now seemed to tire of the military. Patton was demoted to his permanent rank of Captain and subsequently advanced to Major. No one seemed interested in tanks. The total authorization of the Tank Corps was beggarly.

For a warrior, the period after a war is extremely demoralizing; Patton was particularly affected. It took time for him to settle in, to find a kind of niche. Concerned and alarmed about the future of the tank, he began writing articles for submission to military journals. He would contend that the tank is new, and for the fulfillment of its destiny, it must remain independent, not desiring or attempting to supplant Infantry, Cavalry, or Artillery. He continued to hammer away at the premise that the tank should not be incorporated into the infantry.

More senior voices than his concurred, and urged the retaining of an independent tank arm. But General Pershing was to say that the "Tank Corps should not be a large organization, and ought to be placed under the Chief of Infantry." That in essence killed the Tank Corps.

Despite his now-junior rank, Patton was permitted to continue in command of the 304th Tank Brigade at Fort Meade, Maryland, but austerity had set in. The life-blood of tanks is gasoline. At Fort Meade gas was so restricted that Patton had barely enough to crank up his tanks, and not nearly enough to take them out for training. Most of the time they just sat in the motor pool. His situation was emblematic of the post-war Army. Even then, if he were asked, he would have declared that of all the jobs open to him, he would still place service in the Tank Corps at the very top.

But Patton was a realist and, as always, very ambitious. He recognized that there was now no future for him with tanks. Being with a small force of tanks in the infantry would have proved not only discouraging but insufferable. He had to decide where his future lay, and realized full well that the decision would be painful and difficult. The most obvious choice left for him would be a request to transfer back to the Cavalry, where he had already "earned his spurs." That request was approved in September.

He became a Cavalryman once again on October 1, 1920. He was soon ordered to report to the Third United States Cavalry Regiment at Fort Myer, Virginia, where he would command the Regiment's 3rd Squadron. Fort Myer would over the years become his family's "home" in the Army, as its members were exceedingly fond of the post.

Patton would continue to keep a foot in each door. He would constantly remind his listeners of the value and role of the tank, and its tremendous battlefield capabilities. Yet, he thoroughly enjoyed being back in the saddle, and the unique and colorful life of the Cavalryman. *(When I, a brand new second lieutenant, joined the 3rd U.S. Cavalry Regiment, he would be my first Regimental Commander. It would be my first association with Patton, with more to come.)*

Cavalry, his branch, had a long, glorious, eventful history during our nation's pioneering and development. It had spirit, élan, mobility, aggressiveness, and audaciousness (*audace* was one of his favorite words). In its employment it applied speed, firepower, shock action. Its primary tactic was to turn flanks and exploit the rear.

Patton epitomized his branch. He would endeavor to bring the Cavalry spirit to his tanks. They would become his iron horses. He would always believe that the tactics employed by his tanks were definitely similar to those of the Cavalry.

But now a big, black cloud had descended upon the earth. World War II had recently begun. And as has been discussed, British General Montgomery had already played an active, prominent role during the period of May 1940 – November 1942. During those many months, he had been deeply involved in combat and in the planning for combat operations.

But what of Patton? Where was he and what was he doing in comparison to Montgomery? In May 1940 at Dunkirk, Gen. Montgomery was already the Commanding General of an Infantry Division which had been in combat with the Germans. By contrast, in May 1940 Colonel Patton was still at Fort Myer, but now the Regimental Commander of the Third United States Army Cavalry Regiment (horse). Radical changes would soon take place. On July 24, 1940, Col. Patton relinquished command of the Regiment. Shortly after, in August, he was transferred to Fort Benning, Georgia, where he assumed command of the Second Armored Brigade of the Second Armored Division. So it was farewell to the Cavalry, and it would now be tanks all the way. There would be no Cavalry to return to, as it would be phased out as a branch of the Army. (Our leaders belatedly realized that there would be no role for horses in Europe, so as late as the spring of 1942 I, still a Cavalry Officer, participated in the loading of horses in rail cars at Fort Oglethorpe, Georgia. This activity ended the 3rd Cav. as a horse Regiment, and graphically signaled the end of the oldest branch in the Army – the Cavalry.)

After 31 years of military service, Patton, finally, became a General Officer at Fort Benning: He received his promotion to Brigadier General. Events began to move rapidly for him, and many changes took place during the last five months of 1940. He became acting Division Commander of the Division in September, and permanent Commander in December. As Division Commander, he would be deeply involved in training, maneuvers, and combat exercises. For a variety of reasons, although he was not yet a household name, he was becoming a nationally known figure.

In January 1942 he was selected to command the I Armored Corps.

That forced him to say farewell to his beloved 2d Armored Division, with which he had been so deeply involved for so many months.

Just two months later he was picked to command and *create* a new desert training center in the desolate Mojave Desert in southeastern California and a portion of Arizona. The War Department had astutely determined that it was essential to train American troops in desert warfare. As established by Patton, it turned out to be a superb training area. *(I heartily agree, for I spent over seven months there.)* Several divisions and many separate units received extremely valuable training there. Although it gave him a great deal of satisfaction, with the world at war Patton believed that this assignment would sidetrack him and take him away from a possible field command. His concern was unfounded, for in July of 1942 he was summoned to Washington, told of an operation called "Torch," which would be the invasion of North Africa, and informed that he would command the Western Task Force of that operation. The prevailing sentiment was that the actual invasion force should appear to be entirely American, and, thus, should have an American Ground Commander. The job fell to the colorful, aggressive, and World War I- experienced General George S. Patton, Jr.

Much had to be done in a short period of time. There were always built-in problems of a hurry-up operation; juggling a myriad of details, changes of personnel, lining up the command structure. Training took on a frantic pace.

During the early stages of Torch planning, Patton's mission was to invade Oran, but as late as early September, it was changed to Casablanca, which left Patton with but sixty-four days to train his invasion force.

With Patton commanding the Western Task Force, the invasion of North Africa took place on November 8th. (This was just five days before Montgomery's battle at El Alamein ended.) The battle for Casablanca consisted of a series of spirited actions in three widely scattered locations. Amazingly, the war in Morocco was officially over three days later, on November 11th (Patton's birthday). For Patton it was as much his diplomatic as combat skills that brought the battle to a rapid conclusion. Once again he exulted, and had every reason to do so. He had said that he would take Casablanca by D+3, and he kept his promise. Remarkably, the battle for Casablanca had been won with extremely low casualties – 337 killed, 637 wounded, 122 missing, and 71 captured. Patton was most pleased and proud of this aspect of the operation, and did not hesitate to remind Gen. Eisenhower that his troops had "achieved the impossible," with the intimation that he did, too. In assessing his low casualties, he was heard to state that either "proverbial luck or more probably the direct intervention of the Lord was responsible."

Militarily "Operation Torch" was a success. As a result, Patton's star shone brilliantly. His picture would be splashed over the front pages of newspapers all across America. His extremely successful command of the land forces in that operation solidified his reputation as an outstanding battle Commander.

It has earlier been mentioned that after El Alamein Montgomery became a "name" to the British people. It is safe to say that after Torch, Gen. Patton had definitely moved from being "known" by the American people to being a "name" in America.

It was in North Africa that the press began to use the term "Old Blood and Guts" (a name to which his World War I tankers would immediately take violent exception.) Lt. Gen. Leonard T. Gerow, who served in WW I, would be told by Gen. Marshall, "Patton is by far the best tank man in the Army. I know this from the first World War I watched him closely, when he commanded the first tanks we ever had...."

With the brief campaign in Morocco at an end, Patton found himself now a restless, discouraged, rear-area soldier with no battles to fight. He would spend his days trying to stay busy and productive. He became particularly disturbed as he watched his troops being withdrawn from Morocco and sent to join the combat taking place in Tunisia, while he was being left behind.

The most frustrating experience for a true warrior during combat is to be forced to sit. Little did he know then that many months in the future, and most unfortunately, he would again have that experience.

CHAPTER 3

GENERAL BERNARD LAW MONTGOMERY –

GENERAL GEORGE S. PATTON, JR.:
HEAD TO HEAD,
TUNISIA

General Patton's first taste of combat since WW I had been very brief. It ended quickly, abruptly, and successfully. And because his operation went pretty much according to plan, and accomplished its mission, he could not help but feel somewhat euphoric. The long-awaited excitement, however, had dissipated. It was not easy for him to sit on the sidelines while American troops were engaged in combat.

Fate would finally intervene, and there would be an abrupt and radical change in his fortunes. On the afternoon of March 4, without any warning, he received an urgent message from Eisenhower directing him to depart early the next morning for what was termed "extended field service." An astute Patton was immediately seized with great excitement, and knew this had to be an answer to his prayers, for he sensed that he would soon be returning to combat.

But what had happened to Montgomery, and where was he located on this date? The last mention of Montgomery had him glorying in his defeat of the "Desert Fox" at El Alamein, in far-off Egypt. During the weeks that Patton idled, Monty continued to be deeply involved in leading his Eighth Army.

After the El Alamein battle and defeat, Field Marshal Rommel retreated as fast as he could to Tunisia, in high but very unrealistic hopes that he could somehow eventually defeat the recently arrived American and British forces. Montgomery moved out to take advantage of the vacuum left by the departure of Rommel. The German General had received orders from Hitler to stop, hold, and defend an especially good defensive position at Marsa el Brega on the extreme western edge of Cyrenaica. General Montgomery and his Eighth Army approached this area on December 13, 1942, but Rommel chose not to defend it and continued his withdrawal. German Field Marshal Kesselring, an excellent tactician, believed that Montgomery's advance could have been delayed for weeks, perhaps months, if he had been made to fight for the hundreds of miles between Marsa el Brega and the Tunisian town of Gabes on the gulf of Gabes. As it turned out, Montgomery would have virtually a free ride from Egypt, across Libya, and into Tunisia, but even then it took him a considerable amount of time to accomplish that.

In the meantime Axis forces were building up their defenses along the Mareth Line, south of Gabes in Tunisia, which they knew Montgomery sooner or later would have to attack.

By March 4, (the day Patton had received his summons from Eisenhower,) Montgomery had for some days been massing his Eighth Army for its assault against the Mareth Line.

Meanwhile, Patton's intuitive belief that he would be returning to combat was quickly confirmed by Chief of Staff, Gen. Walter Bedell (Beetle) Smith, who strongly intimated that Patton would be relieving Gen. Fredendall of the II Corps. That was confirmed by Eisenhower on March 5, and on the morning of March 6 Patton arrived at II Corps to assume command. (On this date Rommel attempted a desperate spoiling attack from the Mareth Line against Montgomery's forces. He tried to turn the British flank, but failed. The maneuver was quickly broken up).

Patton found II Corps Headquarters anything but a tight ship. "Route order" would be a better term for it. Military discipline and courtesy were not only lacking – they seemed non-existent. Uniforms were anything but uniform – men seemed to be wearing anything they chose. There was a laid-back attitude – no sense of urgency. The staff appeared weak, undoubtedly because of youth and lack of leadership.

Patton arrived at II Corps after it had, in recent actions under Gen. Fredendall, lost 7,000 men and 235 tanks. He had an almost impossible deadline. He had only *ten days* to impose his leadership upon the corps, and to effect a radical turn-about. During his first whirlwind inspection of the corps, Patton found some units in good shape, while others needed a quick and dramatic improvement. He became a whirlwind, moving incessantly, being everywhere. Even within the first hours there were radical changes and improvements, and tangible evidence that things were beginning to shape up. His biggest challenge was to instill into the men, virtually overnight, the missing fighting spirit, for in just ten days the Corps had to be ready for more combat.

The mission of II Corps would be to attack east toward Gafsa and El Guettar, to divert Rommel and threaten his flank, while Montgomery launched his *long awaited* attack against the Mareth Line, which would have him advancing north, parallel to the Gulf of Gabes.

So after a great length of time and many comparisons, Montgomery and Patton would, finally, be together – in the same battle and on the same battleground.

On March 12, Patton learned that he would be promoted to Lieut. General. His official orders reached him a couple of days later, so by the date of the Corps attack, he was wearing his third star (an appropriate rank for a Corps Commander).

It was after only ten days with Patton in command that II Corps, now sporting a completely new face, a positive attitude, and a new fighting spirit, moved into the attack on March 16. The offensive would be known as the Battle of El Guettar. Patton's forces moved surprisingly quickly and aggressively and seized Gafsa the next day, March 17. Patton continued his aggressive push, and his forces seized El Guettar, Maknassy, and Sbeitla before the end of March. During the days of that operation, Patton was almost a carbon copy of the much younger Patton of WW I. He was constantly on the move, drove himself incessantly, took all kinds of risks, and spent endless hours visiting front-line troops.

He was shot at by an Arab, and was almost killed by German artillery, as he sat on a hillside watching an engagement down below. He walked through a minefield that was not cleared, and dived for cover as he was strafed by low-flying Messerschmitts.

On March 20, four days after Patton launched his attack, Montgomery's Eighth Army began its final push from Mareth to Tunis. Montgomery's frontal assault, well supported by artillery, was followed by an attack of the British XXX Corps along the coast. Montgomery's mission was to make a dash for the Gabes gap and the plains beyond, but he was hit hard by the enemy and by nature's elements, which together bogged down his assault. He was bedeviled by appalling weather, swollen rivers, and determined, effective enemy resistance. It was not until March 26 that the attack, greatly aided by the desperately needed and fierce air support from the Desert Air Force, was successful by breaking out at El Hamma, slightly southwest of Gabes.

At this point a most interesting and somewhat startling development occurred in the Axis defense. On April 5/6, the British XXX Corps again attacked Italian Gen. Giovanni Messe's positions. But after initial reverses for the British at the hands of the Italians, the XXX Corps found, to its great surprise, that the enemy was retreating. It was later proved that Gen. Messe had wanted to continue to hold his position, but was overruled by Col. Gen. von Arnim, who reportedly "knowing that the fearsome General Patton was approaching the Italian Army's right, had decided to pull Messe's force back to regroup for what promised to be a major battle."

This was quite remarkable. The Allied battles of WW II were barely underway. Patton had made only a brief appearance as a Combat Commander, yet he was already feared by the German Army. This was the first time, but most definitely would not be the last time, that Patton's name and reputation alone would have repercussions and an effect on battlefield operations.

Now Patton was ready for what would turn out to be a most significant event – his first direct battlefield contact with Montgomery. He joined up with the Eighth Army on April 8. He would be part of the link that helped create a unified arc of Allied forces from the US II Corps to the British 1st Army, through the French 19th Corps to the Eighth Army. That set the stage for what was hoped to be the final Allied victory in Africa by pushing the Axis forces back to Tunis and Bizerta.

In implementation of that plan, the US II Corps was moved the following week to the right of the British 1st Army at the center of the attack.

Patton's El Guettar Battle lasted a mere eight days. As battles go, particularly when compared to those which were yet to come in Europe, it could be termed, at best, a lesser engagement. However, it was a most significant victory for Patton's Corps. It had successfully accomplished an important mission. It was the turn-around point for them. Now they were winners; they were redeemed. Hereafter, they knew that they would be able to handle any opponent. They proved that they had regained their combat spirit. Patton was credited with giving the U.S. Army its first major victory against German troops, and he emerged from that battle as the Army's top Combat Commander.

In the weeks and months ahead Eisenhower would more than once be credited with "saving Patton's bacon." Yet in North Africa Eisenhower had bungled politically, and suffered militarily with the Kasserine Pass debacle. Consequently, he appeared to be operating under a dark cloud, and the ground seemed shaky under his foot. Patton, by his dramatic success with the II Corps and his El Guettar victory, might well have saved the day, and with it Ike's job and his future.

The days and minor engagements which immediately followed El Guettar were anti-climactic, and brought periods of inactivity for Patton. By the middle of April, with Patton's II Corps in position for the attack when it resumed, Eisenhower believed that the situation in Tunisia had stabilized: Patton could now return to his permanent command in Morocco. Patton had been under no illusions. From the outset Eisenhower had made it clear that the assignment to II Corps would be a special, temporary one. It appears that as far back as February 1943, Ike had selected Patton to command the American assault force in the invasion of Sicily, which was planned for the middle of the summer.

Patton was, apparently, unaware of his projected new assignment, for on April 13, two days before he was to leave II Corps, he still appeared uncertain of his status.

On April 15, at a Change of Command Ceremony, Patton turned over II Corps to the man who had been his Deputy, Gen. Omar Bradley. During the final weeks of the Tunisian campaign, II Corps proved equal to the challenges imposed upon it. Gen. Marshall was fulsome in his praise of the Corps' accomplishments.

Patton's remarkable and unprecedented achievement has to be considered at least a minor military miracle. When he assumed command of the beaten and bedraggled Corps, it was reminiscent of, and not unlike, the challenge that Montgomery faced when he took command of Eighth Army in August, 1942. However, the results would be vastly different. As has been pointed out, Montgomery informed Churchill that it would take him two months to get ready for that "tricky Rommel." Yet, that Army under the "Auk" had recently stopped a long retreat and was readying itself to go on the offensive – it was not an organization on its knees needing to be picked up. Patton only had *ten days* to get ready for his first battle. During that brief period, he had to rid the II Corps of its losing mentality, to wipe out the unfortunate legacy of Fredendall and the apathy that existed, and to convince his troops that they could perform better than they had up to that time.

Patton's astounding achievement spanned a mere 41 days. All of this was accomplished in two weeks less than the two months that Montgomery had declared he needed to get his Army ready. One cannot help but be impressed by the remarkable difference in the approach and manner of meeting a similar challenge exhibited by Montgomery and Patton.

While Patton was leaving II Corps and out of combat once again, Montgomery was still pushing his Eighth Army to the north. Even during this final operation, he would be criticized for allowing the British 1st Army to shoulder the entire burden of that final drive to Tunis, while later claiming credit, nevertheless.

In the next Allied offensive soon coming, those two combatants would again face off in the same battle, on the same battlefield.

CHAPTER 4

GENERAL BERNARD LAW MONTGOMERY – GENERAL GEORGE S. PATTON, JR.:

HEAD TO HEAD, OPERATION HUSKY, SICILY

While the fighting was still going on in North Africa, plans were already underway for the next major offensive operation. Thus, the Allies were fighting one campaign while planning another. The operation being planned was called "Husky," and it would be the invasion and conquest of the Italian island of Sicily. The impetus for this operation came from the British. By undertaking this military action in Sicily, the British hoped that they would knock Italy out of the war.

Husky would prove to be an almost totally British operation. It would have virtually the same command structure as existed during the Tunisian campaign. British General Harold Alexander had been the Land Force Commander in Tunisia, and he would play the same role in Husky. Naval and Air Forces would be commanded by senior British officers. That would mean that the only senior American members involved would be Generals Eisenhower and Patton. Eisenhower's involvement would be anything but a critical, deep one. It would be a "run it by me" participation. He would be kept informed, would confer with Alexander, and nod his head – but essentially he would let Alexander run the show. Eisenhower would actually have little influence on the operations, and his role would approach that of a chairman of the board, or that of an interested but not deeply involved by-stander.

The designated invasion Commanders were Gen. Montgomery and Gen. Patton. Montgomery's Eighth Army was designated the Eastern Task Force, while Patton's invasion element was designated the Western Task Force. Thus, Patton would be the one and only American with a significant role in the action in Sicily.

The planning for Husky was a perfect example, a case study, of what planning should not be. It was not Allied planning; it was British planning. It was the worst possible example of planning by committee. Every senior British Commander had input, a position to uphold, an angle that he was trying to promote, to advance. There were intense inter-service rivalries, bickering, squabbling that went on for three months with not yet a plan on which there could be general agreement. Although Patton would be a principal, an exceptionally vital element in the invasion, he sat on the sidelines, a non-participant, as the British argued and debated among themselves.

With the effort going nowhere, Montgomery to his great credit and at great career risk — proposed a compromise upon which all were finally able to agree. Thus, the invasion and operations on Sicily were based on a plan developed by Montgomery. It was his plan. And, as was certainly to be expected, it was geared so that he would play the leading role. It was like a playwright authoring a play, and giving himself the leading and dominant role in it. Amazingly, Alexander had let the planning unfold without the development of a master plan for the conquest of Sicily. Even more amazing, the two invasion Commanders, the two Ground Commanders, Patton and Montgomery, had not met a single time to discuss strategy or coordination.

Montgomery, naturally, was to make the main effort. Patton's mission was to conduct an invasion by landing around the Gulf of Gela along Sicily's southern coast, and then to seize Gela's airfields. Once that was accomplished, Patton's only other mission was to protect Montgomery's left flank as he drove north. Alexander accepted this strategy, which would have Patton acting "as a shield in his left hand, while Montgomery would serve as the sword in his right hand." It was clearly evident that because of the U. S. Army's early misadventures in North Africa, Alexander still had little trust and confidence in the fighting abilities of the American soldier, so he considered it only appropriate that they be awarded a secondary role. Patton was deeply resentful and seethed at being what he considered a second-class citizen. But he held his tongue, undoubtedly because he did not want to provoke Eisenhower.

Montgomery would behave as if the campaign were a British war with the Americans on hand merely to lend their support. His arrogant and imperious demeanor advertised his belief that only his British troops could win the important battles in Sicily. Sometime during the planning, Air Chief Marshal Sir Arthur William Tedder said of Monty, "He is a little fellow of average ability who has had such a build-up that he thinks of himself as Napoleon."

To understand better the actions that would unfold, one should visualize the island of Sicily to be an irregular triangle lying on its side, with a rather short base facing east and the two elongated sides roughly peaking slightly to the northwest.

The shortest way home was north along the base, the east coast. The ultimate objective, the prize, was Messina. That city was the closest point in Sicily to the Italian mainland: the two were separated only by the very narrow Strait of Messina. The German and Italian troops, if overrun, would have to flee to Messina in order to be evacuated to the mainland.

So Montgomery chose for himself, as his axis of advance after landing, the shortest, most direct route to the city of Messina.

The final approved invasion plan directed the Eighth Army to land four divisions and one independent Infantry Brigade along a fifty-mile front in southeast Sicily, from the Pachino Peninsula (southeast corner of Sicily) to the city of Syracuse, and to capture that key port. The Eighth Army would consist of the XIII Corps under Lt. Gen. Miles Dempsey and the XXX Corps commanded by Lt. Gen. Oliver Leese.

Along the south coast and to the west, Gen. Patton's forces would make their primary landings at Gela and Scoglitti, employing the 1st and 45th Divisions of Gen. Bradley's II Corps. To the west, Gen. Lucian Truscott's 3rd Division would land at Licata to protect the American left flank.

The object of the American landings was to seize a bridgehead in the Gulf of Gela, between Licata and Scoglitti in southeastern Sicily and west of Sicily's southernmost tip, and to capture the key port of Licata and the airfields near Gela. Having accomplished that, they would penetrate inland to the north.

D-day for the operation was July 10,. 1943. On July 6, aboard Admiral Hewitt's flagship, the *Monrovia*, the admiral conducted a brief, simple, but emotional ceremony. He presented Gen. Patton with his first Seventh Army flag. So from that moment on Gen. Patton was an Army Field Commander, and the American troops who would play a major role in invading and conquering Sicily would be members of his 7th Army. The motto of his 7th Army would become, "Born at sea, baptized in blood."

On invasion day LSTs (landing ship tanks) and LCTs (landing craft tanks) in great numbers were utilized to place tanks on the shore along with the infantry.

The invasions were eminently successful. The landings were well established, coastlines captured and drives inland began. Eight divisions had landed, and the front was about 100 miles long.

Most surprisingly and amazingly, Montgomery seized and occupied Syracuse and Augusta without a single shot being fired against him. He was handed all that on a silver platter. By controlling Augusta, he, in one fell swoop, was already a third of the way to Messina.

One day after D-Day, the Americans received a severe enemy tank counterattack. A Canadian account relates, "The day after the landings, the German counterattacks began in earnest. However, those were directed primarily at the Americans to the west of us. One of these assaults involved 60 Panzerkampfungen Mk. IV tanks. During the attack, the Americans were able to hold their ground and destroy 43 of the enemy tanks."

Although Gen. Patton had a difficult time restraining himself from leaving his ship and landing on D-Day, he decided that he just HAD to be there on the 11th. This was a most timely decision. He would be much in evidence and deeply involved during the German tank counterattack. His personal presence at the front lines is credited with having much to do with the thwarting of the German major tank effort.

Once again, Patton would make bold headlines in the papers back home. They credited him with leaping into the surf, and personally taking command to turn the tide during the fierce tank battle.

Within the first 48 hours, the Allied effort was so successful that they were poised to exploit the absence, at that point, of a coordinated Axis defense of the island. Patton's 45th Division was making particularly good progress in its advance to the north. Suddenly, without warning and to his great astonishment, Patton received a totally unexpected blow. Gen. Montgomery, on July 12, had decided that his Eighth Army should make the main effort to cut Sicily in two, and so proposed to Gen. Alexander, who readily agreed. However, there was a "petite" problem. The 45th was already ideally positioned to encircle the German defenses facing the Eighth Army. Montgomery's proposed route of advance would take him across the inter-Army boundary, and directly across the route of advance of the 45th Division. For Monty to go ahead with his plan, the troublesome boundary would have to be shifted farther to the west. Gen. Alexander ordered Patton to turn over the required real estate to the Eighth Army. But doing so, would force Bradley to withdraw the 45th Division back to the Gela beaches, and restart them. They would still be committed to advance to the north, but this time their positions would be on the left (west) flank of the 1st Division. This was an astounding, incomprehensible, and devastating decision and development. Gen. Patton, at that point, should have screamed like a "mashed cat." Apparently still careful not to excite Eisenhower's ire, he remained uncharacteristically silent, which stunned and dismayed even his closest associates.

Earlier, when it was perfectly obvious that he would be playing a decidedly secondary role in the Husky operation, crusty British Admiral Cunningham urged Patton to protest his limited role. Patton emphatically refused with the comment, "No, goddammit, I've been in this Army thirty years, and when my superior gives me an order, I say, 'Yes Sir!', and then do my goddamnest to carry it out." But in this case, things certainly went too far. That superior, Alexander, in this situation appeared to be merely a "yes man" for Gen. Montgomery.

Events immediately proved the decision to be extremely flawed. What the better-positioned American infantry with the advantage of close artillery support could have accomplished relatively easily became a costly struggle for the Canadians. All this as the 45th stood by helplessly.

In the long term, Montgomery, by being greedy, committed an unpardonable military sin – he split his main forces. He did not just split them; he split them widely and badly. He would have Gen. Dempsey's Corps attacking up the coastline toward Messina; Gen. Leese's Corps would be operating in the west. And amazingly, the Mt. Etna massif, which was indeed massive, would be between them. The two Corps would be fighting separate, independent wars with no coordination or mutual support, if required.

By his decision Alexander could not have helped the Germans any better, or any more; he played right into their hands. He gave to a suffering opponent one of battle's most precious ingredients – time. Now the Germans could call upon their ingenuity and cleverly reorganize their defenses. They were now eligible to set the timetable for the remainder of the campaign.

Meanwhile, Montgomery would have an extremely difficult time on the eastern plains of Sicily. He had captured Syracuse and Augusta by default. Staring him directly in the eye was the open, coastal plain, favorable for tanks, across which he must attack in order to reach and seize the port of Catania. Once this was accomplished, he would encounter a totally different and most challenging problem – the assault through the foothills of Mt. Etna. This was a most formidable obstacle. It had to be overcome, if Montgomery were to have any hope of reaching Messina.

But first things first. Montgomery would encounter fierce resistance all the way to Catania, and amazingly, would not be able to capture that port city until August 5 – only five days less than a month after he had landed at Syracuse and Augusta – with Messina not much more than 50 miles down the road.

The reasons for Montgomery's overall lack of success were quite uncomplicated and easily explained. He was fighting separate Corps battles. Because of the wide frontages and harsh terrain over which his troops fought, each of the Eighth Army Divisions was fighting its own independent battle. The offensives for all four divisions would go badly because the Germans savagely and successfully resisted all attempts to crack their defenses. But this time even the confident, cock-sure Monty recognized that for him the jig was just about up, and he would not have the quick victory which he had earlier predicted.

For Patton it would be a completely different story. The change of boundary situation had left him more resentful than ever, and he was charged up enough so that he was now ready to determine the course of the campaign and on his own terms, if necessary. No one was more aware of Montgomery's situation than he. By July 17, he knew full well that Montgomery's separate offensives had been virtually stopped by the clever and tenacious German defenses, and were in serious trouble. His Canadian Corps had been slapped hard in the rough, difficult, mountainous terrain of Central Sicily.

The other Corps was totally bogged down in its advance to Messina by the determined, vicious Germans who were defending the critical Plain of Catania.

Finally Patton decided to make his move. On the afternoon of July 17, he cornered, and had his show-down with, Gen. Alexander. Patton pressed him to concur and approve his plan to let Bradley's II Corps drive to the north to cut Sicily in two. Such a maneuver, except for being farther to the west, is precisely what Montgomery had earlier demanded, and which caused the boundary fiasco. But now even Alexander recognized that Montgomery was failing badly in that effort.

By receiving Alexander's concurrence, Patton now knew that he had successfully placed his foot firmly in the door. He was aware and exulted that he had hit Alexander at the right time and had out-maneuvered him. After an uncharacteristic period in a bit of hibernation, the real Patton now emerged. Despite stiff German resistance all along the way, he would begin the rapid, impressive progress that was his trademark. He was now the imaginative, audacious Patton once again. He was on his own; he would no longer inform Alexander of what he intended to do. And what he intended to do was masterful, thrilling, and staggering in its boldness.

Unbelievably, he intended, first, to capture the Sicilian capital of Palermo. Incredibly, that would put him as far as he could possibly get from Messina. Then he would turn east and attack along the whole northern coast of the island to the ultimate prize, the strategically significant Messina. What a mouthful! Who but Patton could conceive such an operation? With the capture of Messina there would be no war left. The miles that would have to be covered defied the imagination. If successful, Patton would have advanced around the entire perimeter of Sicily (along both elongated sides of that triangle) with the exception of the relatively short east coast, which was Monty's.

What had started out as a two-man race had quickly become so one-sided that it was no longer a contest.

Patton formed a provisional Corps consisting of the 82nd Airborne Division, the 2nd Armored Division, and the 3rd Infantry Division under Maj. General Geoffrey Keyes.

Palermo was situated on the northwest coast of Sicily. To reach it, the troops would have to attack across appallingly rough and difficult terrain. Incredibly, this was accomplished, and Patton arrived in Palermo on July 22, having overcome the Italian 'Assietta' Division in the process. He had advanced as much as a hundred miles since he had his meeting with Gen. Alexander. The distance to Palermo alone was roughly equal to the entire distance from Monty's most southern landings to Messina. The capture of Palermo was the turning point of the battle for Sicily. And Patton was just getting started.

By this time even Montgomery recognized his desperate plight. He was still having difficulty breaking the German defenses facing him. So it finally happened! Montgomery took the initiative and invited Patton to Syracuse on July 25. Here we have a great irony. Patton had three days before captured Palermo, while Montgomery was still sitting in the city that he had occupied on D-Day. The purpose of the meeting was to discuss a common strategy that would bring the campaign to a rapid conclusion. Amazingly, this was the first time that the two Army Commanders had met since well before D-Day. By instigating this meeting Montgomery seemed to concede that it was Patton who was winning the fight.

From Palermo to the east along Sicily's entire northern coast, Patton continued his aggressive, demanding campaign. He pushed his troops hard, unmercifully, and himself even more. He used every possible and imaginable tactic and strategy. When held up by fanatical German defenses, he resorted to small-unit amphibious operations, which placed his troops behind the German defenders and broke their spirit. Finally, on the evening of 16 August, while a small British task force was still some miles south of Messina, an American 3rd Division patrol became the first allied troops to enter that all-but-abandoned and ruined city. That same morning a British armored and commando force was landed ten miles south of Messina. This was Montgomery's last desperate stroke. The purpose of this force and its sole mission was to make an all-out move to beat the Americans to Messina.

Their best efforts, however, were to no avail. They were astonished and disappointed to learn that the Americans were there before them.

But, undoubtedly, the most stunned, disappointed, chagrined, and furious individual was Montgomery. From the outset, during the planning and before the operation was launched, Montgomery had virtually reserved the right to take that all-important city all for himself. His own plan, he believed, guaranteed that. But the US troops which were expected to be the perpetual shield for the Eighth Army's sword were, instead, the victors.

Patton arrived in the city at 10:00 AM on August 17, some hours ahead of Montgomery. Patton won the race. For Montgomery it must have been humiliating and galling to realize that even with the cards originally stacked decisively in his favor he had come in second.

The Seventh Army Commander deservedly gloried in his triumph. An intense and even bitter rivalry had developed between him and Montgomery, which would last through World War II. Patton desperately wanted to beat Montgomery to Messina. Of course, he did this for personal glory. But more importantly, he had deeply resented what had persistently been the condescending attitudes of Generals Alexander, Montgomery, and the other senior British officers. He wanted to prove to the world once and for all that the American soldiers were not only every bit as good as the British – but, indeed, better.

So, Sicily had been conquered. The war there was over. Those two antagonists – Montgomery and Patton – had climbed into the same ring together. They would be eye-ball to eye-ball, head to head. Those two gladiators and competitors would mix it up furiously for 38 days. At the conclusion of the bout the judges' scorecards were collected. What did they say of the operation and the two fighters?

The operation:

1.) Sicily characterized bitter battles over terrible, harsh terrain against a determined enemy.

2.) There never seemed to be a master plan for the conquest of Sicily, and the capture of Messina.

3.) General Alexander never seemed willing to take control, even during the campaign's most critical moments.

4.) Alexander's indecisiveness invited, at times, competing and divisive courses of action for the Eighth and Seventh Armies. The result was that the two Army Commanders seemed to be conducting their wars independently.

The two fighters:

The campaign in Sicily offered a sharp contrast between the proper and improper uses of armor. Montgomery's traditional approach, which served the British so well in the Boer War, did not work nearly so well for him in Sicily. The proper use was exhibited early under the individual already labeled the Master Tanker, Gen. George Patton, when he quickly pressed his armor into action shortly after landing at Lisata and Gela.

While Montgomery slugged it out along the east coast on the short track to Messina, Patton raced northwest along a lengthy part of Sicily to Palermo. From Palermo he charged east along the whole northern coast to Messina.

Montgomery sustained 11,843 casualties, while Patton lost 8,731, a quarter fewer casualties. Yet, he covered a distance $3\frac{1}{2}$ times greater than Montgomery's with greater exposure to the enemy.

It has been generally agreed that Montgomery's conduct of the Sicily campaign was, as would be his later actions in Italy, at best "uninspiring." On the other hand, Patton was not only successful in North Africa, but performed even more brilliantly in Sicily, and has been credited with conducting an operational campaign that was "absolutely extraordinary."

Gen. Eisenhower would cite him for exemplary performance in battle. Ike attributed the Allied victory to Patton's "energy, determination, and unflagging aggressiveness." He would say, "The operations of the Seventh Army are going to be classed as a model for swift conquest by future classes in the War College." Eisenhower recognized that Patton had superb Corps and Division Commanders, but he stated that without Patton those Commanders could have done nothing. And one more rare bouquet from Eisenhower – "Patton is indispensable to the war effort – one of the guarantors of our victory."

So the fight in the ring in a sense was "fixed," for the contest was fought under the rules largely established by one of the two antagonists. But the "fix" became unraveled, for even with that great advantage the odds-on favorite was soundly defeated by his opponent.

If one word could best describe the actions of Patton and Montgomery in Sicily (and later in Europe) it would be *audace* (audacious) for Patton and "plodding" for Montgomery.

This narrative will continue to follow the actions of those two individuals in the months ahead, and will keep comparing them during the events of World War II in Europe. Montgomery and Patton would continue to occupy the spotlight and generate great interest. Both were described as consummate actors whose actions in public were performed with an eye on the troops whom they hoped to impress. Let's see what happens next.

CHAPTER 5

GENERAL BERNARD LAW MONTGOMERY:

SICILY TO NORMANDY, D-DAY

After Sicily, when the British Eighth Army moved into Italy, Gen. Montgomery remained in command. As in Sicily, his performance could best and most generously be termed slow, unimaginative, and undistinguished. It appears that this performance was recognized, for he was subsequently relieved of his command, and returned to England. After arriving in England, he replaced Lt. Gen. Frederick Morgan, who had been deeply involved in the 1943 preliminary planning for the assault into Normandy.

And once again, as he had in the past and would again in the future, Montgomery used adversity as a launching pad to even better circumstances. Amazingly, when he returned to England after his performances in Sicily and Italy, he had suffered no black mark; there was no blemish, no stigma. Beyond comprehension, he returned to England still a hero, and with the added and most favorable reputation as a Commander who was most prudent with the lives of his troops.

Subsequently, he would learn that he had been selected for one of the most important and critical assignments for the Normandy operation – Ground Commander for the cross-channel invasion, and for the initial assault and establishment of the bridgehead.

This appointment surely had to be a mistake. There must have been more qualified choices, and Eisenhower knew one in particular and wanted him. It was General Sir Harold Alexander, who had been the Land Force Commander in Tunisia as well as in Sicily, and was now commanding the Allied Armies in Italy. Eisenhower regarded him as an outstanding strategist. But the word that was passed on was that he was so valuable that he could not be spared from his command in Italy. This begs incredulity, for it suggests that the operation in Italy over which he had command was more important that one of the most vital roles in the Normandy invasion. The real reason, for the choice of Montgomery must have been a political decision. This would not be the last time that Monty would luck out in this manner. Churchill must have believed that he had no other choice. He undoubtedly sensed that had he done otherwise, the British public would have showered him with wrath. Montgomery was considered by this time to be the savior of England, the Messiah, since El Alamein. It seemed that he could do no wrong. So Montgomery's appointment pleased the British public and the British soldiers who looked upon him as a true national hero. However, it bewildered and dismayed a number of senior American Commanders (and some British) who continued to find the man, among other things, abrasive and egocentric.

With his planning responsibilities and now his invasion command, Montgomery was indeed in "fast company," and would hold membership in the highest of councils. He would sit at the table as part of Gen. Eisenhower's most senior Anglo-American staff. This was an extraordinary group of men who had already played decisive war roles. They were Deputy Supreme Commander, Air Chief Marshal Sir Arthur Tedder; Chief of the Allied Naval Expeditionary Force, Admiral Sir Bertram H. Ramsey; Commander Allied Expeditionary Air Force, Sir Trafford Leigh-Mallory; Lt. Gen. Walter Bedell Smith, Chief of Staff; Ground Commander of the Allied Armies during the initial assault and establishment of the beachhead, General Sir Bernard Montgomery; and Lt. Gen. Omar Bradley.

At the table, Sir Arthur Tedder, Eisenhower's Deputy, appropriately sat to Ike's immediate right. Montgomery, of course, could be found to the immediate left, shoulder to shoulder with the "big guy." Just before Operation "Husky" Eisenhower found Montgomery, "A very able, dynamic type of Army Commander, who needed only a strong boss to keep him in line." One can only wonder if, after Sicily, that was still Eisenhower's opinion. It was Eisenhower who was that boss, and would have to be the strong one to keep him in line. Would he?

On April 7th, at his Headquarters at St. Paul's School in West London, Montgomery made an absolutely splendid presentation of the invasion master plan which was completely approved by Eisenhower. Gathered to listen to him was the entire British/American high command – land, sea, air – all the individuals who would play prominent roles on D-Day. There was no question – his was a remarkable performance, and he had very prominent witnesses. But Montgomery got carried away by delivering highly optimistic expectations, which he could easily have avoided. What occurred that day would haunt him forever. In a sense he shot himself in the foot. For the rest of his life he would be challenged by some statements he had made, and he would have great difficulty explaining and rationalizing them away.

The map which he had exhibited showed hastily sketched "phase lines" depicting goals to be reached up to 90 days after the invasion. Gen. Bradley, who would command the American 1st Army in the invasion, was furious. He refused to commit himself to Monty's "phase lines."

The last of the lines, D+90, stopped along the Seine, just short of Paris. This seemed acceptable, so it did not become an issue. But Montgomery made a fatal mistake. He had a line, D+17, which showed the British firmly in possession of Caen. As is so well known, it was after considerable fighting and beyond D+40 before the British were actually in control of that very critical French city.

The great tragedy is that Monty did it to himself. His staff stressed that the lines had been intended to be flexible, but as presented they stuck, because of Montgomery's rigid commitment to those lines. Monty opened himself up to an historical controversy that appears to be unresolved to this day.

His actions during this period opened the window to two of his great failings – his inability to get along with his contemporaries, British and American, and, as would be very evident in the weeks ahead, his insistence that he was always right – that all had gone according to plan (his plan), even when it was perfectly obvious that it had not.

The complete plan for OVERLORD was set forth in one final briefing three weeks before D-Day. Attending were the King of England, the Prime Minister, Winston Churchill, Eisenhower, and the senior Commanders and staff. Again, Gen. Montgomery was much in evidence and in his element. He arose to explain the plan of battle for the initial assault phase of OVERLORD, which was Operation NEPTUNE – the cross-channel movements and airborne landings. Following that, Montgomery went to the next phase, which was the securing of the beachheads. Once again his presentation was most impressive.

Then Montgomery said in conclusion, "We shall have to send the soldiers into this party 'seeing red.' They must see red. We must get them completely on their toes, having absolute faith in the plan and imbued with infectious optimism and offensive eagerness. Nothing must stop them. Nothing. If we send them into battle in this way – then we shall succeed."

At best those could hardly be termed emotional, inspirational words. While the planner and briefer was at work, his new and pivotal role was rapidly developing. In the south of England his troops of the 21st British Army Group were assembling, as were the troops of the American 12th Army Group. Montgomery would soon assume command of the 21st, and would again become a Field Commander. General Bradley would lead the 12th American Army Group.

Fate surely plays some strange tricks. Here was an individual who was completely bested by Gen. Patton in Sicily, and who was subsequently brought home from his command in Italy, and who now occupied one of the most lofty of military positions. How could that be? His most recent performances apparently did not matter, had no obvious negative impact. Montgomery still seemed to be leading a charmed life.

Between Sicily and D-Day he had solidified his position as a major player, a force to be reckoned with. On the compass of events his course was firmly set. But what of his rival?

With major combat about to be resumed, where was that great Field Commander, Patton? He had not been heard from. What had happened to him?

CHAPTER 6

GENERAL GEORGE S. PATTON, JR.:

SICILY TO NORMANDY, D-DAY.

Where was Patton?

He had just conducted an extraordinarily successful campaign all across the island of Sicily. Another Patton triumph. For him, euphoria. Then suddenly, the glow disappeared, and just as suddenly, a dark cloud closed in overhead. The bubble had burst, things had turned sour, and the taste of victory was now replaced by bile.

The weeks and months which followed would be for Patton wilderness weeks and months. He had had ups and downs, triumphs and disappointments, but this would be one of the most depressing, frustrating, demoralizing periods of his military career and of his life. He was in the dog-house and in limbo. His situation would mirror exactly the dictionary definition of limbo – "one in a state of neglect and oblivion."

What caused this stunning, dramatic, unbelievable reversal of events?

Patton had visited in Sicily, a week apart, two evacuation hospitals filled with the wounded. The purpose of his visits was to show his concern, to console, to express his admiration and appreciation for their courage and feats, and to pin onto the worthy decorations that they had so recently earned. However, he had at each hospital –shockingly and unbelievably – slapped a soldier. This, of course, was an absolute no-no – a totally unforgivable sin.

Although this just could not be explained away, there were factors that may have led to these provocations. Patton had been under tremendous stress, much of it brought onto himself by his great eagerness to succeed (for example – first to Messina). He had driven his troops very hard, at times even unmercifully, and himself even harder. He later said that Commanders of invasion troops are under great tension, and may do things that they later regret. In looking at, talking to, and decorating soldiers as they lay in bed, tears came to his eyes, and he became very emotional, for he recognized that he was in the presence of genuine heroes. He saw men with terrible wounds, still bearing up positively and proudly, and even pointing out that others had it worse than they. Moments later, at each hospital, he confronted a soldier whom he considered a malingerer, a marked contrast to the soldier heroes whose beds he had just left, and in that agitated state slapped the soldier. This, of course, was absolutely unheard of – a very senior officer slapping a low-ranking enlisted man.

Those two incidents, as might be expected, sparked a remarkable chain of events. The "word," like a rumor, swept quickly throughout the military, but as a kind of challenge to loyalty was pretty well kept "within the family." However, as was inevitable, the civilian media learned of it, and found themselves "forced" as their civic duty to spread the word back home, spear-headed by a well-known and sometimes controversial columnist. And they did it effectively. As they full well knew would happen, there was a great uproar in the country, consternation in the USA, the populace shocked, a storm of criticism moving swiftly led by irate representatives, senators, and mothers. Forgotten was the hero, it was time for his head.

To Eisenhower's great credit, despite intense and severe pressure from all sides to send Patton home in disgrace, he firmly resisted that pressure. He knew full well, and he recognized it better than anyone else, that he would need the tactical genius of Patton in the fight across Europe, if he were to win the war.

Before either Eisenhower or Patton had left Sicily, the strong bonds of friendship that over a period of many years had linked the two were beginning to unravel. In somewhat of an understatement, Eisenhower informed Gen. Marshall that Patton continued "to exhibit some of the personal traits of which you and I have always known."

Patton had entered Messina on August 17. Five months later, on January 18, 1944, he was still in Sicily. It was on that day when he learned that Eisenhower, who had recently arrived in England, announced that General Omar Bradley would command all American Ground Forces in the forthcoming cross-channel invasion. This was a real shocker, and rocked Patton back on his heels. He was stunned, acutely disappointed, dismayed, and deeply hurt. He knew immediately that Bradley was now destined to command the Army Group that would be established in France after the invasion. Deep down, even under the shadow where he now lived, Patton had held out hope that it would be he who would get the command. Commanding the invasion force was the one job that he had desperately hoped he would have.

The selection of Bradley meant a radical change in their relationship. Bradley was now elevated over Patton. Particularly crushing was the realization that the officer so recently a subordinate Commander would now be his superior Commander.

He just could not understand, and would always have a difficult time accepting, the selection of Bradley to command the American Army designated for operation OVERLORD. This action, he believed, completely ignored his experience in conducting amphibious operations. He had demonstrated conclusively in Morocco and Sicily that he was the most experienced, the pre-eminent American in conducting amphibious operations. Further, he had already demonstrated his great worth as a Combat Commander in an Allied Theater with British and French troops.

Patton, of course, did not realize or recognize that Eisenhower truly valued his ruthless driving power, but thought Patton best suited to an exclusively American Theater as an Army-level Commander. He would never understand, as well, that Eisenhower preferred a Commander who might never win a spectacular battle, but who would not cause him serious problems or embarrass him.

But it is certain that Patton clearly recognized as far back as North Africa that Eisenhower had and continued to have a growing admiration for his West Point classmate, Gen. Omar Bradley, whose steady demeanor had won Eisenhower's respect and confidence. Of Bradley Eisenhower said, "He exhibited a fine capacity for leadership and a thorough understanding of the requirements of modern battle." Apparently, of prime importance to Eisenhower was the fact that Bradley had "never caused me one moment of worry." (In sharp contrast, apparently, to the mercurial Patton.)

So from North Africa through Sicily, Bradley's star was rising, while Patton's was dipping and dimming.

Thus, it was not really surprising that Eisenhower nominated Bradley for the most important American Army Command, and sent him to England to form that new Army Group, and to participate in the Normandy invasion planning.

By late January 1944, Patton would join Eisenhower and Bradley in England. His arrival was quiet, certainly unheralded, with only a tiny, undistinguished group to greet him. After his arrival, he learned that they finally had plans for him. He was told that he would have command of the American Third Army. When he received his appointment, his Army was merely a title, a designation. The troops and units that would make up his Army were beginning to arrive in England, but most were still forming up in the United States. So for a time he would be figuratively "unemployed."

Even though he was now an Army Commander, he would still have some disappointments. His Army would not in any way participate in the invasion of Normandy, or in the initial drive out of the beachheads. The First Army would do the initial fighting. Patton's Army would have to sit by at the ready, and would not begin its operations until the invading forces had widened the bridgehead sufficiently so that the ground seized could absorb the many hundreds of men and their vehicles that would comprise the Third Army. Even more disquieting for Patton, at this point, was the realization that the mission of the Third Army was left vague, and that the time and date of the activation of his Army and commitment into action was very loose. It would depend on the situation, on how events would unfold.

During the weeks ahead in London and throughout England, there would be furious and frenzied activity. Many men would devote endless hours to all aspects of the planning for the upcoming invasion. When the top council met, it included the two top Ground Commanders – Montgomery for the British and Bradley for the Americans. Yes, once again, it was Bradley and not Patton. There has been much sentiment that one of the great mistakes of the war was Eisenhower reversing the roles of Patton and Bradley.

So once again Patton would be in limbo, and would find it most difficult to be gainfully occupied. He said at the time, "It's hell to be on the side-lines." Patton must have agreed with John Adams, who in a much earlier era had said, "To be wholly overlooked, and to know it, are intolerable."

There is no question but that Patton during the weeks before the invasion was somewhat of a mystery. No one seemed to know what he was doing or where he was. Pretty much under wraps was where he was. He would from time to time emerge to give his famous speech to the troops now assembling in England that would serve under him in the Third Army. He would tell them, "Don't forget, you don't know I'm here at all. No word of that fact is to be mentioned in any letter. The world is not supposed to know what the hell they did with me. I'm not supposed to be commanding this Army. I'm not even supposed to be in England. Let the first bastards to find out be the goddam Germans."

Patton emerged momentarily and very innocently on another occasion, which he would deeply regret, for it provoked another totally unexpected firestorm about him. He was being the "good guy." He had been invited to Knutsford, England and had accepted an invitation to make a few remarks to open the Welcome Club for American soldiers in that community. His comments that day included the statement, "the evident destiny of the British and Americans, and of course the

Russians, is to rule the postwar world." The press, as was expected, were there. Patton and Eisenhower had both expressed a strong desire, and the press well understood, that Patton's presence in England should not be reported upon. But to the press, always looking for "the story," Patton's reference to the Russians, which seemed to be merely an afterthought, was immediately seized as an indiscretion, and pounced upon with a vengeance. Overnight, Patton's innocent comment – his brief unthinking moment, which at the very worst was a "local boner," instantly became an Affair of State. With anyone but Patton, it never would have been an issue. But anti-administration forces played it up hard, and it rapidly became another Patton sensation back home.

As the wag stated, it was *deja vu* all over again. Patton's continued presence in England was pointedly questioned. The great irony: while people back in the States were clamoring for his relief, wanting his scalp, the Germans, as will be described, so feared him and were so terrified of him that his name alone would in the near future tie up many of their divisions, in fact an entire Field Army.

As before, Eisenhower stood by him, but not without consequences. On May 2, just a month before the invasion, he formally rebuked his Third Army Commander, and reminded Patton that he was "once more taking the responsibility of retaining you in command in spite of damaging repercussions resulting from a personal indiscretion. I do this solely because of my faith in you as a battle leader and for no other motive."

For Patton, another irony would emerge. Long before his Third Army was organized, long before it became operational, before it ever got its first look at the Germans, Patton, without lifting a finger, without a single shot being fired by his Third Army, would indirectly have a tremendous influence, effect, and impact on the Normandy invasion, and on operations for a period after the invasion. That tremendous influence required no overt actions on his part; they were based solely on his name and reputation. It would turn out to be an incredible story.

Many in the German high command firmly believed that the Allied cross-channel invasion would occur at the Pas de Calais. Such a crossing made very much sense. Here the Channel was at its narrowest point, making for easier transport of the invasion force. Most importantly, a landing here would be a greater strike than in Normandy, would outflank the defenses of the Seine river, and would place the troops 150 miles closer to Germany than if they had landed in Normandy. The beaches were also better. Side benefits: Allied fighter aircraft would have a much closer operational range, and there would be a good chance of over-running the sites of the "V" weapons which were being launched from that area against England. Calais had much to offer to the Allies, and the Germans knew it.

So the Allies decided that they would exploit and capitalize on German expectations and fears. The Allies came up with an amazing deception plan called FORTITUDE. To begin with they created the fictitious First United States Army Group. It was made up mainly of non-existent units with a few real subordinate units included. To make it a powerful, believable fighting element it would consist of two U. S. Armies, the 9th and 14th, and one British, the 4th To make it even more believable, they chose Gen. Patton to be its Commander.

The total thrust of FORTITUDE was to try to keep the Germans focused on Pas de Calais. Radio and all message traffic had to be extremely realistic, and had to reflect exactly the procedures that would be expected of a huge Army Group assembling in the English fields, and preparing itself for a huge invasion operation. German aircraft flying over the area had to be convinced that armies were, indeed, assembling there. Thus, very realistic dummy tanks, vehicles, and equipment were scattered across the supposed assembly areas. It was an imposing and formidable operation.

But one of the most convincing aspects of this mammoth undertaking had to be Gen. Patton. Of all the Allied Generals, he was the one most respected and feared by the German military, and the one whose fighting qualities they most greatly admired. Consequently, they closely monitored his activities and whereabouts. Yet, he seemed to have faded from sight. The Germans just would not buy the information that they had picked up that Eisenhower was greatly upset with Patton, and had shown his great displeasure by severely admonishing and punishing his valued Commander. The Germans, with their military culture, just would not and could not accept the report that the greatest and most successful Allied Commander was in the dog-house because of such minor, trivial, insignificant transgressions as slapping a couple of soldiers. They suspected subterfuge on the part of the Allies. They remained totally convinced that Patton, the most distinguished and successful Allied Ground Commander, would be commanding the First United States Army Group, and that he would lead the main effort across the Channel to Pas de Calais.

FORTITUDE was a huge success; it accomplished exactly what it was designed to do. It effectively tied up major German units in the Pas de Calais area. Had these same units been deployed and in position to react immediately, they could feasibly have blunted critical portions of the invasion, and most seriously affected its results. So convinced were the Germans that Normandy was a side-show that those units remained anchored even after they had reports that Patton was in France, and until it was too late. There is no way that the extent and effectiveness of the Patton name and reputation in the success of FORTITUDE can be accurately measured. Suffice to say, it was more than substantial.

Patton's active role was, at the moment, considerably less substantial than the cover role he had been playing. He was not part of the great gathering of OVERLORD Commanders in Portsmouth before D-Day, when Ike made his famous decision to launch the invasion. For a great many days Patton had been merely a spectator, and more in the dark about what was happening than many soldiers who were ready to board their ships and craft for the trip across the Channel.

On June 4, he was very restless and attended church, and later dreamed that he was leading the assault. He had been having recurring nightmares about not getting into the war before it ended. Repeatedly he thought, "I hope I get in before it's over."

On June 6, Montgomery was commanding invasion troops and Bradley was commanding invasion troops. Where was Patton? Like the rest of the world he learned of the Normandy landings at 7:00 AM, June 6, by listening to the BBC (British Broadcasting Corporation) on his radio. One can only imagine this old warrior's depth of disappointment, disillusionment, discouragement, and desolation to find himself on the wrong side of the Channel at one of the most critical periods in history.

However, little did he know at that moment that destiny would soon be beckoning to him from a wide-open door, and that in a few action-packed weeks his reputation would be not only restored but greatly enhanced. More than that, his exploits and successes would electrify the world.

CHAPTER 7

GENERAL BERNARD LAW MONTGOMERY:

D-DAY – AUGUST 1, 1944.

It had generally been agreed during the planning for the operation that a key to success of the Normandy invasion was the early capture of the old university town of Caen. In fact, there was strong sentiment that failure to take Caen on the first day would dangerously compromise the invasion.

The importance of Caen was readily understandable. It sat nine miles inland from the seaside resort town of Riva Bella, at the confluence of the Orne River and the sea. It was Normandy's major road and rail center, and control of the vital road junction meant control of all lateral movements. So it was extremely vital and valuable to Allied strategy.

But even more important, the capture of Caen would present Montgomery with an exciting opportunity. It would immediately open the door to the southeast and to the Plains of Falaise. That flat land was ideal, perfectly suited for armor operations. Tanks reaching it could move at once into the exploitation phase. The terrain was ideal, as well, for the establishment of airfields. The city of Falaise was merely 32 km. down the road, with Argentan about an equal distance beyond. When elements reached Argentan, they would be perfectly positioned to swing east to head for Paris, which was only 195 km. from Caen. That meant that Montgomery's forces were by far the closest invasion elements to that great city. The invading American forces, on the other hand, were a significant distance to the west, and instead of flat, open country they were contending with flooded fields and the abominable hedgerows which presented difficulties beyond comprehension. The hedgerows seriously impeded the advance of the American infantrymen, and were discouraging not only to them but to their leaders, as well. Under such circumstances, Montgomery could easily have been the "White Knight" of the invasion.

At this point it is well to recall that, significantly, Montgomery many weeks before the invasion, over a relief map at St. Paul's School, predicted an *early* tank "knockabout" from Caen to Falaise. He continued to emphasize the importance of the thrust toward Caen. He, himself, made Caen an important symbol, and promised to win it.

Before the invasion, ULTRA code-breakers had determined that Rommel had positioned the refitted 21st Panzer Division (which had been destroyed in North Africa and had been reconstituted with mostly inexperienced troops) southeast of the city of Caen. It appeared to be the only significant obstacle facing Montgomery's forces, other than light beach defenses. Before testing the 21st the British, however, faced one totally unexpected and unpredicted major obstacle that came close to destroying them, and over which they had no control. It was the weather which struck the English Channel on June 4, two days before the invasion. The tides from the storm surge would be extremely high.

Gen. Bradley and the American forces decided to launch their assault on Omaha and Utah Beaches at 0630 on June 6. For the British and Canadian forces, Montgomery decided that it would be an hour later, at 0730 hours. The reason for this decision was that it was hoped that the difference in time would provide them with a higher tide and less beach to cross before reaching the dunes. Montgomery received more from the beaches than he had expected and bargained for. Where the beach at Riva Bella is normally 30 yards wide at high tide, this day the beach was barely 30 ft. This was hardly enough maneuver room for a Sherman tank debarking from a landing craft. Understandably, vehicles of all types were soon milling around the tiny beach, and it was beset with problems and much confusion.

Consequently, disaster number two was not long in coming. After the vehicles landed on the beaches and began moving inland, a traffic jam of horrendous proportions developed. Tanks which had been put ashore successfully by their landing craft now found themselves completely stalled in long lines of supply vehicles. This was incredible, a nightmare. Tanks, the prime fighting element, the ones which had been destined to lead the assault on Caen, were buried – not moving to the front.

According to Montgomery's plan, three armored brigades were committed to take Caen before the 21st Panzer Division would be able to counterattack. To do this, the tanks most certainly had to move out quickly and aggressively. Not anticipated in his plan was an unexpected stroke of good fortune, which would almost have insured the success of his mission. On this day, not only were the British and Canadians confused, but there was great confusion and uncertainty, as well, in the German high command. Most of the day was spent by the time the Germans reacted. This explains why the 21st Panzer Division did not counterattack until 1400 hours, and why it took so long to remove the restrictions on the 12th SS Panzer Division which had been stationed nearby, so that it could join in the battle as late at 1500.

Now, one of the battle's great ironies. When the Germans counterattacked, it was not against British tanks, it was against British infantry. Tragically, on their own, without any help whatsoever from tanks, the British 3rd Infantry, although moving cautiously, advanced successfully to within three miles of their objective, Caen. Needless to say, once German armor hit the division, it was no contest, and the infantrymen were stopped dead in their tracks.

Unbelievably, an absolutely golden opportunity had been ignominiously squandered. The late reaction by the Germans had almost guaranteed a British victory, if they had implemented their original plan. With tanks supporting the infantry or, much better yet, with tanks attacking ahead of the Infantry, the D-Day mission and objective of capturing Caen on the first day of the invasion could readily have been accomplished. One can only conjecture on the tremendous impact such an achievement could have had on the breakout from Normandy, and the subsequent battles across France and into Germany. So instead of being taken on the invasion's first day, Caen would remain an elusive target for Montgomery, until several weeks later. The city would not be taken until after Bradley's Operation Cobra, when tanks of what would be Patton's Third Army were freed from the tentacles of the hedgerows, and would go charging to the south.

The defining element on Montgomery's first invasion day was to have been his armor – his tanks. He desperately needed them to capture the city of Caen, and immediately to position themselves for the quick thrust into the open plains of Falaise that beckoned to him invitingly. That would have been his tank "knockabout" from Caen to Falaise, which he had much earlier predicted. (Patton would have salivated at such an opportunity.)

It boggles the mind that Montgomery's three armor brigades were "no shows," "missing in action," that they never entered the fray. Where were they? What happened to them?

At last reading, the tanks were "milling around" with supply vehicles. Because they were never in the battle, it can only be assumed that they were not able to extricate themselves in time to be a factor in the battle, with predictable results. That is, undoubtedly, what happened to them. At the same time, it is particularly important to reflect on what *should* have happened. *(This is the view of the writer who, as will be later developed, was a Commander in the Armored Division which led Patton all across Europe.)* It is totally and completely incomprehensible to this tanker that the three British armor brigades never engaged in combat on that first day. To an aggressive and experienced tanker the solution was quite simple.

Yes, the tides were high and the beaches narrow, but the beach defenses had been eliminated by commandos who had operated earlier. The tanks should not have hesitated once their treads had hit the sand, and should have charged forward. There were several points on Sword Beach that could readily have served as tank exits, and knowledgeable, skilled, and aggressive Tank Commanders would have pushed their tanks over the embankments and into the village streets. One way or another, they would have gotten out of the crowded beaches and escaped from the jammed roads. It was clearly evident that Montgomery had committed a cardinal sin. From what transpired, there appeared to be no evidence that priority on the roads had been given to armor. Unbelievable as this is, such a fundamental lapse would not have stopped aggressive and determined Tank Commanders. If supply or other vehicles had not given way voluntarily, the tanks with much more muscle would have forcibly and even ruthlessly shoved them aside, and pushed on determinedly. After all, they had been assigned a mission, and that was the capture of Caen. That is the way it could and should have happened.

So the apparent factors in this failed mission, in addition to the lack of road priority for his armor, was Montgomery's continued treatment of his tanks as "step-children," the lack of aggressive action by his Tank Commanders, because they appeared to be hand-cuffed, and there was no demonstration of initiative because they, apparently, were not permitted to take action on their own. This combination of factors is an invitation to anything but victory. No wonder that claims were consistently being made that Montgomery had no "feel" for armor.

His attack had been stopped, but with both the 21st Panzer and 12th SS Panzer still at strength, it could have been an even more calamitous loss – a "wipe out." Unfortunately, the "filing away" of his tanks on the beaches and roads would have severe consequences on the entire invasion, and on subsequent breakout attempts.

On June 8, two days after the invasion, Montgomery instructed his Gen. Dempsey "to develop operations with all possible speed for the capture of Caen." An opportunity to encircle the city from the west shortly after D-Day was botched by the 7th Armoured Division, the most famous of all the constitutional formations of the old Eighth Army. This must have been another blow to Monty, for it was one of his veteran desert divisions, which he had handpicked for an important role in Normandy. Nothing seemed to be working.

And for Gen. Dempsey there would be no capture of Caen "with all possible speed." Instead, his Second Army would suffer a totally unexpected, puzzling and radical change in mission. There now comes a most interesting, intriguing episode that at the same time remains incongruous, bizarre, and surreal.

For the next three weeks Montgomery used Gen. Dempsey's Second Army to make repeated frontal and futile attacks to capture Caen. Dempsey rammed his troops again and again against the Panzer elements, which had been gathering opposite him. The only results that these attacks produced were heavy losses. The irony was that the harder he rammed the more difficult was his situation. The Germans, of course, knew the importance of Caen and the area to the southeast as well as the Allies. They knew that they had Montgomery cornered. They recognized, all too well, that if they kept him boxed-in they were delaying and making it much more difficult for the Allies to break out of Normandy. To ensure that they kept him cornered they continued to reinforce the forces surrounding him. In football parlance that would be called "piling on." So the harder Montgomery hit, the more Panzers he had to hit.

It was not long before there was mounting criticism that Montgomery was losing control of his campaign. But once again, as had happened before and would again, the Montgomery magic took over. The negative again became positive; victory was once more snatched from the jaws of defeat. Montgomery was taken off the "hook" by no less a personage than Gen. Omar Bradley. That distinguished officer had been at the very center of OVERLORD planning, had commanded an Army during the invasion, and would be an Army Group Commander involved in the Allied actions all across Europe. Yet he made some puzzling assertions. He would write that while American General Collins was hoisting VII Corps' flag over Cherbourg, Montgomery had been spending his reputation in the bitter siege against Caen. Bradley records that for three weeks Monty had rammed his troops against those Panzer Divisions which he had *deliberately* drawn toward that city as part of the Allied strategy of *diversion* in the Normandy campaign. Bradley reminds us that Caen contained an important road junction that Montgomery would eventually need, but for the moment *"the capture of that city was only incidental to his mission."* Monty's primary task was to attract German troops to the British front so that American troops might more easily secure Cherbourg, and move into position for the breakout. Bradley continued by commenting that in this diversionary mission Monty was more successful for, as has been mentioned, the harder he hammered toward Caen, the more German troops he drew into that sector. And while this diversion was *brilliantly achieved*, Montgomery, nevertheless, left himself open to criticism by *previously over-emphasizing* the importance of the thrust toward Caen. Monty's achievement, Bradley opined, should have been measured in the number of Panzer Divisions the enemy rushed against him.

After the war, Montgomery himself would join in attempting to revise some history. In 1946 Monty would allege that the OVERLORD planning always contemplated only a holding action in the British sector around Caen.

He stated that the Allies would "threaten to break out of the initial bridgehead on the eastern flank – that is, the Caen sector…draw the main enemy reserves into that sector…keep them there…. [and] make the breakout on the western flank, using for this task the American armies under Gen. Bradley." He went on to say that "strong and persistent action in the Caen sector would achieve our objective of drawing the enemy mobile reserves onto our eastern flank. This was my original conception of the manner in which the Battle of Normandy was to be developed. From the start it formed the basis for all our planning, and was the aim of our operations from the time of the assault to the final victory in Normandy. I never had cause or reason to alter my plan."

By 1948, he recalled that his plan was, "so to conduct the land battle that the British would draw the main German strength…to fight it and keep it there." Among Montgomery's many avowed talents, Master of Rationalization must be added to them.

There are several aspects of his story that are most difficult to reconcile:

1.) It had been understood before the invasion that a key to success of the Normandy invasion was the early capture of the city of Caen. Yet, some days later while Montgomery's troops were butting their heads against the German Panthers, it was contended that, "for the moment the capture of that city was incidental to his (diversionary) mission."

2.) If Caen had actually been seized on the first day as planned, Montgomery would have, undoubtedly, broken out to the southeast during subsequent days. He would have been out somewhere on the Falaise Plains, during the period when his "diversionary" efforts were actually taking place. It appears that such an eventuality was, in fact, anticipated. Planning as early as February 26 still showed the British Second Army, not at Falaise, but beyond Argentan and all the way to Alencon (directly west of and well on the way to Paris) by D+25. If this was, indeed, "on the books," it certainly assumed a major offensive by Montgomery on the Allied Eastern Front. Yet, as has been claimed by some, the OVERLORD plan supposedly assigned Montgomery the containment mission. If this is so, is it not a concession well ahead of time that Montgomery was not expected to seize Caen during the early days of the invasion? Once again – more interesting and confusing contradictions.

3.) Some claimed that the diversionary effort of Montgomery was brilliantly achieved. Yet, in the minds of many, successful military operations are measured in the rate and length of advance. Thus, it is difficult to comprehend that Montgomery could be considered successful because he stirred up resistance that would more tightly box himself in, and make it less and less likely that he would be able to pull out and advance at a time of this own choosing.

4.) It is hard to imagine that the strutting, cocksure, egotistical, publicity-hungry Montgomery would willingly consent to a role that would diminish him, and conduct an operation that would evoke criticism and tarnish the luster of his reputation. It would have been completely out of character for Montgomery to have used himself as a sacrificial lamb.

The "diversionary operation" strains credulity, and is difficult to swallow. Even while Monty's frontal assaults were at their heaviest, Eisenhower was expressing his disappointment at the delay before Caen, and kept urging Montgomery for the early capture of the city, and more to the point – the exploitation after.

Eisenhower, who always seemed to handle Montgomery with "kid gloves," a month after D-Day, in a July 7th Communication, said to Monty, "It appears to me that we must use all possible energy in a determined effort toward a breakthrough." Air Chief Marshal Tedder, Eisenhower's Deputy, would say that Eisenhower's purpose in writing was simply to "tell Montgomery tactfully to get moving."

And "get moving" he, finally, did. Shortly before midnight on the evening of July 7, 460 night-flying Wellington bombers of the RAF Bomber Command began a 40-minute drop of 2,300 tons of 500 and 1,000 pound bombs on a carpet 4,000 yards wide and 1,500 yards deep. Six hours later, just before dawn on July 8th, three British and Canadian divisions of the 1st Corps attacked directly across the carpet and into Caen, with three armored brigades in immediate support and a fourth in reserve. By this time the city was stunned and cratered. More than 14,000 buildings had been destroyed and damaged. Unfortunately, the heavy bombs had so cratered the area that bulldozers had to fill in holes, before the troops could advance over them. Through many of the Germans were, likewise, stunned by the aerial bombardment, most continued to resist with their customary tenacity.

Elements of the 1st Corps had advanced well enough to capture the section of Caen west of the river during the next day, July 9. Thereupon, this thrust bogged down like all its predecessors. It carried no further than the Orne. And, of course, there was still no break-out.

Now there was no longer a "diversionary" effort to "occupy" Montgomery. At some point he would have to cease what American troops disparagingly called his "pivoting" around Caen, and launch a determined offensive effort to "break out."

Finally, on July 18, nearly six weeks after D-Day, the day he had been scheduled to capture Caen, Montgomery kicked off a massive attack aimed at that ravaged city. It was still partially occupied by the Germans. Monty's mission was not only to complete the conquest of Caen, but also to break out to the southeast. The operation would be called GOODWOOD.

The instructions to Gen. Dempsey, commanding the 2nd Army, charged him to prepare a "massive stroke" from Caen to Falaise. Montgomery, himself, promised that "the whole eastern flank would burst into flames" in a "decisive" victory. Yet, later, after this bold pronouncement, his caution about explicit commitment again reasserted itself, and he ordered Dempsey to erase even the name of Falaise from the 2nd Army plan.

Before he launched his attack, he had a thunderous preparation. More than 2000 heavy, medium, and fighter-bombers dropped over 8,000 tons of bombs. This was over three times the weight that preceded the July 8th attack. This massive effort from the skies cratered the area. It would be reminiscent of the surface of the moon, and not unlike the battlefields of WW I. The scarred surface would subsequently back-fire and would hamper and haunt, and be a severe impediment to the attacking tanks and other vehicles.

This time Montgomery remembered that he had tanks. Also, he would not limit his attack to a single corps. On this one he would go "full bore." His 8th Corps would attack with three Armored Divisions. The 12th Corps would open with a diversionary attack. The Canadian 2^{d} Corps would attack simultaneously with the 8th Corps, which, it was hoped, would complete the conquest of Caen.

The Germans astutely concentrated much of their strength on Bourguebous Ridge, which they anticipated would overlook the projected battlefield. They had three main defensive lines and a reserve line. Cleverly, they established a gun line studded with 88mm's (one of the very great weapons of WW II) and with other guns, as well. Two favorable factors helped insure that the ridge would be potent and deadly. The first was that there were not enough planes available to the British in their massive attack to extend the preparation bombing carpet far enough to include that line, so the ridge was relatively untouched by air. Secondly, the gun line also happened to be at the extreme range of most of Dempsey's artillery.

Not long after the battle kicked off, Montgomery's first dispatch of that offensive, in typical Monty style, announced: "Early this morning British and Canadian troops of the Second Army attacked and *broke through* the area east of the Orne and southeast of Caen."

The attack was aimed at the German gun line. But by the time the spearheads had advanced that far, most of the British forces had fallen well behind, entangled in congested village crossroads (*deja vu*). Without support, the spearheads faltered against thunderous fire from the 88's. Early in the afternoon a decision was made to hurl everything available head-on against the ridge, casualties be damned. However, unexpected difficulties arose. Routes open to armor proved to be too narrow. The tanks were mostly strung out beyond supporting distance of the spearheads. Consequently, the forces were severely punished and badly bloodied. That day, July 18th, alone cost the Second Army 270 tanks and 1,500 men without cracking the Ridge.

The next day, July 19th, the British confined themselves to mainly local attacks. By the third day, July 20, these efforts had considerable success, and drove the enemy from most of the northern slope of the Bourguebous Ridge. But the Germans clung to the crest. Some time later a thunderstorm erupted, and quickly made a quagmire of the area of the bombing carpet and the area of operations. This unexpected strike from the heavens doomed the operation and effectively spelled the end of GOODWOOD. It was sealed, and punctuated with an exclamation point, by a German counterattack on the 21st

When the action had finally stopped, the Germans were still holding the high ground at Bourguebous Ridge. The British suffered 5,537 casualties and lost 400 tanks, 36 percent of their tank strength in France. 2nd Army had, finally, after many weeks, completed its occupation of the ruins of Caen. However, the gains were extremely minor when placed against the promises and expectations. To put it bluntly, GOODWOOD turned out to be another Montgomery disaster.

Once again, in typical fashion, Montgomery would arrogantly claim to be satisfied with the latest attrition of German strength (how about British attrition?), and the diversion of attention from Bradley's front. (Same old refrain.) He never explained why he used the words "broke through" in his initial dispatch if, as he subsequently insisted, although a breakthrough failed to occur on the Allied left, such a breakthrough was never intended.

Eisenhower had been growing disillusioned and moody because of Montgomery's lack of progress. Now he, at last, was angered and dismayed by Montgomery's performance. To Eisenhower and his senior staff, GOODWOOD was a real disappointment. Questions quickly arose at SHAEF (Supreme Headquarters Allied Expeditionary Force) regarding Montgomery's competence, and the sentiment was that it was time to send the British General packing. Staff members even began wondering who would be Montgomery's successor. It was said that Eisenhower was pressed by his own British Deputy, Air Chief Marshal Sir Arthur Tedder, and others to replace Montgomery. There were indications that Tedder was ready to write to the British Chiefs of Staff about Montgomery's deficiencies. Rumblings of discontent were heard in London and Washington. From all this it was clearly evident that consternation about Montgomery was widespread – coming from all directions. Such a ground swell of critical opinion was bound to take a heavy toll. So what happened to Montgomery? The answer – nothing, absolutely nothing.

He may have been bloodied, but was unbowed; he may have been nudged a bit, but was still standing steady as a rock. Montgomery magic was still at work. He was still a master of rationalization. As far as he was concerned, under the circumstances, he had done all that could have been done.

As has been mentioned, in British eyes, he was still credited with Britain's come-back in the war; he was a symbol of victory. Consequently, he remained cherished by the British people. But beyond the affection of the British people was the magic effect he had on British soldiers. His slight, erect figure excited great assurance among the soldiers. He could stir his troops to rapture. He was now a figure of legend. The black beret was his trademark, was recognized everywhere, and invariably aroused great enthusiasm.

He, himself, made a virtue of and capitalized upon his reputation as the forever careful planning General, the supreme authority of the set-piece. He was well aware of his reputation, and played upon it like a violin virtuoso. A close aide to Gen. Bradley is quoted in late June, "Went to tea with Monty and found him oppressive. Monty is beginning to believe in the Monty legend; that he is a great man of history, fully convincing himself of his godlike role … the word *my* recurs in his conversation."

Hero worship has been with us over the ages. It will ever remain a puzzle, an enigma. Who among us will earn, be singled out, be chosen for the praise, veneration, adulation that will be heaped upon him, for whatever reason? What event, achievement, act of courage, contribution to our society, or personality will endear him to hundreds, thousands, millions – even a whole nation, as in Montgomery's case? Some become heroes for good reason – instantaneously, understandably, unquestionably. Why others are so elevated is, often-times, a puzzle. Montgomery was such an enigma. He was not a physically imposing figure. To many who knew him, he was brusque, opinionated, cold, egotistical, and rigid. He was anything but an attractive personality. Many of his "credits" were dubious, suspect. He even traveled under "false colors" with his trademark, his best-known affectation – the black beret. That head-piece traditionally was the proud stamp of the British tanker: he wore it with great pride, and it provided him with instant recognition, distinction and prestige. Now he shared it with Montgomery, who was *not* a tanker. Those who really "knew" Montgomery found it incomprehensible that he would have and maintain such a "hold" on the British people.

Now the final question, how did Montgomery survive relatively unscathed his performance during the horrendous six weeks from D-Day to GOODWOOD? Once again, as before and as would happen again, the decision to "keep" Monty was obviously anything but a military one – it had to be politically motivated. Prime Minister Churchill, naturally and understandably a politician, certainly must have recognized that it was in his best interest to continue not to tinker with an icon. It is, thus, assumed that he decided that the British hero should remain in position to continue to be a British hero. So once again it appears that Churchill must have "leaned" on Eisenhower, and Monty continued, "to go about his business."

Thus, as the operations in Normandy were nearing a conclusion, Monty would appear unperturbed, undaunted, unsullied, unscathed, and untouched. He was still the 21st Army Group Commander, and the Allied Ground Commander. He remained one of the important Allied leaders in the drive to push the Germans back to their homeland and to defeat them. When the war was ended, he would still be there with his feet planted firmly on the ground – *irrepressible* to the end.

CHAPTER 8

GENERAL GEORGE S. PATTON, JR.:

D-DAY – AUGUST 1, 1944.

The spotlight had constantly and glaringly been on Montgomery in France from D-Day on. He had been chest-high in all the action taking place. But where was George Patton? Nowhere in sight. The contrast between Montgomery's and Patton's activities could not have been more remarkable or dramatic.

Patton was in England. He had arrived in that country with some carry-over in key personnel from his Seventh Army in Sicily. Now they were members of the Headquarters of his new command, Third Army. He, with his staff, had settled down most inconspicuously in the Midlands, near a place called Peover, far away from the hustle and bustle of D-Day preparations and the invasion traffic of southern England. From the leisured, quiet life he was living, he might as well have been just another English burgher. His Third Army was simply an Army Headquarters without troops. It would be so until its commitment in France at some date not yet known and apparently not immediate. Because of that, the Third Army was assigned to the ETO (European Theater of Operations). In that capacity it had, in a sense, become a ward of Eisenhower, and would remain so until activated and inserted into action.

Patton was the forgotten man. Like millions of people all over the world, as has been mentioned, he had first heard of the D-Day invasion on his radio. It was the stunning announcement from BBC (British Broadcasting Corporation). For a man like Patton, a long-time distinguished soldier with an already spectacular combat record dating back to WW I, it was a humiliating, shattering experience.

It seems that everyone who was anyone in the military was in some way directly involved in the D-Day planning or its operation. But not Patton. He had absolutely no influence on, nor had he contributed in any way to, the planning of OVERLORD. Of course, his role as the big decoy in FORTITUDE was substantial, absolutely extraordinary, with results that were far more amazing than anyone had anticipated. Yet that role was a passive one. It did not require him to lift a finger, only to keep out of sight. So American's greatest Field Commander, a proven warrior, and a superlative offensive weapon, was on the sideline, in limbo, and, in football parlance, not even on the roster.

During the days of June, Patton chafed while the war went on without him. He lamented that, "Time drags terribly. I am nervous as a cat … [and] full of gloom." His great and abiding fear was that the war would end, while he sat uselessly and helplessly in Peover. He had always wanted to be a hero. He believed that his opportunity was out there now, but his great concern was how to get there before that opportunity vanished. Also, by becoming that hero, he could at least redeem himself for the indiscretions that had placed him in Eisenhower's dog-house. His Army staff was every bit as anxious as he to get him into action, for he had become extremely irritable, hard to live with.

One bright spot was that even though he had been out of action, out of the spotlight for some months, he was still well remembered and highly regarded. Proof of that was the fan mail he occasionally received in batches. One of his fans even wrote urging him to run for president.

For some time after the landings, he received no official dispatches. Thus, he had only the vaguest idea of what was really happening in Normandy. From his sixth sense, his well-known battle sense, he surmised correctly that things were not going well with the Normandy bridgehead. This bold, aggressive Commander sensed that the leaders on the ground there seemed to be content to be merely holding on and not advancing.

To try to end the stalemate, he even went so far as to propose a plan that would land a Corps of two Infantry Divisions and one Armored Division on the north coast of Brittany. He had his close friend and West Point classmate, Everett S. Hughes, a senior assistant of Eisenhower's, slip the material into Ike's reading file. Nothing came of it. But it was another example of boldness, vision, the ability to see and think ahead, which he would apply many times with his Third Army in the weeks that followed.

By the end of June, Eisenhower was growing impatient and edgy at the slow pace of the Allied advance. On June 27th Everett Hughes brought him more discouraging news centering around the delay of the

American First Army. In utter frustration Eisenhower was heard to say, "Sometimes I wish that I had George Patton here."

Finally Patton made his move from England to France. He crossed the Channel on July 6th, exactly one month after D-Day. He traveled under tight security wraps and with the greatest of secrecy. It was critical that the cover not be blown on FORTITUDE. The deception that Patton was still in England, readying his Army Group for the "real invasion" in the Pas de Calais was, amazingly, still working. The best evidence that the Germans continued to believe this cultivated hoax was that most of the German Fifteenth Army was still waiting for Patton to lead the main invasion there.

Patton drove with his small personal staff to an airfield near Salisbury, where they boarded a C-47 transport, which was escorted to France by four P-47 fighters. They flew over the port of Cherbourg and the recently invaded beaches to a landing strip near Omaha Beach.

As soon as his feet hit the ground, he was surrounded by soldiers, sailors, and newspaper correspondents. So much for tight security! Here, apparently, was an already established legend, and he still had a war to fight. He warned them all that he was still a secret. However, news of his scheduled arrival in France must have spread like wildfire, for everyone, it seems, wanted to see him. The magic was still there. Some days later, as he stood on the beach watching tanks that would be in his Third Army disembark, a Navy lieutenant said, "And when you see General Patton … you get the same feeling, as when you saw Babe Ruth striding up to the plate. Here's a big guy who's going to kick the hell out of something."

He remained overnight at First Army Headquarters to be briefed. There was no doubt that there was a war on, and he, finally, was very near it. Artillery fire was so close and boomed so loudly and so frequently that the briefing was constantly being interrupted.

With Patton in France his Third Army Headquarters had also been relocating. He was assigned a bivouac area in the Cotentin, where he was to await commitment under the yet-to-be-formed 12th Army Group. His command post was established on July 6 and settled in at a place called Nehou, not too far from the resort town of Barneville, which sat on the west coast of the peninsula. Nearby was the swollen Douve River.

He would be located behind Gen. Middleton's VIII Corps. With him there would be two Corps Headquarters without troops, awaiting their assignment to and commitment with Third Army. A third Corps would soon join.

It was not long before an impatient Patton began pacing back and forth like a caged tiger. His staff was only too aware that he desperately wanted to get the bit in his teeth, and move on into the fray.

For Patton the days dragged on until July 20. That was two days after Montgomery had launched GOODWOOD. That day some startling news was heard that cheered everyone, and momentarily brightened an atmosphere which had been so gloomy. It was learned that there had been an attempt on Hitler's life. Most wondered about the implications of such sensational news. George, however, wondered most about how it would affect the life of Patton. When the news of the assassination attempt reached him in the Cotentin, he bounded down to Bradley's command post at Colombieres, "For God's sake, Brad," Patton pleaded, "You've got to get me into this fight, before the war is over. I'm in the dog-house now, and I'm apt to die there, unless I pull something spectacular to get me out."

How Patton got into the war requires considerable discussion of organization and reorganization. The Commander of all Ground Forces for the D-Day landings and Deputy to Eisenhower was Gen. Bernard Montgomery. He was in command of the 21st Army Group. Under this command was the British Second Army with two Corps and the American First Army, also with two corps. The British Second Army under the command of Gen. Dempsey landed at Gold, Juno, and Sword beaches. The American First Army under Gen. Bradley landed at Omaha and Utah beaches. Although the American First Army was under Montgomery's command, that command could best be described as a "nominal" command. Gen. Montgomery was so involved and so preoccupied with the difficulties and travails of the British Second Army that, fortunately, he was forced to leave the American First Army pretty much alone. He provided little guidance, and the First Army, happily, operated relatively independently.

The U.S. Army on the continent had grown steadily in strength, and by July 25 it would number 21 divisions. In anticipation of this, and as had earlier been planned, Eisenhower on July 14 gave Bradley the go-ahead to establish an Army Group. The U.S. First Army now had many more than the prescribed number of divisions for a Field Army, and its maintenance and overhead services were being badly taxed. A second Field Army was absolutely essential. So the authority granted to Bradley included the activation of the Third U.S. Army which, of course, would be commanded by Patton. When the reorganization took place, the divisions and other resources would be split between the two armies. Bradley would relinquish command of First Army to Lt. Gen. Courtney H. Hodges. At this point Bradley would step up to command of the 12th U.S. Army Group.

When Eisenhower flew to France for a conference concerning Bradley's upcoming Operation COBRA and saw the First Army map crowded with divisional tabs, he asked Bradley when he would expect to bring the Army Group into the picture, and activate Third Army. Bradley answered Eisenhower's question by suggesting the date – August 1. Eisenhower readily agreed.

But even after the 12th U.S. Army Group became active, Eisenhower would not be ready to cut the Americans free from Montgomery's 21st Army Group. The result would be anything but a clear, crisp, non-controversial chain of command.

Eisenhower's SHAEF Headquarters, and thus Eisenhower himself, were still in England. Sitting in that country, Eisenhower could not, as he should, function as day to day Commander of Allied Ground Forces in France. It was for that very reason that Montgomery had been named Eisenhower's Deputy for the invasion. The establishment and commitment of the 12th Army Group would put them on an equal footing with Monty's 21st Army Group. It had been anticipated that when this occurred, Eisenhower would take over as *the* Ground Commander, and assume direct responsibility between the two.

U.S. equality of command with Montgomery's Army Group had been agreed to in England months before the invasion as part of the Overlord plan. At no time had there been any intention of continuing Montgomery as Eisenhower's ground Deputy.

However, an especially awkward situation presented itself. If Eisenhower assumed direct command from across the Channel, it involved a great risk in communications. Another great risk – if Eisenhower were urgently needed in France for a critical decision, he might find himself grounded in England by the ever-temperamental weather. Such problems would be eliminated once SHAEF was established in France. But the Allied forces had not yet uncovered a city extensive enough to house and accommodate the widespread activities of SHAEF. Therefore, until SHAEF was permanently established in France, Eisenhower directed that Montgomery would again act as his agent, exercising *temporary* operational control over the U.S. Army Group.

These decisions were kept under wraps, and SHAEF censored news of this command line-up. However, as might be expected, before the announcement was officially made, a newspaper reporter ignored censorship restrictions and filed a story, which stated that the U.S. Army Group had been granted co-equal status with that of Monty's 21st Army Group. The report instantly caused an uproar in England, where the parity of command was viewed as a deliberate affront to Britain's war hero. The British press alleged that Montgomery had been slurred. Some newspaper writers even went so far as to denounce it as a demotion for Montgomery, and a rebuke to the British people.

Eisenhower should have met the issue head-on by relating that the command structure had been agreed to months before the invasion.

Thus, he could have stopped the recriminations which instantly followed before they ever got started. Once again it appears that he feared to offend the British people, so he withheld such an explanation. The best person to squelch the ruckus, of course, was Montgomery himself. He could have arranged for a hasty press conference, and provided a satisfactory explanation to the newsmen. But Monty was well aware of his reputation, and enjoyed the sympathetic support which he instantly received, as he believed it to be his due. As on other occasions, he was not about to stand in the way of a favorable wind, and he chose not to lance a festering boil.

It would not be until the last day of August that the American 12th Army Group was pulled from Montgomery's command, and this time, finally, granted co-equal status with the British Army Group. The next day, September 1, Eisenhower was, at last, in practice, the Allied Ground Commander. Apparently to console Montgomery on his somewhat diminished status, the British promoted him to the rank of Field Marshall, as the change was being made and announced.

The advance in Normandy, if it could be called that, moved at a snail's pace. The operations were already well behind its established timetable. There was pessimism, gloom, and even a wisp of desperation at the highest levels. The specter of a World War I stalemate hung like a cloud over their heads.

Montgomery's Second Army was still boxed in at Caen. His GOOD-WOOD attempt at a breakout had failed miserably. The American infantry was bogged down in the hedgerows. These formed a natural line of defense across the neck of the Normandy Peninsula, and were more formidable, even, than a defense that could be contrived and constructed. Some insisted that they were every bit as formidable as the jungles of Guadalcanal.

Bradley decided that it was urgent that something be done to shake loose from the stalemated hedgerows, and to effect, finally, a breakout in Normandy. So he set about doing just that; he devised a plan called COBRA. This would kick off later in July, after a great aerial bombardment similar to that of Montgomery's GOODWOOD. Hopefully, it would be followed up by an operation more successful, with significantly greater results.

The operation, after some delays, was launched on July 25. It began with the planned aerial bombardment. *(I was an eyewitness; I stood on the deck of a Sherman tank. The action that unfolded before me was so close that I felt that I could almost reach out and touch it.)* I watched in awe as wave after wave of twenty-five hundred heavy bombers, medium bombers, and fighters dropped thousands of bombs and thousands of tons of explosives. The target was a tiny doomed rectangle of French soil; five square miles of Normandy pasture that became an inferno. As I watched, the smoke and debris obscured the sun and turned day into night. My 35-ton tank actually bounced on the ground – the concussions were that great. The generals had depended upon, and expected much from, the carpet bombing. It was hoped that the massive air bombardment would provide an open door through which our troops could pour, and, thus, effect a break-through, so desperately needed. Euphoria at first, then gloom. Because of several unfortunate factors, a considerable number of the Fortresses' and Liberators' bombs had struck outside the target area. This caused a considerable number of casualties among the front-line troops, and disrupted units ready to attack. Among those killed was Gen. Lesley J. McNair, head of U.S. Ground Forces, on a visit from the U. S. to witness the attack. Dejection "settled in over us like a wet fog", said Gen. Bradley.

Several hundred U.S. troops were killed and wounded, and the planned advance had been dislocated. What had momentarily been believed to be on the brink of a break-through now looked as though it might fail. But the mood soon shifted to optimism. There was rapid re-organization on the battlefield, and the U.S. troops began to advance.

And now Patton, finally, would make his way upon the stage. In a matter of days he would become the most prominent character on that stage, and would remain in the spotlight and dominate the action in the weeks and months ahead. (For the first time since the public revelation of the soldier-slapping incidents, and beginning in late July, there would be much for Patton to relish.)

As was mentioned, Patton's bivouac was behind Middleton's Corps. He had known for some time that, when his Third Army was activated, VIII Corps would be part of his command.

With COBRA pending, Patton had been barely able to contain his impatience to join the action. Despite Patton's eagerness to aid Bradley on the COBRA attack, Bradley was anxious, for ease of control, to re-strict it to First Army until the Third Army was actually activated. But later he apparently had a change of heart. He now recognized that when the hour had arrived for COBRA'S breakout, that hour was the unique opportunity for the very rashness that would have made Bradley distrust Patton under different circumstances. Thus, when Bradley became aware that Middleton's Corps had an opportunity to leap forward and join the break-through effort, he telephoned Patton's Headquarters on the afternoon of July 27 to authorize Patton to take immediate control of VIII Corps, *for the time being.*

The relationship which followed was unprecedented, and would result in a highly unusual command arrangement. Here was the awkward situation of Patton commanding a Corps that was not yet under his command. That did not stop Patton or Middleton. They soon had their heads together, planning the attack of the VIII Corps early the next morning. That was a strange *tête-à-tête*. Gen. Middleton was the Commander of VIII Corps of the First Army commanded by Gen. Bradley. Gen. Patton was the Commander of the Third Army, which at that moment did not exist. So Patton was directing the actions of VIII Corps, even though he did not officially have direct command. This posed no difficulty, for Middleton clearly recognized that he was dealing with the individual who would be his boss, his direct Commander, in just about four days. Bradley placed some legitimacy on this arrangement by improvising a title for Patton. Bradley declared that for the moment Patton would be his Deputy Army Commander.

Patton's influence was immediately felt. He and Middleton agreed that, despite reports of a wide variety of mines up ahead, it would be VIII Corps' tanks that would lead the attack. And as events would soon prove – what a momentous decision that turned out to be!

Middleton ordered Major General John S. Wood's 4th Armored Division to move out at five in the morning on July 28 to drive south on the Periers-Coutances highway, where Wood was to coordinate the advance through Coutances with the oncoming VII Corps on his left, before barreling further southward. (This Division would gather many nicknames – among the best-known would be "Patton's Spearhead" and "Patton's Best." The 4th Armored Division would in the days and weeks ahead be the leading and dominant player in every action of Third Army. The two could not and would not be separated. Of Third Army's 281 combat days, the 4th Armored was in that Army for 280 of them. I was the S3 (operations officer) and later Commanding Officer of the 8th Tank Battalion of the 4th Armored Division. Thus, the actions of that division and that Army which I will describe are described not from the perspective of an historian, but from that of a participant.)

A second Armored Division participating in the attack was Major General Robert W. Grow's 6th Armored Division, which Gen. Bradley had given Middleton during the afternoon of the 27. The 6th Armored Division's mission was to move south from Lessay, by-pass Coutances on the west, and drive on to Granville.

It was my Eighth Tank Battalion of Combat Command B of the 4th Armored Division that quickly demonstrated its professionalism on July 28. That is the day that it broke out of a depressingly stalemated situation among the hedgerows of Normandy, and by slashing aggressively seized the city of Coutances before the end of the first day. The capture of Coutances by the Eighth Tank Battalion was most significant. Its reaching Coutances first meant that Gen. Collins' VII Corps, which had a head start, as its own history put it, "lost the race to Coutances."

Of far greater significance, the capture of Coutances was unmistakable evidence that the Normandy breakout had finally occurred and was a success. There was a definite exclamation point the next day. Without slackening their pace, the troopers of the 4th Armored, led by the Eighth Tank Battalion, continued their attack to the south. The enemy defenses had been penetrated, and their troops disorganized. However, there were constant pockets of determined and even fanatical resistance. The tanks of the 8th powered over or by-passed that resistance. Prisoners were being gathered up in ever-increasing numbers. We were already learning a valuable lesson. It was amazing how quickly the enemy lost its will to fight when they realized that we had gotten around them and behind them. We would experience that many times in the days ahead.

On the third day the Eighth reached Avranches, and on the fourth day, July 31, elements of the 4th Armored seized that tactically and strategically important city. It was ours! Avranches sat at the base, at the bottom of the Normandy peninsula. It was the door, the gateway to all of France – to Brittany on the south and west, and Le Mans, Chartres, and Paris to the east. What is amazing and most reassuring about this breakout operation is that the Patton "touch" became immediately evident. On a few hours notice he had planned the strategy of the VIII Corps attack. By having the VIII Corps attack with two Armored Divisions he instantly made things happen. Overnight he had turned a slow, dreary offensive into a dramatically successful one. He would exhibit that touch many times in the future.

There was a bit of irony in this operation. Patton and Middleton had expected Wood's 4th Armored Division to cross the See and seize Tirepied, east of Avranches, shielding the key crossings of the main highways, but yielding the honor of first entering Avranches to Gen. Grow's 6th Armored Division. But the 4th advanced with so much flair and speed, as well as skill, that by the evening of July 29th it was decided that it was in a better position than the 6th to capture Avranches, and it was awarded that prize. Both Patton and Middleton could take great satisfaction for their flexibility and for the 4th's performance.

Early the next day, forces of the 4th Armored Division, now led by Combat Command A, started their drive towards Rennes, the capital of Brittany. Four days from breakout in Normandy to breakout *from* Normandy. Incredible!

Later the U.S. Army Official History would have these words, "the sensational success of Gen. Wood's 4th Armored Division had exploded the nightmare of static warfare that had haunted the Americans so long in the Cotentin. Under Gen. Wood… the style of fighting was set in this, the first of the division's many breakthrough operations. It was a daring, hard-riding, fast-shooting style. The division's front was as wide as the roads down which it sped. The recon men out front kept going until they hit resistance too hot to handle. Teams of tanks and armored infantry swung out smoothly in attack formation under the protective fire of the quickly emplaced artillery. The division broke the enemy or flowed about them – cutting the German lines of communication and splitting apart the units."

And now the long awaited day had arrived.

CHAPTER 9

GENERAL GEORGE S. PATTON, JR.:

HIS 4TH ARMORED DIVISION LEADS THE WAY

AUGUST 1 – AUGUST 15, 1944

Combat Command A of the 4th Armored Division moved out with typical aggressiveness at 0500 on 1 August, and drove south. The division would become the first American and Allied element to enter Brittany, and by early evening it had advanced forty miles and neared the outskirts of Rennes, the capital. This was another most impressive, significant achievement.

However, its actions were overshadowed by even more dramatic events of the day. For quite some time there had been on many calendars a big circle around the date – *August 1*. This was a day to which many individuals had looked forward with great eagerness, anticipation, and, for some, great impatience. Now it had, finally, arrived. Of all those who looked forward to this day, no one came close to exhibiting as much restlessness as George Patton. He was the one who was most guilty of chomping on the bit – much more so than even Omar Bradley. For Patton this day would mark the turning point in his fortunes, and would be one of the most electrifying, rewarding, and satisfying moments in his tumultuous life.

By noon his Third Army had become operational. Patton was once again in command of a powerful fighting force, and engaged in yet another pivotal war. He was impatient and extremely anxious to demonstrate, once more, exactly what he was made of. He acted as if he had just been pardoned and released from jail. Almost instantly he was a whirlwind – he was everywhere, prodding, cajoling, exhorting. HIS Third Army would soon be moving so rapidly that it would soon become necessary to relocate his command post almost every night in what were quickly referred to as one-night stands.

Now for a humorous sidelight to this most eventful day. There was another dramatic way in which Patton established his presence on the battlefield. A simple order from him that day, which I vividly remember, required every individual in Third Army to, "Put on your necktie." We in the ranks were thunderstruck, disbelieving. Why? Our uniform was a woolen shirt and trousers. We were operating in the hot, French, August sun. To gain some relief our shirts were open at the throat. Why now, of all times, for such an order? The tie was a narrow black string one which had not been worn in a long, long time. In my case it was somewhere in the deep recesses of my tank, and had to be resurrected. It took some "remembering" to give me a clue as to where it might be. It was eventually found and put on. It is safe to say that every individual in Third Army bitched and griped loudly, as I did, some with very colorful expletives. The "why," however, can be easily explained. There is no question but that when each man retired that night, whether it be in a tank, in a truck or on the ground, he knew without doubt who his Army Commander was, and that the "old man" commanding him was Lt. Gen. George S. Patton, Jr. This was another example of Patton's unique style of leadership.

On this day, as scheduled, the 12th Army Group also became operational. From the lofty position of Commander of this Group, Bradley would now become Patton's superior, and his Group would include his First Army, whose command he had passed on to Gen. Hodges. As was planned, Gen. Middleton's VIII Corps became a member of Third Army, and Patton automatically inherited that Corps' 4th Armored Division. Compared to the significant events of the day and in the general scheme of things, having the 4th Armored in his command appeared to be anything but earth-shaking. After all, this was but one of many divisions that would serve under his command in Third Army. But as events would unfold in the weeks ahead, acquiring the 4th Armored would be one of the most fortuitous things that happened to George Patton on that eventful and memorable day.

It is a truism that a military unit is a reflection of its Commander. There is not a better example than the 4th Armored Division, which was truly a reflection of its Commanding General, John S. Wood. The main reason that the 4th would work so smoothly, effectively, and successfully as part of the 3rd Army team was the unusual, unique relationship that existed between the Army Commander and his Division Commander. It is appropriate at this time to describe briefly that relationship.

On this day a wedding took place, an act that joined in close association Gen. Patton and his Third Army with Gen. Wood and his

Fourth Armored Division. It was a marriage made in heaven, and time would develop it into an absolutely splendid union. Patton on that day acquired a rare, invaluable possession, one that would have historic implications for him.

That became quickly evident, for very soon Gen. Patton would make his stunning, momentous sweep across France. It was a tremendous, incomparable military achievement about which historians still salivate. It is universally agreed that the accomplishment ranks as one of the most sturdy pillars upon which Patton's immortality rests. For that operation, as it would be all during the war in Europe, the 4th Armored Division was Patton's spearhead.

Patton and Wood were tankers. They understood mobility, speed, and firepower. Gen. Patton was already a widely known figure. His actions in North Africa and his masterful handling of armor on the restricted island of Sicily had gained for him a very broad and even heroic reputation. He was a daring, imaginative, audacious, visionary. To continue to be successful in the broader, more demanding battle in Europe he would need just the right tool. He found it in Major Gen. John S. Wood's 4th Armored Division. Gen. Wood, unlike Patton at this point, was unknown. Now, many decades after the war, he, among the great captains of that war, still, tragically, remains an unknown.

Gen. Patton graduated from West Point in the class of 1909; Gen. Wood in the class of 1912 (Eisenhower graduated later – 1915). Patton was Wood's Academy senior by three years. Patton, thus, would be Wood's mentor, and Wood would be Patton's *protégé*.

Service in Europe during WW I came not too long after their graduations from West Point, and their friendship and association continued. Wood was in the same class as George Patton at the Staff College in Langres, France. Throughout their careers the paths of these two men crossed and crossed again.

They were both products of the old Army, students of military history, and schooled in audacity. John Wood, like Patton, was bred as a horse soldier. However, with Wood it was Horse Artillery, not Cavalry. Like Patton, Wood was outspoken and did not suffer fools gladly. Their relationship can be best understood by quoting from personal reflections of Gen. Wood:

"Those were… years in which there was time for study and quiet reflection on the nature of war and the shape of wars to come. George Patton, with whom I served at Leavenworth (formerly a Cavalry post and site of the Army's Command and General Staff School) and Hawaii, possessed a splendid library of military works, and we read everything from the maxims of Sun Tsu and Confucius to the latest articles in our own and foreign publications. We often sat, glass in hand, arguing loud and long on war, ancient and modern, with its battles and Commanders. George's delightful wife, Bea, used to stand it as long as she could, and then retire, saying she had never heard two people argue more vociferously on the same side of all questions."

It is perfectly obvious from the above that Patton and Wood were extremely close, perhaps as close as any Army Commander and subordinate Division Commander could ever be. It is important to know more about this individual who played such a critical role in Patton's Third Army successes.

Major General John Shirley "P" Wood (the "P" for professor, a nickname acquired at West Point, and also known as "Tiger Jack," reportedly because he paced back and forth, and also for fearlessly standing up to Gen. Patton) was a bold and daring Commander, as his division's actions had already demonstrated. He would prove to be one of the brightest, most aggressive, and brilliant of the WW II Division Commanders. He would be willing to take risks, and was really the architect of the later rampage by Third Army across France. For weeks, as the 4th Armored went, so went Third Army. Wood's vision set the pattern for armor operations in Europe. He was a Commander who took the bit in his teeth. He never needed prodding. If anything, he needed, on occasion, merely a check rein. Patton understood him.

Much of the fame that Patton would enjoy as a result of his Third Army's sweep across France belonged rightfully to Wood and the 4th Armored Division. To Patton's credit, he acknowledged this debt throughout the summer and fall.

Wood was one of the very few officers in the Allied Armies whom military critic, B. H. Liddell Hart, eminent British historian, military writer, and critic, found alert to the possibilities offered by Hart's own strategic theories of deep armored envelopment and the indirect approach. Hart declared that Wood was, "The Rommel of the American Armored Force, one of the most dynamic Commanders of armor in WW II, and the first in the Allied Armies to demonstrate in Europe the essence of the art and tempo of handling a mobile force."

Some time later, Patton would declare of Wood's 4th Armored Division, "The accomplishments of this division have never been equaled. And by that statement, I do not mean in this war, I mean in the history of warfare. There has never been such a superb fighting organization as the 4th Armored Division."

And so Gen. Patton plotted the strategy, and Gen. Wood executed it. Accomplishing the impossible became routine. They made a great team. As already mentioned, of Third Army's 281 combat days, the 4th Armored was in that Army for 280 of them.

The days and weeks ahead would prove that Patton with a 4th

Armored Division had a distinct and unbeatable advantage over Montgomery, who was without one. The great irony is that even if Monty had had a 4th Armored Division, based on past performance, he would have been at a loss to understand and interact with General Wood and to employ the division effectively.

The 4th Armored Division continued its aggressive sweep south. The Army's official history later put it most succinctly, "A naturally headstrong crew became rambunctious in Brittany." The division quickly and vividly lived up to that portrayal. After reaching the outskirts of Rennes, two combat commands swept around and beyond the city, making it considerably easier for the following infantry to enter and clear the city.

Gen. Wood immediately recognized that he should move out of Brittany as quickly as possible, so as to place his division in position for the main action, which would take place in Central France. Combat Command "B," with my Eighth Tank Battalion leading, made an especially wide sweep around Rennes. During this speedy advance, there was no semblance of organized German forces. Their units had been badly mauled. However, there were pockets of determined and even fanatical resistance, as well as road craters and blown bridges at critical locations. These caused but temporary delays, and the Eighth, after pushing hard and fast, stopped at a location near Chateaubriant, which was well southeast of Rennes. It was exciting to realize that we were now perfectly poised and positioned. We had a clear corridor all the way to the Loire. What a glorious opportunity for a wholesale blitzkrieg operation to the east! We just knew that our next orders would have us thrusting and hurtling rapidly in the direction of Germany.

But on August 4 the heavens caved in upon us. We were stunned, staggered and shocked. Gen. Wood received unbelievable, and, to him, incomprehensible orders. He was told to turn his back on the east, and drive to the southwest. Astonishing! He was ordered to have his Combat Command "A" move and seize the port city of Vannes, and Combat Command "B" was to advance further west, with its objective the well-known port of Lorient. *These were port cities on the Atlantic.* At the same time, the 6th Armored Division was to make the long dash to the westernmost port of Brest.

The decisions to effect these moves were illogical and alarming. The Normandy breakout was highly successful, the capture of Avranches was a strategic and tactical triumph, the seizure of Rennes a vital necessity, and the sweep around Rennes to the environs of Chateaubriant masterful. All this led to the next obvious step – attack full steam ahead to the east.

There appeared to be no question that higher Headquarters was blindly following the OVERLORD script for that western turn into

Brittany. They were doggedly sticking to their pre-invasion plans of capturing the Brittany ports. Their claim was that they needed Brest's port facilities, as well as those of the south Brittany ports of Vannes and Lorient. They considered these vital to the maintenance and supply of the anticipated Army movements through France. However, those plans were based upon a scenario which predicted a slow, orderly German retreat across France, with the Brittany ports as bases for supply.

The breakout at Avranches, however, changed all that. The plans no longer applied. Rigidly sticking to those plans was a major mistake, a costly blunder. In one fell swoop it seriously disrupted the momentum gained after the Normandy breakout. Many voices later claimed that it was one of the most colossally stupid decisions of the war.

To his senior Commanders, Gen. Wood immediately protested such employment strenuously and vehemently. He reminded them in no uncertain terms that the enemy was located to the east, and that the war was not going to be won by going west. He declared, "We're winning the war the wrong way, we ought to be going toward Paris." He predicted that the Germans would be well dug in, and would strongly defend the ports; that the ports would be destroyed, before they were over-run or surrendered; and that once in American hands, they would be unusable. He pointed out to them that he could have the 4th Armored Division at Chartres (175 miles NE of Rennes) in two days. Further, that by blazing a path for Third Army, the 4th Armored could open the way to *cutting off the Germans at the Seine*. But it was not until August 15 that Wood was, finally, permitted to turn the division to the east. By that time two weeks were wasted, and the glittering opportunity was long lost. Suffice to say, the high command did not appreciate being reminded by a lowly Division Commander that they were winning the war the wrong way.

But in all of this, where was the shrill, squeaky voice of Patton? *(And his voice was high and squeaky, as those of us who had heard him speak were aware)*. Its silence was deafening. This is exactly the kind of scenario that would have had him charging out of his corner with both arms flailing away. He would have ranted and raved, and rightfully castigated his superiors for their stupidity. Instead, he remained silent, and let his subordinate Commander do the "heavy lifting" by protesting alone. His conduct is understandable when one recognizes and understands that in those early and crucial days in Brittany, Patton was dealing from a position of weakness when it came to challenging the authority of Bradley, Eisenhower, and Ike's senior staff. Patton, after long weeks under wraps and in the dog-house with his military career in jeopardy, well understood that he was extremely fortunate to find himself commanding anything. He was only too well aware that another serious mis-step and it would be all over for him. He just could not take such a chance with less than a handful of days under his belt in his new war. It was the case of burnt child dreads fire.

Wood, on the other hand, was sticking his neck out, but did not care. He was speaking up for something that he definitely believed had to be aired. It was reported that he raged at Patton for not fighting for this golden opportunity to exploit to the east, and for, apparently, failing to grasp the array of possibilities open to the 4th Armored Division, including a thrust through the virtually unprotected Orleans gap. Patton, on the other hand, was concerned that Wood was being too aggressive, and ordered him to ease up and toe the line. Alone and disillusioned, Wood even began to regard his friend and Commander as "one of them."

So, two powerful, valuable Armored Divisions, the 4th and 6th – the backbone of General Patton's recently activated Third Army – would turn their backs to the enemy and their ultimate objective, and drive as fast as they could *away* from the main war.

Combat Command "B" led by my Eighth Tank Battalion began its drive to Lorient early on the morning of August 6. We continued to apply the tactics that had thus far worked so well for us. The enemy defended as best they could with pockets of heavy resistance, blown bridges, and road craters, but we were relentless. By the afternoon of the 7th we were already at the gates of Lorient, only 3 km. away, when we were stopped absolutely dead cold. We were hit by the most powerful, massive, accurate fire of the war, thus far. The enemy rolled a carpet of fire from the city right to our forward elements. The fire came from long-range artillery pieces, powerful naval guns, and high-velocity direct fire from leveled anti-aircraft guns. It was murderous, and caused numerous casualties. We discovered later that forward observers hidden in trees out from the city were responsible for the responsive and accurate fire.

It became instantly evident that Lorient was dug-in and ready to fight. It would be heavily defended. The city was a classic built-up area. An attack upon the city would require house-to-house, street-to-street fighting, which was absolutely not a mission for an Armored Division. So we pulled back, out of range, and waited to see how much time it would take for the high command to reorient its thinking, and send us back to where we belonged. In the meantime we laid siege to the city. Nothing could get in or out. We played havoc with trains and trucks trying to get in. They carried men, supplies, and equipment, and their losses were tremendous.

It took nearly a week, but we were, finally, relieved. We were ordered to move back to a location not too far from where our odyssey began. Without hesitation we mounted up, turned 'em over, and headed east. It was late on the afternoon of August 14. when our tank tracks began to move. Little did we know then, as we moved away from Lorient, that the city which had been only 3 km. from our advance elements, and which we estimated and predicted was dug in and ready to fight, did exactly that. The Germans in the city kept American forces at bay for ten months, *and held out for the remainder of the war.*

However, our minds at that point were concentrated on the task ahead. Darkness came soon, but instead of slowing down, we pushed ahead. We had embarked on what would be an historic forced march. Except for brief stops, we moved relentlessly until the afternoon of August 16th. We finally stopped near Chateau Renault. We had traveled (this in tanks) 264 miles in 24 hours. It would turn out to be the longest sustained march of the war. A few days later, Gen. Patton would tell his staff that elements of this Third Army had advanced farther and faster than any Army units in history.

Not long after our historic march had ended, we heard electrifying news. Combat Command "A," which had been withdrawn from the vicinity of Vannes before we left Lorient, and had a shorter distance to travel, took advantage of this jump start and had on that day captured the large, historic and critically important city of Orleans. The city was approximately fifty miles to the northeast of our position, and nearly directly south of Paris. By holding Orleans, Third Army and the 4th Armored Division had a firm toe-hold from which to kick off, when it resumed its offensive to the east. We, at Combat Command "B" would, thus, have a "free ride" for many miles, until we came abreast of Combat Command "A."

The units of Combat Command "B" needed a brief breathing spell to recover from their grueling Lorient experience. Vehicles and weapons badly needed maintenance, and the troops required a bit of a rest. But, they were soon closed up on CC "A's" current position.

Our Lorient "adventure" was a tragedy. It was extremely costly, and accomplished absolutely nothing. Men and machines had been badly punished, precious time was spent, and already half of the glorious days of August were gone. Tanks had made a needless round trip of approximately 500 miles – 500 miles of wear on tracks, 500 miles of wear on engines. Thousands of gallons of scarce and precious fuel were consumed, thousands of rounds of ammunition expended, men wounded, precious lives lost, vehicles damaged and destroyed. Yes, the enemy suffered much heavier casualties, but they would not have been in the main fight, anyway.

Now we were in virtually the same location from where it had all started. All for what? If they were honest with themselves, it must have been galling for members of the high command to recognize that Gen. Wood's protestations had been perceptive and with complete foundation.

There was one great, big bright spot. Gen. Patton now knew that he had exactly the right troops for the challenges ahead. They had demonstrated that they could pick up quickly with a minimum of instructions, move in any direction, advance rapidly and relentlessly, roam far and wide, leave destruction in their wake, exhibit stamina and endurance, and get the job done. Now Gen. Patton and those troops would be facing new trials and challenges. Little did they realize that in a remarkably short time they would spearhead the Allied advance by making an absolutely unprecedented sweep across the widest part of France, and move close to the German border. It would be a masterful campaign. Historians would label it one of the great achievements in military history, and another Patton triumph. It would gain for him a big step toward military immortality.

CHAPTER 10

GENERAL BERNARD LAW MONTGOMERY – GENERAL GEORGE S. PATTON, JR.: AUGUST 1 – AUGUST 15, 1944, HEAD TO HEAD.

The actions just described feature my 4th Armored Division. From reading that account it might lead one to assume that Third Army was merely a one-division Army. The actions that will be described for the second two weeks of August would appear to confirm that impression. Yet, on the contrary, Patton's Third Army was a broad, powerful force. The 4th Armored Division had fought under VIII Corps (Gen. Middleton) from the breakout in Normandy to, and then all the way across, Brittany. When the 4th Armored turned east and left Lorient and Brittany, it also left behind the VIII Corps. That organization would command and control the forces left behind in Brittany. For the 4th's subsequent offensive operations it would be in XII Corps, commanded initially by Maj. Gen. Gilbert R. Cook and subsequently by Maj. Gen. Manton S. Eddy. Also under Patton's command was the XX Corps, commanded by Maj. Gen. Walton S. Walker, and XV Corps, commanded by Maj. Gen. Wade H. Haislip. During August, Gen. Patton would have in his Army nine divisions, of which six would be infantry.

While the 4th Armored and VIII Corps were engaged in Brittany, tanks of Patton's XV Corps emerged from the bottleneck at Pontaubault, just south of Avranches, and headed southeast in typical American armor fashion. Their initial objectives were Mayenne and Laval. In less than half a day they advanced 30 miles against virtually no resistance. Without pausing even for a deep breath, they continued to push hard, and three and a half days later they had advanced another 45 miles. On August 8, XV Corps took Le Mans, which had been the Headquarters city of the German Seventh Army. This put Gen. Haislip directly south of Alencon, and he was now perfectly positioned to turn north to that city and beyond to Argentan. He was now 85 miles southeast of Avranches, and was ideally located, as well, to make an encirclement to the east that could threaten two German Armies.

On the 8th, while Haislip was taking Le Mans, my Eighth Tank Battalion and other elements of Combat Command "B" were holding onto the outskirts of Lorient on the Atlantic, which we had reached the day before. Patton's Sixth Armored Division was closing in on the big port of Brest.

Gen. Patton's other two Corps, the XII and the XX, would be operating farther south of Haislip's XV Corps. They would be heading east with parallel sweeps along the Loire River.

Events were occurring in Normandy that would become critical, and would force Patton to turn his head away from the 4th Armored in Brittany and his other two corps, as well. The actions taking place in Normandy now required his full attention, and then some.

Hitler had ordered an attack to the west through Mortain in an effort to reach the coast at Avranches. If it were successful, he would have separated the First and Third American Armies, and by turning north could have driven some of the Allies into the sea, and trapped some divisions in the south. He had quickly gathered up four Panzer Divisions, and they on August 6 were poised to strike toward Avranches. Then out of the darkness on the night of August 6/7, they attempted to do just that. Without the warning or benefit of an artillery preparation, the Germans attacked and achieved tactical surprise.

Earlier, Gen. Montgomery, still tasting the fruits of the Allied successes in Normandy, felt sure that the next decisive battle would be fought for the crossings of the Seine, and he had other Allied Generals sharing his opinion. Because he believed that there would be no German counter-attack, he was planning for one more assault on August 8. upon that most formidable and completely frustrating obstacle, the Bourguebous Ridge, which still stood between Caen and Falaise. His operation would be called TOTALIZE. His rationale for predicting no counter-attack was his belief that the German concentration north of Domfront, about 25 kilometers southeast of Mortain, was insufficient to produce a counter-attack strong enough to reverse the battle in Normandy. Patton was not quite ready to accept Montgomery's forecast, and was uneasy, and on August 6. his well-known battle sense warned him that the enemy was "genuinely up to something."

That "something" was the counterattack that overran Mortain from the north and south and plunged southeastward. That advance had nearly reached St. Hilaire du Harcouet by noon. At that point the Germans were within 15 km. of reaching Avranches. Panic!! However, the enemy was repulsed by heroic infantry actions, and driven back. They were battered all the while by the magnificent American artillery, and they had absolutely no surcease from American air support which had the Germans constantly in their sights, and pounded them mercilessly. American forces were soon back in control, and the alarming threat was temporarily blunted.

Although the immediate threat to Avranches had been stopped, the battle was far from over. The fighting continued around Mortain all day long on August 8. There appeared to be no decision, as both sides held on to their positions. However, Field Marshal Gunther von Kluge, the senior German Commander, was a realist, and recognized the futility of still trying to push ahead in the Mortain area. He feared that his forces would become too deeply entangled, and he decided that it was time to pull back, or face the possibility that all of Army Group B would be trapped and destroyed. The senior officers on the ground were appalled when, on August 9, Hitler ordered an even stronger attack toward Avranches. Kluge, dragging his heels, postponed renewing the attack from August 9 to the 11 Hitler, in the meantime, pulled Gen. Heinrich Eberbach from the Falaise area, and sent him to lead a new charge toward Avranches.

When Eberbach made his assessment of the situation at Mortain, he declared that he could not be ready to follow Hitler's desires until August 20. Hitler still insisted on August 11, but the new attack was never able to unfold.

By the evening of August 10, the Germans were well aware that the American XV Corps was now heading north out of Le Mans, which made plain the threat of a double envelopment. The German generals on the ground agreed, and tried to convince Hitler that continuing efforts toward Avranches had no prospect of success, and had to be terminated. They had to get into position to blunt the XV Corps spearhead, which would soon be threatening Alencon, and after that – Argentan. There were heated discussions by Hitler and his generals all day long on the 11th, after which Hitler approved only a minor withdrawal around Mortain, but still insisted that there would be a later renewal of the counterattack to Avranches and the waters of the English Channel. Kluge had already alerted his troops for a withdrawal, and was pushing his forces to block the 5th Armored Division of XV Corps below Argentan.

While heavy fighting continued at Mortain on August 8, Montgomery on that day launched his operation TOTALIZE. For the operation Montgomery gave the mission to Gen. Crerar of the Canadian First Army, who in turn assigned it to the most experienced officer, Lt. General G. S. Simonds. He developed a considerably different plan. He opened operation TOTALIZE on August 8 without the heavy aerial bombing in front of the attack as in GOODWOOD, so that his attackers would not be handicapped by the craters and rubble which immediately followed heavy aerial bombing. His plan had his forces attacking during the darkness of 7/8 August. The reason for this choice was to make it more difficult for German artillery on Bourguebous (yes, the very same ridge), which had stopped the forces in GOODWOOD, to cause extensive damage to forces once again attacking it.

And as with GOODWOOD, there were some wrong turns and traffic jams. Despite this, the attack gained its first objective, and by dawn on the 8th the attackers had advanced five kilometers. Alack and alas, as before, a ground mist in the early daylight hours delayed further advance, and gave the enemy time to reorganize for a counterattack. What had initially been a good possibility of turning the penetration into a COBRA-like breakthrough, never happened.

However, the usual errors which continued to plague and bog-down British/Canadian operations were very much in evidence. The forces stopped to deal with strong points, rather than by-passing them (could learn a lesson from the 4th Armored Division), and they stopped the attack completely overnight on August 8/9, after gaining some thirteen kilometers.

There was short bombing by an air attack, causing casualties; time was provided to the Germans to withdraw to a line of prepared positions; and the period August 9/14 was utilized for regrouping and mounting diversionary attacks.

Crerar was, finally, ready on August 14. Simonds attacked again as he did to open TOTALIZE, but this time, rather than using darkness, he used smoke. At last, the Canadians were able to advance, and moved within five kilometers of Falaise. Through August 15 and 16, the Germans hung tenaciously to the last ridge before the town. On the 16th a Canadian force made a flank attack from the west. After a long day's fight on August 17, Falaise was at last secured.

Back to the Mortain action. On August 11, three days after TOTALIZE had kicked off, the Germans were heatedly debating their next courses of action, especially how to keep the Allies from effecting a double envelopment. Conversely, Montgomery was considering all the factors that would enable him to do just that – to complete the double envelopment which the Germans so feared. It must be remembered that Montgomery, at that time, was more than just the 21st Army Group Commander. He was also the overall Allied Ground Commander, and would be until Eisenhower assumed that role at the beginning of next month.

It was in this role that he made some decisions that would later haunt him, and be difficult and awkward for even him to explain away. He now had two pincers moving, XV Corps moving north, and his Canadians attacking south from Caen toward Falaise and Argentan. Montgomery believed that the Germans would react to the threat of the Allied pincers by shifting forces from Mortain or committing troops from farther east. He decided that the Americans would encounter more difficult terrain, reminiscent of that found earlier in Normandy, in the Alencon/Argentan area. He believed that, because of this, the Germans would throw their strength against the American threat, and the result would be that the Americans would make less progress in the next few days than his Canadians. With this reasoning, he assumed that the Canadians would reach Argentan from the north, before the Americans were able to reach it from the south.

He made another fateful decision. He decided to retain the existing boundary between his own 21st Army Group and Bradley's 12th Army Group, and ordered the Americans to stop XV Corps just south of Argentan. Even as he was making his decisions, events to the north provided a strong indication that what he had decided was unsound and already a cause for great concern. The Canadian attack had been bogged down for three days. So much for Montgomery's prediction that the Canadians would beat the Americans to Argentan.

As early as August 12, Bradley's staff were grumbling that "the British effort ... appeared to have logged itself in timidity and succumbed to the legendary Montgomery vice of over-caution." The Americans, on the contrary, were on August 12. streaking past Alencon, and the next day were on the outskirts of Argentan. They had already been sitting at that town for more than a day, before Crerar even began his attack along the River Laison, still a few kilometers from Falaise. Haislip was convinced that he could continue his rapid advance all the way to Falaise, where he could link up with the Canadians, and together they could seal the German escape route, and trap those two German Armies. On August 16, while Crerar was closing in on Falaise, there was an open door of about 25 kilometers through which Field Marshal Kluge's Armies would be racing, to escape being trapped by the Allied enveloping forces.

As early as August 8, Bradley had recognized the exciting possibility that the Germans could be trapped and destroyed. That it was more than something that had just crossed his mind became clearly evident when he talked to a distinguished visitor that day at his Headquarters. He was called upon by Secretary of the Treasury, Henry Morgenthau, Jr., and during their chat, he really opened up. He told the Secretary that he had "an opportunity that comes to a Commander not more than once in a century. We're about to destroy an entire hostile Army."

It turned out that Bradley, like Montgomery, "blew it." He would be every bit as responsible, as culpable, as his British counterpart for what happened and what did not happen. He, too, would have great difficulty explaining away his decisions. They were difficult to understand then, and are still debated today. The fact remains that the two Army Group Commanders squandered an unprecedented opportunity. As a result, a surprisingly large portion of the German Army that was to be destroyed somehow slipped through the noose that never was completely tightened. Not only were the decisions extremely controversial, but, more than that, they constituted one of the very great blunders of WWII in Europe.

There have been many recriminations, rationalizations, explanations, admissions. Simply stated, the reasons the gap was never closed were that Bradley initially ordered Haislip's XV Corps stopped at Argentan; that Montgomery subsequently insisted that the Army Group boundaries hold; that Haislip's forces not cross that boundary; and that Bradley did not fight against, or even object strongly to, Monty's decision. The British General insisted that it would be the Canadians moving from the north that would close the gap.

Patton believed that Montgomery was using this situation as a kind of redemption. By the middle of August, British prestige had suffered greatly. While the actions of the Americans from the breakout in Normandy bordered on the sensational and were monopolizing the headlines, Montgomery had been confined to his tiny corner at Caen. Here was a grand opportunity for his Army to gain some respect and some of the glory at last.

Of all the senior Allied Generals, it was Patton who seemed to have the best grasp of the situation, to be on top of it. Early on, it was he who seemed to have the vision, who viewed "the whole playing field." He was again exhibiting his sixth sense, his great "battle sense." As early as August 11, Patton doubted Montgomery's ability to move south through Falaise fast enough to close the Falaise-Argentan gap, before the Germans slipped through. So that day he told Haislip to be ready to push his XV Corps through and past Alencon, to seize Argentan, and then press on to Falaise. Patton recognized that with XV Corps moving out so rapidly they might at some point be over-extended and be out on a limb, and that they might need to be reinforced. So on that date he reached all the way back deep into Brittany for his favorite division, the 4th Armored. He called Gen. Wood to alert him for possible movement to the east to become part of Haislip's pincer. He also directed Gen. Walker to move his XX Corps from the Mayenne/Le Mans area toward Carrouges, so as to be able to cover Haislip's left flank. He also had his XII Corps positioning itself so as to move parallel to the Loire, heading in the direction of Orleans. But it, too, could swing north, if needed. So his three Corps were widely separated, but moving, moving. This, obviously, was not a General who was content to sit on his hands. Furthermore, there was nothing promising about the actions of the Canadians to the north that would cause Patton to erase his skepticism about their ability to close the gap. So Patton ordered his XV Corps to push on through Argentan and on to Falaise. He told his Chief of Staff to instruct Haislip to "push on slowly in the direction of Falaise, allowing your rear element to close. Road: Argentan-Falaise your left boundary inclusive. Upon arrival Falaise, continue to push on slowly until you contact our Allies."

To get official approval for what he was doing Patton called Bradley and reported, "We now have elements in Argentan. Shall we continue and drive the British into the sea for another Dunkirk?" Bradley immediately answered, "Nothing doing. You're not to go beyond Argentan." Bradley's orders were so firm and unequivocal that Patton immediately halted all movement to the north.

In the late morning of August 13. the 12th Army Group Chief of Staff, Gen. Allen, called Gen. Gaffey, Patton's Chief of Staff, "to reiterate and underline Bradley's decision to restrict Patton to the inter-allied boundary. Under no circumstances was the boundary to be crossed. The XV Corps must halt at once." Here was a case of more than one pair of hands tugging at the reins of an unruly, unpredictable mount to keep him from charging ahead.

But Patton was not yet finished. He tried to get to Bradley with one more plea. Bradley, however, was not available, as he was at SHAEF Advance Headquarters. Not being able to talk to Bradley, Patton pleaded that Allen urge Bradley to speak to Montgomery. When Allen reached Bradley, he was with Eisenhower. *Bradley urged that the Army Group boundary continue to be observed.* Once again, as in North Africa and Sicily, Ike appeared more like a bystander than a Commander. He rubber-stamped Bradley, and *agreed to let the halt order to Haislip stand.* Allen was instructed to provide Patton with the decision.

While this was unfolding, Bradley's G3, General Kibler, had telephoned the Chief of Staff of Montgomery's 21st Army Group to seek Montgomery's permission for an advance beyond Argentan. The Chief of Staff, also, flashed the red light in front of the Third Army. And that was that.

Soon after, Patton told Gaffey, "*The question why XV Corps halted on the east/west line through Argentan is certain to become of historical importance.* [How right he was!] I want a stenographic record of this conversation with General Allen included in the history of Third Army."

Three days later, Patton, writing in his diary, had this to say, "I believe that the [halt] order ... emanated from the 21st Army Group, and was either due to the jealousy of the Americans, or to utter ignorance of the situation, or a combination of the two. It is very regrettable that XV Corps was ordered to halt, because it would have gone on to Falaise and made contact with the Canadians northwest of that point, and definitely and positively closed the escape gap."

By this time Panzers and SS troops leading the withdrawal were already slicing through the gap. The foot-dragging of Montgomery's forces totally dismayed and infuriated Patton, who watched helplessly and with disbelief as his enemy continued fleeing. Patton raged at Montgomery's failure and his blunder, but was especially incensed that he had been prohibited from closing the gap himself.

It did not help Patton's composure to receive frequent reports from his intelligence officer describing the numbers of enemy that were escaping the trap. At some point he was seething, and told Gen. Bradley, "Hell, by now they've all gotten out."

But as was so typical of Patton, he did not stop to cry over spilt milk. He was once again looking ahead, shrewdly gauging his next move. He told Bradley, 'There is nothing out front, nothing at all between me and the Seine." He was envisioning a second, wider envelopment. Bradley seemed to agree, for he began to shift the main effort of his armies to the east.

Although Patton decried the circumstances that permitted so many of the enemy to escape, he was realistic enough to know that there were very, very many of the Germans who were not able to make it out.

The gap never closed, but it had narrowed. The retreating Germans were under constant fire. Eisenhower later described the pocket as "one of the greatest killing grounds of any of the war areas." The official U.S. Army report later related, "The carnage wrought during the final days as artillery of the two Allied Armies and the massed Air Force pounded the ever-shrinking pocket was perhaps the greatest of the war. The roads and fields were littered with thousands of enemy dead and wounded; wrecked and burning vehicles; smashed artillery pieces; carts loaded with the loot of France, overturned and smoldering; dead horses and cattle swelling in the summer heat."

The defeat suffered by the Germans was one of their worst. The numbers of men who were caught in the pocket, and those who escaped, can be only roughly estimated. Figures compiled by the Allies, as can be expected, vary from those of the Germans. The best guess on the casualties are that there were about 10,000 Germans killed and approximately 50,000 captured. Other losses included more than 220 tanks, 860 artillery pieces, 7,130 miscellaneous vehicles destroyed, and 2,000 horses killed. These figures can be debated and adjusted, but by any measurement they are just plain appalling.

It is even more difficult to arrive at a figure for the number of troops who escaped. The Germans have claimed that 40 to 50 percent of the trapped forces made it out safely. That appears quite high when placed against the backdrop of the carnage that choked the roads and fields. A figure that appears acceptable is that about 40,000 Germans escaped through the noose that was never tightened and the gap which so easily could have been closed.

It is absolutely amazing that with the "tornado" resulting from Allied fire, and the slaughter for which there was no discrimination, that among those who escaped were one Army Commander, four Corps Commanders, and twelve Division Commanders. These were senior leaders who were running, but who would turn to fight another day in critically important leadership roles.

On the subject of leadership roles, it is appropriate to pause for a moment to examine, highlight, and summarize briefly the combat accomplishments of our two principals – Montgomery and Patton – during the first two weeks of August. Montgomery had a tremendous combat head start on Patton. As is well known, Montgomery's combat began on D-Day, June 6, and continued without pause to August 1; that meant that Monty already had 56 combat days under his belt on the day that George was facing his first.

On August 1, as has been described, Montgomery's forces after those many combat days were still confined to the area in and around Caen. It was not until eight days into the month that Montgomery would make another major effort to free himself from the shackles of Caen and move toward Falaise. It would take his forces until the 17th. before they had control of that city.

But what of Patton? What did he accomplish by August 8, the day Montgomery's TOTALIZE kicked off? What he did was just plain incredible! On August 8, Patton's VIIIth Corps had forces along the Atlantic. His XV Corps had seized Le Mans, was 85 miles southeast of Rennes and about 115 miles southeast of Avranches, and was poised to turn north toward Alencon and Argentan. His XIIth and XXth Corps were south of XV Corps, parallel to the Loire, and advancing to the east to position themselves for the big drive soon to come across the wide part of France, and were ever ready for the radio transmission that would turn them north, if XV Corps needed help.

What is stunning and difficult to comprehend—soon after the 1st of August, Patton had forces simultaneously streaking *west and east*. In a little over a week he had his elements flying in all directions—"all over the landscape." It was truly amazing and completely without precedent that in a matter of days he was fighting a two-front war 500 miles apart, and at the same time protecting his 485-mile right flank.

Astonishing!

Less than a week later, on the 13th, Haislip's XV Corps reached Argentan, the southern handle of the pincer, while Montgomery's forces would not take control of Falaise, the northern handle, until the 17th, leaving the gap between.

The contrast between the accomplishments of Montgomery and Patton during this brief period could not be more starkly defined and delineated – a remarkable difference.

In a very few days the Argentan-Falaise battles would be finished. The British, Canadian, and American units, like unfettered colts, would surge eastward. Normandy would be behind them, and a large part of France in front of them would stand liberated.

CHAPTER 11

GENERAL BERNARD LAW MONTGOMERY –
GENERAL GEORGE S. PATTON, JR.:
HEAD TO HEAD,
AUGUST 16 – AUGUST 31, 1944.

On August 14, after a staff conference, Gen. Patton discussed, briefly, the accomplishments of Third Army up to that point. In recalling those achievements it seemed incredible that they spanned a mere *two weeks*. Yet, two weeks was the extent of the life of that Army, since it had been committed to action. Patton was justifiably very proud, and no one could challenge him when he boasted, again, "the Third Army has advanced further and faster than any Army in the history of war." He could have added "and in the shortest period of time."

Never one to be content to pause and rest on his laurels, he was soon driving, advancing once again, and always looking well ahead. Now the Seine River was in his sights, and was his next significant objective. He had his XV Corps with its 5th Armored Division headed for a crossing of the Eure River at Dreux. His eyes were focused, as well, to his south. There, Gen. Walker's lightly manned XXth Corps had captured Angers on the Loire. The arrival of the 7th Armored Division served to "soup up" XXth Corps, and Patton had them heading for the Eure as well, toward the large cathedral city of Chartres. Units newly arrived in France were quickly absorbed into XIIth Corps, and that corps, led by elements of the 4th Armored Division with the 35th Infantry Division in close support, were aiming at Orleans. His Army, recently restrained by the Argentan-Falaise episode, had been released from Bradley's "stop order" and was again a free spirit, and was charging hard once more in all directions. By the 16th of August, Third Army held those important prizes, Dreux, Chartres, and Orleans.

Not long after, on the 18th, forces of Haislip's XV Corps reached, with little difficulty, Mantes on the Seine. Yes, the first of the Allies were established on the Seine, and they were from the Third Army. That location was some forty kilometers on a bee-line northwest of Paris. What is striking, once again, was the expansiveness of Patton's Third Army. His was still a broad, broad Army front.

By reaching the city of Mantes, XV Corps had already entered the zone of the 21st Army Group. Because he could not argue with success and had nothing better to offer, Montgomery this time did not object, and his mood was described as "expansive." To advance further would carry Haislip squarely across the paths of the British Second and Canadian First Armies. The senior Allied Commanders agreed that Haislip should exploit his capture of Mantes by establishing a bridgehead on the right bank, as well.

Patton and General Wyche of the 79th Division, XV Corps, had together been wondering if they should seize that opportunity to cross the Seine. During the evening of August 19th, Wyche received the order to "Go," and on that night. The division was eminently successful, and by the next afternoon there were trucks, tanks, tank destroyers, and artillery across the river. *The first units across the Seine were elements of Third Army.* Patton immediately directed his other two corps, the XIIth And XXth., to pass through the Paris/Orleans gap to the Seine south of Paris. Walker's XXth Corps was ordered on August 21st to push to Melun and Montereaux. From Orleans the XIIth Corps was given the mission of leaping 100 kilometers to the east, with its objective Sens on the Yonne River. As was so characteristic of him, Patton was still thinking big.

Back in the action at Mantes, XV Corps was ordered to make a sharp left turn, and drive down the Seine with its objective Louviers, another big jump – this time 50 kilometers. When they reached Louviers, they would not be too far from that major city, Rouen.

It had been Patton – Patton, with little mention of the American First Army, or the British and Canadian armies. On August 20, the day that XVth Corps was heading for Louviers, the senior Commanders recognized that the American First Army had been squeezed out of the northern front. They now deemed it wise to move XIXth Corps of First Army into action, and to commit it alongside XVth Corps to reinforce that corps' left flank in its drive down the Seine toward Rouen.

At this time a significant change took place in Patton's XII Corps. Its Commander, Gen. Cook, had to be replaced for medical reasons – apparently a circulatory problem. His successor was Maj. Gen. Manton S. Eddy, who had distinguished himself in the successful employment of the 9th Infantry Division. Eddy was a doughboy, and had had no experience with armor. Patton later related that Eddy, upon assuming command, apparently, quickly recognizing that the right flank of his Corps was open and unprotected, asked Patton how much concerned he should be about that flank, as he moved east out of Orleans. Patton said, "I told him that depended on how nervous he was." Then Patton added, "He had been thinking a mile a day was good going. I told him to go fifty, and he turned pale." As events would unfold in the weeks that followed, Eddy, on occasion, would have difficulty understanding and accepting his orders from Patton. He would also have a hard time predicting the actions of, and trying to rein in, that aggressive and ebullient subordinate Commander, "Tiger Jack" Wood, of the 4th Armored Division. Wood, on the other hand, believed that he was eminently successful *despite*, at times, his Corps Commander.

By August 22, elements of Gen. Corlett's U.S. XIX Corps captured Elbeuf. This placed his forces a relatively short distance southwest of Rouen. During their advance, XVth and XIXth Corps drove all the way across the British Second Army front, and into the zone of the First Canadian Army.

The British and Canadians, finally, made their presence known. Elements of Canadian General Crerar's Army began attacking eastward across the Dives River near the coast on August 16. He had a difficult fight with units of the German Fifth Panzer Army. On August 22, the Canadian Army, about 28 miles northeast of Falaise and with about 40 yet to go to the Seine, finally reached and crossed the Tougues.

It was not until August 26th that the Canadian Army made contact with the American XIXth Corps in the vicinity of Elbeuf, nearing the Seine and southeast of Rouen. The British, at last, got into the picture, with Gen. Dempsey's British Second Army also connecting with the XIXth Corps, along the Risle River.

However, it appears that the British could not have pressed too hard, for the Germans, using every means at their disposal and plenty of ingenuity, were still successful in fleeing across the Seine with substantial numbers of men, vehicles and equipment. They used a surprisingly large number of ferries, as well as pontoon bridges, and rafts improvised from cider barrels and limbs lashed together. Their final major crossings took place during August 26. and 27, with some ferries still intact and functioning.

It was certainly time for the American elements to pull back to the south and return to the American zone, which they did. With the Americans gone, the British and Canadians closed up toward the river. By the last week in August they would be sitting on the Seine all the way from Vernon to the coast.

Sometime later, British Gen. Dempsey, apparently stung by some criticism he had received, and endeavoring to rationalize what appeared to be a lack of aggressiveness of his troops and less than spectacular achievements, strongly complained that his advance to the Seine was delayed because the Americans got in his way. Bradley quickly countered by pointing out that when the British Second Army started its advance to the east, the German elements had been forced to the north. Thus, Dempsey was able to advance rapidly and without opposition, because the movement of the British forces was through territory that had already been taken by American forces.

XVth Corps was now, and had been for quite some time, a long way from the other two corps, the bulk of Patton's Third Army, and they were near First Army and had already been operating with one of its corps. So it made a great deal of sense to shift command of XVth Corps from Third Army to First Army. The effective date of this change was August 24.

With the XVth Corps gone from his command, and the VIIIth Corps "out of action" in Brittany, Patton could now concentrate on the actions and objectives of his two remaining Corps, the XIIth. and XXth. The Mortain-Argentan-Falaise episode was about to close, and it is safe to say that there was not too much glory to be passed out among the Allied leaders. Patton had to be an exception, for he certainly deserved some plaudits. His forces had been continually on the move and "accomplishing," because of his inspired leadership and vision.

Montgomery, by contrast, erred over and over by misjudging and over-estimating the rate of advance of the Canadians, and by failing to have forces in place to envelope the retreating Germans. If Eisenhower needed an invitation to take over as Allied Ground Commander, Montgomery certainly provided him with one, because of his role in fumbling the closing of the Argentan-Falaise gap.

Even as early as August 21st, before he knew that he would lose his XVth Corps, Patton, the visionary, was, again, looking well ahead. He recorded in his diary the plans he visualized for an advance well beyond the Seine. He wrote, "We have, at this time, the greatest chance to win the war ever presented. If they let me move on with three corps, two up and one back, on the line Metz-Nancy-Epinal, we can be in Germany in ten days." In a little over a week, after he penned those words, he would be stunned and crushed to learn that he would *not* have the opportunity of moving into Germany, any time soon.

Also on the day he made his diary entries, his XIIth. and XXth Corps set off through the gap between Paris and Orleans, and moved hard and fast toward their next big hurdle, the upper Seine. Their rapid advance was most encouraging to Patton, for it served to make credible his diary boast that he would soon be thrusting his way toward the open door into Germany.

Gen. Wood, once again, had his 4th Armored Division on a tear. They quickly leaped the 110 kilometers from Orleans to Sens, and by August 22, they were through Sens and across the Yonne. Then they moved another 65 kilometers from the Yonne to Troyes. They were already sitting on the objective which just a few days before had seemed a target that was way, way "out there." By the evening of August 25, CC "A" of the 4th Armored had the bulk of its tactical elements across the Seine at that city. It is significant to note that Patton's forces *were the first to cross both the upper and lower Seine.*

It is appropriate to pause briefly once again to examine and appreciate the great significance of the situation then existing.

Sitting at Troyes astride the upper Seine, a sizeable force of the 4th Armored Division found themselves approximately 160 kilometers *southeast* of Paris. On this same day, the 25th, the bulk of the British and Canadian forces were closing in on the lower Seine. Two days earlier troops from Montgomery's 21st Army Group had just begun crossing the Seine at a small bridgehead established by the British Second Army in the vicinity of Vernon. Montgomery's Armored Divisions were still some distance away. As the forces of the 21st Army Group were closing in on the river, the Germans were still successfully withdrawing forces across the river, and would continue to do so for the next two days. It was near the end of the month before the British and Canadians would close up to the Seine from Vernon to the coast, and be ready to launch their major crossings.

Vernon was located about 80 kilometers *northwest of Paris*. That meant that the 4th Armored Division was about *190 kilometers east of the longitude* of Vernon as "the crow flies." That distance would increase most significantly, if it measured the twists and turns in the roads between Vernon and Troyes, and could reach at least 240 kilometers as the actual distance between the two forces. On the 26th., 27th, and 28th., elements of the 4th Armored would continue their rapid advance to the east, which would widen the gap even more between the moving 4th and the British and Canadians who were settling in along the lower Seine. An astonishing difference!

With that great objective, the Seine, in hand, what next?

Bradley set about strengthening the Third Army. He had the 90th Infantry Division from Argentan join Walker's XXth Corps, and he moved the 80th Infantry Division from Orleans to Eddy's XIIth Corps. He was even considering returning to Patton the XVth Corps.

Patton urged Bradley to concur that his next objective would be the Meuse River. Bradley, who the day before had been forced to reduce authorized levels of supplies, particularly gasoline, believed that the closer Marne was a more realistic objective. Third Army was so severely outrunning the major supply sources that its actual stocks were well below the new authorization. Third Army had never slackened in its determination to keep moving to the east. Now its forces were using ingenuity, aggressiveness, and some luck to "live off the land." The 4th Armored Division overran thirty-seven carloads of German gasoline and oil at Sens. This translated to 100,000 gallons. Naturally, and as was to be expected, no one outside of Army was to know of this development. On August 28, at Chalons sur Marne, the irrepressible 4th Armored captured another cache of 100,000 gallons. Thus little did Eisenhower or the Germans know that Patton was still advancing to the east after his tanks were supposed to be dry, because of captured stores of German gasoline.

Patton, even though he knew that it would take some pushing, had all along set his sights on rapidly reaching the Meuse. Now he was there. On August 31 CC "A" of the 4th Armored Division sat on the east bank of the Meuse River, to be followed the next day by CC "B." Other elements of XII and XX Corps were, likewise, closing in on the river. During the spectacular advance from the Seine to the Meuse in one week, Third Army consumed 350,000 to 400,000 gallons a day, but received an average of only 202,382 gallons a day. It is perfectly obvious that without the captured gasoline it would have been impossible for Patton to reach the Meuse, but reach it he did! A runner, when he crosses the finish line, is out of breath. Similarly, when Patton's tanks crossed *that* finish line, they, also, were out of breath, except theirs was spelled G A S.

As Third Army was closing in on the Meuse River, a sensational development was unfolding along the lower Seine, many miles northwest of Patton's location. Word had certainly reached Bradley's First Army and Montgomery's 21st Army Group that Patton was already nearing the Meuse, far to their east, and closing in on the German border. This news must have worked like a trip wire, and resulted in an awakening. The Allied forces along the lower Seine seemed to acquire, and then become imbued with, a fresh resolve.

The elements of the American First Army and the British 21st Army Group seemed to break out of their shackles at about the same time. It seemed readily apparent that Patton had broken the ice for them. He proved that what might have seemed impossible was, indeed, possible. They must have concluded that if Patton could do it, "so could we." They set about convincingly proving that to be the case.

The American First Army sent Gen. Collins' VII Corps through the Melun bridgehead, captured earlier by Patton's XVth Corps on August 26, to attack toward Laon. Collins was able to advance rapidly because he met no strong opposition, perhaps helped by German General Model who, hopefully, had sent his surviving Panzers off to intercept Patton, who appeared to be a German priority.

The American Third Armored Division was across the old Chateau Thierry battlefield on August 28. On the same day the American 7th Armored Division advanced across the battlefield of Soissons. So the Americans now had the bit in their teeth and were definitely on the move.

Following not too far behind would be Montgomery's British 21st Army Group. Monty launched his Group's major offensive across the Seine on August 29. The instructions to his troops at the beginning of the offensive must be quoted, for they were so surprising, so totally out of character, that the name "Patton" could easily have been substituted for Montgomery, as the one issuing the instructions.

These are those instructions: "The proper tactics now are for strong armoured and mobile columns to by-pass enemy centers of resistance and push boldly ahead, creating alarm and despondency in enemy rear areas. Enemy by-passed will be dealt with by infantry columns coming on later. I rely on Commanders of every rank and grade to 'drive' on ahead with the utmost energy; any tendency to be 'sticky' or cautious must be stamped out ruthlessly."

Incredible. Was this really Montgomery talking? Eliminate the words "sticky" and "cautious," which were not in Patton's lexicon, and this could readily have been the American General delivering a pep talk. Whether he would admit it or not, undoubtedly "not," Monty must have been aware of Patton's strategy and tactics, for he was definitely patterning this new operation after those of Third Army. It appeared that he had lifted a page or two out of American armor doctrine, which Patton had so consistently and successfully followed and applied. At least for this operation Montgomery was "singing from the same sheet of music" as Patton, and it was definitely working and he was moving!

Gen. Horrocks, commanding the British XXXth Corps, was a prime example demonstrating that the doctrine was being applied, was work-ing, and would be successful. On August 29, Gen. Horrocks moved out of the bridgehead at Vernon. Bad weather, minefields, and remaining elements of the German Fifth Panzer and Seventh Armies held him to a thirty-kilometer advance. The next day the weather cleared and resistance lessened. With dash, aggressiveness, and even a mite of recklessness, not seen for a long while within the British combat forces, and in true armor fashion, Horrocks' XXXth Corps began advancing and then rolling. As he picked up speed, he found success to be exhilarating, and his mouth must have watered for more. Consequently, he kept his drive alive by moving through the night, and because of his new-found aggressiveness, he reached Amiens on August 31. With the help of the French Forces of the Interior (FFI) Horrocks took control of the city with several of the bridges over the Somme still intact.

When the last day of August arrived, the Allies in the north were advancing rapidly and aggressively across Northern France and headed determinedly toward the Belgian border.

It had been an historic and amazingly and unexpectedly successful and productive month. Astonishingly, in thirty days between D + 49 and D + 79, the Allied Armies had traversed a distance that, according to OVERLORD, was expected to have taken seventy days.

Likewise, it is absolutely incredible what Patton accomplished in just one month from the first day of August, when his Army was activated, to the last day of the month. Many statistics could be produced that would serve as a glowing testimonial to the accomplishments of Third Army – miles advanced; cities and towns overrun; enemy killed, wounded, captured (in great numbers); tanks, other vehicles, locomotives destroyed. The sum of all those would, indeed, be most impressive. One figure stands out. In 26 days Third Army would liberate 47, 829 square miles of French soil – truly impressive.

On the other hand, Montgomery's achievements were far more modest, to say the least. It took Monty from June 6 to August 16 to move from the Normandy beaches through Caen to Falaise. By the last days of August his forces had closed up on the lower Seine, crossed the river, and launched their major offensive to the east. As the month was ending, Montgomery was endeavoring mightily to close the 185 longitudinal gaps that separated him from Patton, as that American was being halted.

Now September was about to arrive. There had been strong and early indications that it would be a far more eventful complex, momentous, and history-making month even than August. Very shortly it would be known if the month would live up to its advance billing.

CHAPTER 12

GENERAL GEORGE S. PATTON, JR.:

AUGUST 16 – AUGUST 31, 1944.

Patton's reputation as a uniquely bold and successful Field Commander was quickly established during Operation Torch in North Africa. His performance in Morocco was most impressive, particularly because of his extremely low casualties. After the Kasserine debacle in North Africa, he did a masterful job of turning around the demoralized II Corps, and leading it to victory. He left that campaign recognized as the United States Army's outstanding combat leader. His reputation was enhanced, and his star shone even more brilliantly, after his campaign in Sicily was acknowledged as an extraordinary operation. Now this same General Patton was pointed and primed to meet yet another challenge – this one his greatest one by far.

It would be a masterful campaign. Historians universally would label it one of the great achievements in military history, and another Patton triumph. It would gain for him the fame that he had always sought, a great step toward military immortality, and growth and substance to the ever-growing and -developing Patton legend.

He was still busy as elements of his Third Army had reached the lower Seine, crossed it, and were now advancing north alongside it. But he recognized that he was heading for what would for him be a dead end, and that the demands, challenges, and opportunities lay elsewhere. So he looked deep to the south over his right shoulder, and like the starter at a track meet, figuratively, fired his pistol. The XIIth. and XXth Corps in the runners' starting boxes were unleashed at the sound of the shot to drive in the only direction that mattered – EAST!

The XIIth Corps had a brand new Commander, whose background was completely Infantry, so he would not be able to contribute a great deal. But the XIIth Corps had "P" Wood and his 4th Armored Division, already battle-tested, hardened, proven.

As was to be expected, Patton positioned the tanks of the 4th Armored Division in the forefront – they would lead his Third Army (as they would again and again in the future), and would once again be his spearhead. The 4th Armored was my division, and here is how we made history.

As soon as Gen. Wood received his orders from Gen. Patton to move, he deliberately began exercising loose control over his subordinate tactical Commanders. He eased up on the reins, gave them their heads, and, figuratively, with a touch of his spurs and a flick of his riding crop, sent them on their way. His tanks were soon on a tear – a hell-for-leather drive. (Secretary of War Henry L. Stimson, a long-time friend of Patton's, would observe in "delighted admiration," that "Patton had set his tanks to run around France like bed- bugs in a Georgetown kitchen.")

To carry out his aggressive philosophy the division would operate like Cavalry – slashing, side-stepping, with speed as surprise. The tankers were confident and cocky (they had already proved of what they were capable), and demonstrated a daring, audacious, hard-riding, fast-shooting style. The 4th Armored advanced hard and fast, by-passed strongly held centers of resistance with rapid flanking movements and deep penetrations (the battle cry was "by-pass and haul ass.") When towns or strong points could not be by-passed, they were taken in stride with sudden headlong assaults, bruising power, and violent fire, which broke the enemy. We avoided pitched battles, probed for weak spots, and pushed through into the enemy's rear areas. The Division had a "restless ardor" for pursuit of a defeated enemy. Its outstanding characteristics were its ability to move and shoot, but above all to move. Movement became its middle name, constant momentum its trade mark. A German colonel captured during this period, an officer who had commanded units in Russia, exclaimed, "To know the Commander of this Armored Division would explain to me how this Army managed to achieve such a speed of advance, which in many instances caught us completely unprepared."

The division was aided immeasurably by extremely favorable operational conditions. It was almost perfect tank weather, and ideal tank country. The days were long and the nights short. Thus, there were many hours in the operational day. The fields in the predominantly open country were dry, permitting the tanks to go almost anywhere they chose to go. The water in the creeks, streams, and even small rivers was low, and many of their beds were dry – ideal for fording. If a bridge were blown and the water too deep for fording, the engineers, who stayed closed-up, immediately installed a hasty bridge, enabling the tanks to move ahead with a minimum of delay.

Enemy resistance was disorganized. However, there were many who put up a stiff, even fanatical, defense. Key cities and towns were well defended. The Germans installed hasty mines, blew craters in roads, and fired anti-tank guns from strategically placed positions. They blew bridges as they withdrew, and often defended the sites. Great numbers fought ferociously. There were many who stopped their retreat and wanted to fight, but we would not let them. Instead of engaging them, we out-flanked and swept past them. Once we were around and behind them, even the most fanatical recognized that the "jig was up," and it was futile to continue to fight. By this time we knew, and they knew, that our fire from the rear was more deadly and three times more effective than fire from the front. By using maneuver and surprise, we avoided costly frontal attacks and kept casualties very low.

When we saw fresh tracks, it was like the fox after the stricken hare. We were advancing faster than they could flee. When we caught up with them, we destroyed them. Many of the fleeing enemy had no desire to fight. They were hurrying in the direction of their homeland in the hope that somewhere, before the border was reached, they could organize their forces, and present a stiff, organized defense.

To accelerate its advance and to cover more ground, the 4th Armored, in its advance to the east, operated on a broad front. Up ahead to the left would be Combat Command "A" (CCA) and on the right, Combat Command "B" (CCB). Following behind and always ready for employment, behind one of the forward Combat Commands or independently, was the third Combat Command, Reserve Command (CCR). CC "A" and CC "B" operated virtually independently and moved on parallel axes, usually with considerable distance between them; on occasion they were as much as 45 kilometers apart. Until now, such employment had been unheard of. During my military schooling, it was continually and adamantly stressed that attacking units must be mutually supporting. Operating 45 kilometers apart hardly met that criterion, so the 4th Armored was "throwing away the book." The tactics of the division would be unpredictable, unconventional, and opportunistic, so, they habitually would be guilty of not following "the book."

During the advance across France, Third Army was the south flank of the entire Allied Expeditionary Force; the XII Corps, to which the 4th Armored was assigned. protected the south flank of Third Army, the 4th Armored was the south flank of XII Corps, and my Combat Command "B" was the southernmost element of the Fourth. Thus, the right flank of the 4th Armored was wide open—there was absolutely nothing to our right.

Wood never worried about his flanks. He developed a long, amazing, unique, and lasting relationship with the Thunderbolts and Mustangs of the XIX Tactical Air Command, which not only closely supported our operations, but watched our flanks, as well. The teamwork between the XIX TAC and the 4th Armored was probably closer in spirit and superior in quality to that of any similar operation in WW II, and would not be equaled during that war.

During this period, we moved too rapidly and were too widely scattered for the conventional gathering of Commanders for their instructions and orders, or for the traditional, very detailed operations orders, stressed *ad infinitum* at the service schools. Gen. Wood resorted to simple, oral orders, and "mission-type orders." His own orders from Patton came by radio, or on overlays that were jeeped in or flown in by artillery spotter planes. The normal overlay order was quite simple. It usually consisted merely of a line of departure (usually the most forward positions which we held), a broad directional arrow (Axis of Advance), a goose egg with the letters OBJ (objective, always way out front), and the terse order, "Get going at first light." That's all we had, that's all we needed. And in many instances we needed no orders; we continued doing what we had been doing. It is reputed that at one point early on, when a senior Commander, after seizing an objective earlier than expected, requested further instructions from Patton, the answer was, "Go East and go like hell." That was a classic example of a "mission type order."

Our daily output during that sweep was absolutely sensational and unbelievable. Our tanks made daily advances of as much as 37 miles, 51 miles, 30 miles, and 48 miles. Because of lasting daylight, we operated well into the evening. First light came very, very early. There were not too many hours of darkness. During the brief periods we stopped, we utilized the time to refuel our tanks and other vehicles, and to replace our expended ammunition. The only logistical item constantly in short supply was sleep.

During that advance across France, one action best typified the *élan*, spirit, daring, and aggressiveness of the 4th Armored Division. On August 25, a task force from Combat Command "A" consisting of tanks and armored infantry mounted in their half-tracks advanced toward the large, important city of Troyes, which was well southeast of Paris, and sat on the Seine River. Troyes was a particularly good example of a German center of resistance that we had been facing. It was also one that could not be by-passed, but had to be taken head-on. Because of its location, holding the city was of vital importance to the Germans. There was no question but that it would be heavily and determinedly defended. As it turned out, the heavily dug-in and waiting garrison numbered many hundreds of men. In the advance thus far, the attacking elements of the

4th Armored had relied heavily on speed. Before Troyes speed was more essential than ever. Now was not the time to begin a slow, methodical, careful, time-consuming attack upon the city, even though the situation called for just such a maneuver.

So the tanks of the task force quickly spread out in a wide formation, and the armored infantry mounted in their half-tracks dispersed in an irregular formation behind the tanks. Without hesitation and with all guns blazing, they made a bold, powerful, fast-moving attack across three and one-half miles of wide-open ground directly at Troyes. It was a dispersed, spread formation, desert-type move reminiscent of an old Cavalry charge, as well as the actions and formations employed during our training exercises in the Mojave Desert. The enemy quickly opened fire, sending artillery and direct fire rounds at the charging attackers, but the mobile units moved so rapidly that most of the hurried rounds landed behind them and were generally ineffective. As the tanks neared the city, they saw tank ditches up ahead directly in their path. Instead of slowing down, they increased their speed and actually leaped across the ditches. What may have appeared to be a totally reckless, foolhardy maneuver was, instead, so bold, so audacious, so unexpected that it stunned, shocked, and completely demoralized the enemy. The defenders were so shaken that they appeared to be in a trance, and the attackers quickly and successfully overran and seized the city, and most importantly, Third Army troops were across the Seine. Defenders later said that they just could not believe what they had seen and experienced. By the next day the elements of CC "A" were clearing up Troyes, holding the high ground northeast of the city, and effecting systematic destruction of the Germans attempting to flee to the east.

Unbelievably, on August 31 Combat Command "A" was sitting on the east bank of the Meuse River, and would be joined by CC "B" the next day. My tank battalion had advanced an absolutely sensational 328 miles in 12 days. Even more remarkable – we had moved from the Atlantic to the Meuse in only 18 days. It was not only astonishing but exciting to realize that we were now merely 63 miles from the German border, and that the great prize, the Rhine River, which could prove to be the ultimate objective, was, amazingly, only 140 direct miles away. One hundred forty miles? Why, that was less than half the distance we had advanced in the last 12 days!

In less than a month Patton had thrown a 700-mile right hook across the widest part of France. Our tanks had already put nearly 1500 miles on their speedometers. They had advanced down the Normandy peninsula and into the heart of Brittany, taken a side trip to the Atlantic, and then led Third Army's drive to the Meuse. Now euphoria gripped us tightly. The possibilities and probabilities to the east were staggering.

The roads were clear ahead, and the Moselle River would be undefended. From there the avenues to Germany were wide open. The American forces had by now destroyed the bulk of the enemy needed to man the empty fortifications of the Siegfried Line. The remnants just could not retire fast enough to reach, much less organize, man, and defend, those defensive barriers, which had been constructed inside their homeland. And not too far behind that was the Rhine with, realistically, undefended bridges. The possibility was high that the Germans would collapse when the Rhine River was reached.

On the morning of September 2, we were poised, positioned, ready, and eager to continue our push into Germany.

CHAPTER 13

GENERAL GEORGE S. PATTON, JR.: SITTING ALONGSIDE THE MEUSE, SEPTEMBER 1 – SEPTEMBER 10, 1944.

During the last days of August, as we sped east, our daily output was incredible. It was on August 27, after our 38-mile push, that I became convinced that there could be no stopping us, and I believed that the faster we moved the easier it would get. We had learned that elsewhere along the front, particularly in the north, the other Allied Armies were now beginning to push forward, and would continue to do so aggressively and rapidly. Based on our performance alone, I became so convinced of our invincibility that I confidently announced that the war in Europe would be over by Thanksgiving. I believed that so strongly that I told one and all that I had money to wager to back up that belief: several fellow troopers, not as optimistic as I, quickly took me up on it, so I made several bets. The most significant one (i.e. most money involved) was with Capt. Jim Pirie, who commanded the Service Company of our battalion. Tragically, although he would be well aware in just a few days that he had won the bet, he was killed before he could collect.

On the evening of September 1, after we had crossed the Meuse River at Vaucouleurs, we settled in for the night on the scenic and pastoral east bank of the river. We were poised, positioned and ready to continue our push to the east at first light. I reflected with great pride, and gloried in the realization, that to get where we were we had run a marathon race at the speed of a sprinter. It was almost unbelievable that only a month and four days before, on July 28, we had broken out of Normandy, and here we sat on the Meuse, in spite of that 500-mile side trip to the Atlantic.

As I regularly did, I now grabbed for my maps. I wanted to be ready for our next advance when the orders arrived which I expected at any moment. As I examined my maps, I noted quickly that the Moselle River, which was a most attractive and meaningful objective, and for which we had been eagerly reaching out, was only 30 miles away. At the rate we had been advancing, we would surely reach the river at Bayon, and be on the east bank the next evening. Two days after that, as we continued our charge from Bayon through Luneville, Arracourt, Chateau Satins, and then west of Sarreguemines, we would probably cross the German border west of Saarbrucken. From Bayon that was a distance of slightly over 50 miles – two days. After all, our average had been over 27 miles per day.

Our most direct route from Sarreguemines to the Rhine was to drive slightly to the northeast, aiming at Bingen, west of Mainz, or at Mainz itself. We would advance through Saar-Land over relatively open country, flanking to the west the congested areas of Mannheim, Ludwigshafen, and Kaiserslautern. The distance could not be much more than 80 miles. Yes, I had it all figured out. I had difficulty containing myself. I just knew that when our orders came, they would closely approximate the strategy that I had just envisioned.

However, in a very short time I would know that I would never be able to test my theories, for Fate had radical changes in store for us.

When I realized that it was now well past my usual "bedtime," and the orders still had not come, my excitement abated, somewhat. It would be a short night for me, for first light would soon arrive. I was puzzled, for it was most unusual at this late hour not to know what we were to do and where we were to go the next morning. I did not want to doze off, only to be awakened with my orders. Once that happened, in my role as operations officer, I would then issue the orders to the Company Commanders by my tank radio. But because a state of near exhaustion was normal for us tankers, I must have fallen asleep sitting and leaning back in the turret of my tank with my radio just above me. I was awakened by a bright sun that streamed down through my open Commander's hatch into the turret basket. I jumped to my feet startled, for it was perfectly obvious that the morning was advanced beyond first light. For some reason yet unknown to me, it was abundantly clear that the 4th Armored Division had not received movement instructions. For a moment I seemed absolutely lost. For days it had been "up and at 'em" while it was still dark, and on the move and charging ahead by first light. Today, nothing. I called up the chain of command and they were, likewise, puzzled, and confirmed what I suspected, and that was that no orders had arrived from Third Army via XII Corps. I radioed my Company Commanders with the information, and cautioned them that, as always, they were to be prepared to jump when the call came.

I glanced out of my open hatch and saw activity at each of the dispersed tanks. It goes without saying that every tank crew was every bit as surprised as I was. But like the true professionals that they had become, they took full advantage of this unexpected pause. They had their Coleman burners going to make coffee and to warm their breakfast rations. Not knowing how long the respite would be, they were soon cleaning their weapons, greasing the tank's bogie wheels, and opening its engine compartment doors. There had been little time for urgently needed maintenance. Now they would take full advantage of this unexpected opportunity.

So the day passed. It had been another perfect tank day, and now this one was lost, forever. Because it was the beginning of September, the days would be getting progressively shorter. If the weather in Lorraine continued to be normal, the coming of rain could be expected in the not too distant future. The Battalion Commander and I, as always, had our heads together for a time, but he was every bit as puzzled as I. So, although the men were enjoying the break, there were early signs of considerable concern. Supper was eaten; darkness had enveloped us, and still no orders. For me it was another restless night, as I expected at any moment to be awakened with orders to move. But the orders never came, and it was daylight once again.

This was now September 3; another good tank day vanishing. Concern was beginning to move to alarm. Even the lowest-ranking tanker knew that while we sat the enemy was furiously at work out there somewhere. What "bugged" everyone was that we had stopped ourselves. *(We were doing to ourselves something that the enemy had furiously tried to do, but had failed.)* We were giving him on a silver platter the precious time and opportunity for which he had been desperately striving, to reorganize his forces and to select and man defensive positions. What was especially galling to us was the certainty that at that very moment he was doing just that. Many years later there would be a TV commercial advertising automotive parts that cautioned, "pay me now or pay me later." We well knew that every moment that we were not advancing meant that we would be paying later.

Late that afternoon, as we were all wondering what the next day would bring, word filtered down through the "grape-vine" that the reason we were stopped was GAS, or rather, the lack of it. We at the "grunt" level had been completely unaware that individuals above us had been wrestling for days with the problem of gasoline. During our advance across France, we had gassed up each night, and charged off each morning with full tanks, never giving a thought to how our Service Company obtained it for us. We were completely oblivious to the effort, determination, ingenuity, and luck that had produced it for us.

It was not too long before official confirmation of the problem reached us through the chain of command. We were informed that, yes indeed, there was a shortage of gasoline. The explanation that we received was that we had advanced so rapidly that we were far ahead of where the planners had expected us to be, and we were outrunning our logistical support. It was conceded that there was gas at the port and beaches, but the problem was getting it to us. The distances involved had become so extensive, and the round trips for the supply trucks so long and time-consuming, that it was becoming virtually impossible to push forward the required tonnage of gasoline, ammunition, and other supplies. We now had the picture, and it was nothing but bad news for us.

Before we had time to absorb or even to react to this most shocking news, we were hit with the "hay-maker." It was explained that there would be a delivery of gasoline, but not nearly enough to spread along the entire front. A priority had to be established. Then came the real "zinger" that knocked all of us for a loop, back on our heels. A decision had been made to give Monty the gas, as well as top priority for all other supplies. This was incredible news. No, this just could not be! The shock was so great, so difficult to comprehend and accept, that it momentarily stiffened us.

There was no one "out there" who could readily understand our emotions. For days we had given everything that we had, and then some, to keep advancing. It was dark each night before we stopped. We grabbed a quick bite to eat while waiting for the supply trucks, which had been well behind, to catch up. When they arrived, each tank crew wasted no time in engaging in frenetic activity. First came the gas. The crew employed the bucket-brigade system to get the 15 or more five-gallon gas cans from the truck to the back deck of the tank. The individual on the deck had to unscrew – laboriously, in the dark – the gas cap on each can, screw in the nozzle, pour the contents into the tank, hand back the empty and reach for the next full one. This was time-consuming and arduous. The crew performing this task had been moving and fighting since first light – about sixteen hours. With the tank topped off, then came the important Part II of the re-supply operation – the ammunition. Two tank gun rounds had to be removed from their wooden crate, and then from their fiber tubes. They had to be carefully and tenderly handled so as to prevent a dent of any kind on the brass casing. They were passed up to the back deck, as well, and then down to the man inside the turret, where he clamped them upright on the side of the turret basket. While this major supply operation was unfolding, yet another crew-man would receive and store rations, small arms ammunition, and other needed supplies. After all of this, there would be little time for sleep before it was first light again, and another long, demanding day. Small wonder that these were constantly exhausted men.

Now we were stopped, and it had taken not even a single enemy rifle shot to do it. The letdown was instant, visible, and audible. The helium had escaped from our balloon with a loud, brief snort. The men walked about aimlessly, stunned, shaken, disbelieving, as did I. Strange as it was, one of the first thoughts that popped into my head was about the bets that I had made, and there was no doubt in my mind but that those bets were already lost. The conditions that would have made my bet a winning one had already vanished. For us to be successful after leaving the Meuse, it would be **time** that would be the most critical factor. We would have had to continue moving the day after reaching the Meuse – no pause, no delay, absolutely no stop. The widest possible "window" for us would have been no more than five days. *If we stopped longer than that, we could forget about it. It would be a whole new ball game, our great opportunity would have vanished – irretrievably lost.* That window was now almost closed. Without the direct and overwhelming pressure which we had constantly been applying, the Germans were perfectly capable of reorganizing major forces and quickly pushing them into battle.

My emotions had run the complete gamut. My mind was in turmoil. The one overriding, troubling thought that persisted in haunting me, and for which I believed there was absolutely no explanation, was that the choice had been Monty at the expense of Patton. Someone up there must have had clouded vision; else, where was the awareness, reason, logic? During the periods when I attended service schools, we were told repeatedly that you reinforce success, you do not reinforce failure. Looking back over many months of military operations – who represented success and who failure?

In our society we have long believed that you should go with a winner, be it sports, politics, academia, industry, the military. It appeared that such a belief was being disregarded, for this time we were not throwing in our lot with the winner. I just could not believe that this was a purely military decision – politics, surely, had to be involved. My troopers, who had an amazing awareness of how the war was going, were likewise dumbfounded. When the name Montgomery was raised, they knew about the British General. They remembered that it had taken him nearly two months to secure Caen, his D-Day objective. They knew full well that he was careful, cautious, and slow. Most were aware that he had great difficulty mounting a forceful, gainful offensive. So the decision to give the "vote" to Monty was extremely difficult for them to handle.

During the days ahead, whenever I thought of "the decision," and it was very often, I bristled. But life goes on. All of us recognized that for the time being there was nothing more for us to do but sit. So we decided to make the most of this delightful but tragic opportunity.

The weather remained absolutely beautiful – sunny and warm. The river was crystal clear and refreshing, but not cold – ideal swimming temperature. Now we slept later and ate better. We no longer had to eat on the fly, and enjoyed our leisurely and more tasty and nutritious meals. Not knowing how long our pause would be, the highest priority had been given to maintenance – getting our vehicles and weapons, which we had been forced to neglect, back into shape. Now that that had been accomplished, each man could do pretty much what he wanted, and for each of us life would continue to be idyllic.

I swam often in the river, read, wrote letters, sun-bathed, and played touch football. While swimming in the river one morning, I dislodged some wax that completely blocked one ear. The battalion surgeon, with considerable difficulty and limited "tools," was able to remove the rock-hard clinging substance. On another occasion I had a bit of an adventure with the dentist. He filled a tooth for me, but it was a somewhat primitive procedure. He had to utilize his portable equipment. This meant that in order to provide the power for the drill he had to keep pressing the treadle by foot, in a manner reminiscent of the old sewing machine. Thus, he had to be a contortionist, for he had to keep his foot pumping, while at the same time guiding his drill at the affected tooth. It was not easy for him, and anything but pleasant for the patient (me), but the job got done. So the long stop had some unexpected benefits.

It was on the afternoon of September 5 that a batch of late August copies of the *Stars and Stripes* soldiers' newspaper arrived. Voices were soon heard shouting, "We made it!" For the very first time our division, the 4th Armored, received mention in the paper. Our first action was as far back as July 28, when we broke out at Normandy, and captured Coutances at the end of the first day. That was most significant, as was the seizure of Avranches shortly after. Then followed our actions in Brittany, including our dash to the Atlantic, and more recently what the history books would call the historic sweep across France. Yet, until now, there had been absolutely no mention of the exploits of our division. We had not been able to understand why, but had to agree that censorship must indeed be tight. We learned later that our own Army Commander was not only as puzzled as we, but had a different explanation. Patton blamed Eisenhower (and this did not improve his regard for Ike) for SHAEF's apparent refusal to acknowledge publicly not only the achievements but even the presence of Third Army, until almost the end of August. There could be absolutely no reason for this, but SHAEF, when pressed, offered some excuses that were lame and even absurd.

For us the days passed slowly. Life on the French Riviera could not have been better than what we were experiencing. Yet, every moment that passed found us more uneasy, fretful, and very worried. There was virtually no laughter. The overriding item of conversation was, "I wonder when we will start moving, again?" Furrowed brows were the norm when the future was discussed, in hushed tones. We knew that we could move at a "drop of a hat," for we had topped off the evening of the first of September, and had not stirred since. The only units to use gasoline were elements of the Cavalry Reconnaissance Squadron, who in their light vehicles had been out patrolling to the east to provide us security and to determine what was out there.

We knew full well that the Germans were anything but beaten, and were "hard at it." We would later learn that what we had predicted and feared was, indeed, taking place. The Germans took full advantage of our "vacation" and furiously reorganized. Hitler was determined to stop Patton, his greatest threat. The forces which had been withdrawing under pressure now gathered themselves, badly hurt units began to strengthen; reinforcements were being rushed from Italy; new factory-minted Panther tanks were pushed forward; and Hitler put into furious motion the reconstitution of his Fifth Panzer Army. By stopping Patton, Hitler believed that he could establish a winter line along the east side of the Moselle.

There was more reason to be concerned. The almost perfect tank weather was vanishing day by day. Each night after supper when groups conversed, it was inevitable that someone would ask, "If we had not been stopped, where would we be tonight?"

It was morning again; another warm, sunny day – Sunday, September the 10th. After breakfast, I walked back across the river, and attended Mass at a small picturesque Catholic church. After my noon meal, I conducted a training class for my tankers, as I had been doing regularly during the respite. After it was finished, I was contemplating how best to take full advantage of the remaining hours of this gorgeous afternoon. I glanced at my watch and saw that it was 2:00 P.M. Then suddenly with absolutely no warning we were hit by a totally unexpected, staggering bolt out of the blue. The battalion was ordered to move out as soon as it was ready, with our destination to be supplied momentarily. The companies were alerted for instantaneous movement with the order of march to be provided to them when orders were received. They were instructed to report when their units were assembled and ready to move.

I was thunderstruck by this stunning development, and had difficulty comprehending it. We had sat for nearly ten days without the slightest hint that a move was in the offing any time soon. It was now almost mid-afternoon. By the time we gathered ourselves and began to move, the day would be almost spent. Of course we had known that sooner or later, we would be back in action. But we never expected our orders to come this suddenly, abruptly, and mysteriously. What was out there that caused this sudden move? What was waiting for us that required such a radical departure? Was it some sort of catastrophic development?

But these tankers were real professionals. They had been hit on short notice many times before, so they didn't stop to ask questions. They hopped right to it and got ready. Normally, under combat conditions, the battalion was ready to move "now" in any direction. But this was not a normal situation. As has been mentioned before, the sign of a good outfit is the rapidity with which it digs in. In this situation they had really "dug in" to make life as comfortable as possible. As an example, each tank crew, using a tarpaulin tied to the side of their tank, had fashioned a kind of lean-to. It was under this tarp that the bedrolls were placed, and that is where the men slept. It was a vast improvement, to say the least, over the many hours when they tried to sleep in the tight steel confines of their tanks.

On this day, when the movement orders came crashing in, the un-suspecting men were scattered – some were even swimming in the river. Their belongings were, likewise, scattered – uniforms, drying laundry, writing material, books – as well as tank maintenance equipment and weapons-cleaning material. So it was not an easy exercise to tear down their homes, get back into combat uniform, stow in an orderly manner all their gear and equipment within the very tight confines of the tank or on its back deck. It is amazing what the five combat-experienced crew-members of a Sherman tank, working feverishly and furiously as a team, can accomplish. In what appeared to be an unbelievable minimum amount of time tanks were "turning 'em over," and lining up behind their Company Commander. (The tanks had been started each day, and permitted to idle for a brief period, so as to be ready when the "word came.") This day the "word came," and they were now ready. Of course, before moving out, each man, undoubtedly, had about the same thought. "After sitting idle for nearly ten days, and with this day almost spent, what was the reason for the great rush to finally get going again?'

The tanks moved out smoothly, and after a few miles, it was clearly evident that no rust had gathered during the long rest period, and that the tankers appeared to have retained their aggressive combat edge. We were confident that the first few miles should be without resistance, for the Cavalry Recon Units had patrolled out in that direction. Neverthe-less, we never let our guard down, so we moved with our "combat face" in place.

We had been given as our first objective, Bayon, which was southeast of Vaucouleurs, and sat on the Moselle River. We were to cross the river at that location. Although it was now dark, the eager, rested troops in no time reached and crossed the Madon River, and continued east to a location south of Crantenoy, where we bivouacked for the night. A quick glance at my map placed us about 26 miles south of Nancy – that large, provincial city, the jewel of Lorraine.

But before curling up for the night in my usual place on the floor of the turret basket, I studied my map once again. The showdown was about to begin. We were now a mere five kilometers from the Moselle. In the morning we would be there before our breakfasts had time to settle. As we had known for weeks, the Moselle was a major objective, a critical obstacle that had to be breached, before the attack to the east could be continued. Whatever was there was now waiting for us. There was bound to be trouble. This was a juicy spot for the enemy, and militarily, it was so advantageous for the defender that it cried out for a rugged, determined defense. Unquestionably, while we had been sitting along the Meuse, the enemy had had the time to round up scattered forces, to reorganize and dig them in. Surely, they would make their first big stand here. We would know in a very few hours.

Before falling asleep, I still could not help but speculate about the sudden, surprising, unexpected orders, and their timing. It just had to be that word again – gasoline. That is what stopped us, and I was willing to bet that it was gasoline that sprung us. Patton must somehow have obtained enough gasoline to get us moving again. I would not know until much later that, once given the priority for gasoline and supplies, Montgomery had demanded "all," "everything," and in order to have it, wanted Patton stopped "cold." Eisenhower apparently believed that he would have difficulty explaining the total and complete stopping of the highly successful Army Commander who was finally grabbing the headlines and capturing the imagination of the folks back home, so he left the door slightly ajar.

After elements of XII Corps found another 100,000 gallons of German fuel on September 3rd, Eisenhower, himself, was instrumental in having 240,265 gallons of gas delivered to Third Army on September 5. During the next three days, Eisenhower made an additional 1,396,710 gallons available.

Apparently, when George Patton had added up his newly acquired resources, and confirmed that they were at hand, he knew that he could get to the Moselle and beyond. So, characteristically, he must have decided, "Let's go – and now!" How else can one explain the sudden, surprising, totally unexpected orders at mid-afternoon on a warm, sunny Sunday.

We would soon learn how far and how long we would be able to keep going with what appeared to be Patton's final gasoline allocations for some time to come.

Major General John Shirley Wood in a French orchard in August 1944.

Major General John S. "Tiger Jack" Wood, Commanding General, 4th Armored Division

Albin F. Irzyk

Author, 2nd from right, and his light tank crew which was
employed in the Advance Guard of the 8th Tank Battalion
during the historic sweep across France in August 1944.

Below: Battalion Staff: 8th Tank Battalion.
Author 2nd left.

Third Army Patch worn by its members
on left shoulder.

Although in Third Army, the 4th Armored
Division, as all divisions do, had its own patch
worn at point of left shoulder.

Members of the 8th Tank Battalion
were part of the 4th Armored Division
and thus wore the 4th Armored Patch.
But as most Battalion sized units did,
it had its own Battalion Crest.

General George S. Patton, Jr.

General Dwight D. Eisenhower

General Bernard Law Montgomery.
Photo Credit: SFC Jody Harmon, Armor Magazine

Major General John S. Wood C.G. 4th Armored Division
Explains situation to his Army Commander during sweep
across France, August 1944

Above and Top Right: 8th Tank Battalion tanks conquer the
deep, muddy Canal de l'Est, before making history by fording
the Mighty Moselle River — a truly "unclassic" river crossing.
Photo Credits: U.S. Signal Corps

Sherman Tank M4 A3 E8 "Easy Eight," Employed by the
4th Armored Division.

General Patton was decorated by the United States, Britain, France, Belgium and Luxemburg. Colonel Odom was declared the most decorated Medical Officer in World War II.

Taken from page 78 from short book "General George S. Patton and Eisenhower" by Charles B Odom, M.D.

Albin F. Irzyk

Action on the French countryside

Armored infantry mounting a tank before moving into further action.

We got a big one

A big haul

Fording a river

Deployed and moving cross country

CHAPTER 14

THE DECISION

The rapid Allied advance to the east was a totally unexpected, unpredicted development. It was far ahead of the planners' most optimistic projection. The Seine was no longer what it had been planned to be – a goal, an important milestone, a place to regroup, to advance logistical bases to forward positions. No, it was not a place for consolidation; it would not now even deserve a pause – for the name of the game now was the hot, incessant pursuit of a wounded enemy. The remainder of France had been laid open all the way to the Siegfried Line.

As the war opened up in Europe much of the thinking became focused on "what after the Seine?" The planners had early on decided that the first major and critically important target in Germany was the Ruhr. To reach it, they proposed a primary and a secondary route. The primary route (sometimes referred to as the British) they then considered was the most direct shot through the lower Seine, through Amiens and Liege to the Ruhr. The second one, (sometimes labeled the American), was from the upper Seine through Metz and the Saar Basin to Frankfurt am Main, and a swing north to the Ruhr. The OVERLORD planners visualized using both routes, principally to force the Germans to meet a more widespread threat. The British and American planners early on had agreed that both routes should be followed.

As the war progressed and decision time was nearing, it was well known that Gen. Eisenhower still believed that the war would be won by the Allies advancing on a "broad front' – the two Army Groups side by side from the North Sea to the Swiss border.

Typically, as early as August 15, Eisenhower's most immediate and notable subordinate, the overall Ground Commander, General Montgomery, began to muddy the waters. Monty had always wanted, and now began demanding, a single, "full-blooded" thrust through Belgium and Holland toward the Ruhr.

During the following days, he began a campaign which proposed that virtually all the Allied divisions be concentrated for a single thrust into Germany along a northerly route through the Low Countries (with himself, of course, in full command). Bradley, like others, had the impression that Eisenhower had favored the broad plan of using two routes to drive eastward into Germany, rather than directing too much strength over the northern route. Montgomery, however, was not to be stopped, and he continued to insist that all efforts be shifted to the north and to his 21st Army Group amply and appropriately (to him), reinforced by much of the American strength. Monty, by strongly and constantly advancing his views, repeatedly challenged Eisenhower's position, to the point where Ike began privately to question again the loyalty of Montgomery.

But other voices, as well, would be heard. Not one to be outdone by Montgomery, Patton jumped in with both feet. He forcibly pointed out to Bradley just where he was located in relation to the British. He was by far closer to Germany than anyone else. If he could keep moving – and he saw no reason why he could not – he was convinced that he would be to and through the Siegfried Line, before the enemy could man the fortifications. He had succeeded thus far because of speed and aggressiveness, and he would continue that speed and would give the fleeing enemy no chance to pause and regroup.

He confided in his diary that, "No one realizes the terrible value of the 'unforgiving minute,' except me." It was already a "given" that no other Army had moved or could move as rapidly as his.

So he beseeched Bradley for a few more divisions, the gasoline and supplies he needed, and the permission and authority to continue to charge ahead to grab the "*greatest chance to win the war ever presented.*"

Bradley was now convinced. He readily recognized Patton's position in relation to the other Armies, as he had watched at close hand, with admiration and amazement, the Third Army's spectacular performance since the beginning of the month. So Patton's arguments to turn the secondary offensive into the major one flowed into Bradley's receptive ears, and together they were convinced that these arguments were pertinent and persuasive.

General Bradley considered that the principal advantage of the American plan, with dead aim at Frankfurt, was its direct route through

Lorraine, which was the shortest way to Germany, and for that reason had for centuries been a traditional route of invading armies. Such a main effort would not only carry the Americans past the fortifications of Metz and the Maginot Line to the Saar, and beyond the Saar to the Rhine, but at the same time, would deprive the Germans of their critical and important Saar Basin.

But Patton needed some help. He had a mighty small Army with only two light Corps racing toward Germany. His VIII Corps in far-away Brittany did not count. By contrast, the American First Army had four corps. The Third Army had consistently averaged 150 to 200 tanks fewer than First Army. It was amazing that Patton was able to do all that he had done with the little that he had with which to do it.

Montgomery continued to be unrelenting. His proposal continued to call for *all* Allied strength under his command to be concentrated for the thrust from Belgium. That path would be almost twice the distance of the American proposal through the Saar. Monty's northern thrust presupposed the total abandonment of the American advance. The British plan was literally and figuratively a *single* thrust; it made no provision for a secondary effort.

In recommending that Eisenhower devote *all* his resources to his main effort, Montgomery strongly suggested that Patton be stopped for good at the Meuse, and in a sense "interred" along that river, while he raced on to Berlin.

Eisenhower must have found Montgomery's arguments convincing, for it was as early as August 23 when Eisenhower made THE DECISION (Bradley initially thought it a tentative decision). It was Eisenhower's second fateful decision in the battle of Western Europe – the first was when he set in motion the Normandy invasion. This second decision, like his first, was momentous, and like all momentous decisions, it would have lasting and serious consequences.

According to Bradley, Eisenhower on that date sent a letter to Montgomery, which directed him to make the main effort. Bradley was ordered to support the British effort with all divisions in his First Army. Montgomery would not only have priority in troops – he would also have top priority for gasoline and all other supplies.

The role and future of Patton's Third Army was unclear and un-certain. It appeared that it would not quite be put to rest – but almost. Its advance, apparently, would be a day-to-day operation depending on the "leftovers" from the 21st Army Group and First Army. Patton vowed that regardless of the scenario he would keep moving east until his tanks had run completely dry.

But the principals were not yet prepared to fully accept "the deci-sion." From the 23rd. on there was constant "tugging and pulling," "backing and filling." On one side were Bradley and Patton, and on the other Montgomery. Both parties were pointing out flaws in "the decision," hoping for concessions and adjustments that would be favorable to them. This tug of war would make the disputes over Caen and Falaise into minor debates.

The timing of Eisenhower's decision on the 23rd. seemed strange, premature and abrupt. Events that would seem to have an important bearing on such a decision were just beginning to unfold, and were far from having run their full course. In just a matter of days they would be more fully developed, and could have provided Ike with more and different factors for consideration.

On August 23, troops from Montgomery's 21st Army Group had just begun crossing the Seine northwest of Paris, at a small bridgehead established by the British 2nd Army in the vicinity of Vernon. Not an encouraging picture... It would be near the end of the month before the British and Canadians would close up to the Seine from Vernon to the coast, and be ready to launch their major crossings. But Eisenhower, it seems, had already made his decision, before these actions could take place.

Conversely, Patton, characteristically, as has already been mentioned, was already on a tear. His 4th Armored Division had in one fell swoop moved over 110 kilometers from Orleans to Sens. That city was seized by the 22nd, along with a train-load of gasoline. On the 23rd. Patton's tanks were through Sens and across the Yonne, hurtling their way toward Troyes, which sat on the upper Seine, and which they would reach by the 25th. Six days later, on the last day of August, Patton would have forces across the Meuse River. This was, indeed, an historic sweep. But it seems that Eisenhower had already made his decision, before these actions would take place.

It appears that Eisenhower on the 23rd. did not need any more "factors bearing upon the problem," as he, undoubtedly, had his mind made up. By that time he must have analyzed and accepted all the convincing and compelling reasons that he needed in order to make his decision. And for him they must have been convincing and compelling.

As has already been mentioned – Eisenhower had long favored the "Broad Front" strategy. Advancing on a broad front had always been his blueprint. He must have rationalized that it was still being applied in this situation. Montgomery's main effort would be supported by a secondary push in Bradley's 12th Army Group zone. Whereas Bradley's First Army would be providing considerable support to Montgomery, it would be Patton who would be making the secondary effort. Yet, with the preponderance of gasoline and supplies going to Monty, Patton would have to "make do." So Patton's secondary effort would be extremely "secondary." If Eisenhower looked at this as a "broad front" advance, he surely had to be deluding himself, for that front was way out of balance, and tilted heavily to the left shoulder. So in this case "single thrust" was much more apt than "broad front."

There were, indeed, several compelling reasons why the northern thrust had stood out for serious consideration. It is apparent that Eisenhower considered it urgent that his coastal advance overrun the sites of the deadly V-weapons, which had been playing havoc in England, and thus eliminate them. Another critically important reason for selecting the northern thrust was the absolute necessity to gain a deep-water port. The capture of Antwerp would satisfy that need. In fact, that may have been a stronger argument than the V-weapon for the Channel coast offensive.

The big reason why supplies were not reaching the forward advancing units was that the speed of those advances was out-running the ability of logistical support to keep up. Night and day round trips for the supply vehicles had become longer and longer, and now were almost at the breaking point. It was absolutely essential to secure a major port. There just had to be some relief for what was becoming an impossible strain upon the long lines of supply from Cherbourg and the beaches.

Eisenhower needed a port as quickly as possible, but especially one close enough to the German frontier to supply the "go for broke" offensive to the Ruhr. By far the best bet was certainly Antwerp, which also lay directly ahead of Montgomery's Armies. Unquestionably, Antwerp was a most compelling argument for moving rapidly along the French coast and into Belgium. Antwerp was, indeed, a major port. It ranked with New York among the great seaports of the world. It would be a truly significant prize. Eisenhower earlier had called Antwerp "an indispensable prerequisite for the final drive into Germany."

There were other advantages to the northern thrust. Montgomery would have naval protection for his left flank, and the American First Army on his right flank. He would be close to the Allied supply sources – port and beaches. Close air support could be expected, for his advance would be conveniently accessible for medium bombers and fighters still in England.

All of these were, indeed, convincing, compelling reasons why Eisenhower must have believed that the northern thrust was so important and critical. Yet, it was apparent that there remained one over-riding consideration that was the decisive reason for the urgency to head northeastward. It was the *rush to get* to the Ruhr, and then *quickly to capture* that industrial complex. The Ruhr was a direct shot to the east from Antwerp, and at this phase was the ultimate objective. If Montgomery had troops across the Rhine, and if that critically important area was quickly seized, there was every reason to believe that the war in the West would be over before the end of the year. This was an electrifying, mouth-watering prospect, *if it succeeded.*

However, for it to happen much work needed to be done. Two phrases stand out – *rush to get to* and *capture of* the Ruhr. This challenge was hardly a walk in the park. There were many difficult and critical hurdles to be leaped. This was not just an ordinary objective to be seized – another town/city, hill, or crossroad to be captured. The Ruhr was one of the most heavily populated, and most extensive and concentrated, industrial complexes in the world. It was the mechanical heart of Germany, and it had to keep beating. If that heart stopped beating, the war would end abruptly. The Germans could not wage war without it. They, better than anyone, understood the power and criticality of the region. Under no circumstance would they permit it to be snatched away from them. They would defend it ferociously, fanatically, and ingeniously. It would be anything but a juicy plum to pick.

The first big requirement – getting there quickly – would be anything but automatic. The northern axis was much more difficult than Patton's to the south. The terrain across which Monty would have to traverse was so challenging that it would be a perfect excuse for caution and timidity. The straight shot east would cross the Belgian border into the Netherlands, where the advancing forces would encounter multiple water cross-compartments that would have to be negotiated. Furthermore, the terrain off the roads would be wet and muddy, making cross-country movement difficult for heavy vehicles. Then, almost immediately, they would come face to face with the built-up areas.

During this advance, Eisenhower's overriding objective and hope would undoubtedly be to accomplish the destruction of the enemy's field forces well to the west of the Rhine, so that Montgomery could drive into the heart of Germany – hopefully, virtually unopposed. But viewed more realistically it could be expected that German resistance would become progressively heavier the closer he approached the German border. Getting across the border was merely his first challenge. His second big challenge –conquering the Ruhr – would instantly be in jeopardy, for his forces would immediately be confronted with a tight concentration of heavily populated cities even before they reached the Rhine. Heavy concentrations such as Krefeld, Munchengladbach, and then Duisburg, Düsseldorf, Hagen stood in their path. To advance and seize these large cities would most certainly require street-to-street, house-to-house fighting. There would be road-blocks and mined streets, and snipers on roofs. The enemy would be not just the uniformed military, but also every civilian who could cause harm and delay.

So the northern thrust all the way from its onset to the Ruhr was a mammoth, monumental, massive undertaking. It was a breath-takingly difficult, complex challenge, and would strain to the absolute utmost the talents, determination, endurance, resources of all who were involved. Did Montgomery have the horses, sufficient forces for all this? For this tremendous operation to succeed it would require two critically important ingredients: First, troops in sufficient strength that were seasoned, battle-tested and proven, disciplined, professional, aggressive, offense-minded. Second, for these troops there had to be a remarkable, masterful, indomitable, inspiring leader. This Commander, likewise, had to be battle-tested and proven. He would have to have vision; to be able to see the whole battlefield; to be aggressive, offensive-minded, to be capable of surprising and absorbing a surprise; to quickly seize unexpected opportunities; to be flexible, not rigid; to be audacious but not foolhardy; and to be a superb tactician. Did Eisenhower have the troops and the leader that fitted these extremely demanding profiles?

The troops which he had chosen for this critical operation did not, unfortunately, come close to filling the desired profile. The ones he would rely on were basically the British and Canadian armies. (The American First Army would protect the right flank, but their actions would be limited by a paucity of logistical resources.) Their record until now was far from scintillating. They were the ones who had bogged down on D-Day, operated inconclusively about Caen for weeks, participated in the GOODWOOD disaster, had similar difficulties with TOTALIZE, never met the expected and hoped-for timetable in reaching the Falaise/Argentan gap, and more recently were sluggish in their endeavor to reach the Seine. These troops, who would be facing far greater and more difficult challenges, hardly fit the mould.

The extraordinary leader chosen by Eisenhower for this operation – the great knight on his immense white charger, the individual whom Ike believed would "get the job done," the one upon whom he placed all his chips, his marbles, "bet the bank, " "went for broke" was none other than General, and for this operation Field Marshal, Bernard Law Montgomery. This Commander, like his troops, came well short of fitting the prescribed mould. Yet, this was Eisenhower's choice to lead the operation that he hoped would end the war by the close of the year.

How could Eisenhower have made such a decision? He had been with and had observed close at hand the activities of the British General in a variety of situations and operations from 1942 on, a period of over two years. In a sense he had the opportunity to conduct a two-year audition of that individual. It prompts the question – after those many months of observation, did he really not know his oft-troublesome subordinate? Montgomery's long record has already been covered in considerable detail. Yet one must wonder, how much looking back and "weighing" did

Eisenhower do before he decided to go with Monty? What kind of soul searching did he do; what were his considerations, his evaluations?

Ike was certainly well aware that in his "great victory" at El Alamein, Montgomery's WWI-style, set-piece battle of attrition resulted in 13,500 British casualties; that his tanks advanced reluctantly and without any imagination because he knew nothing of tank tactics, and under his command, the tank played a supporting, ineffective role; that 600 of his 1200 tanks were quickly destroyed or immobilized by a mere 200 of Rommel's badly combat-beaten tanks; that Rommel with barely 30 tanks remaining and almost out of gas withdrew. Even his staunchest supporters faulted him for the conduct of his Eighth Army's operation following El Alamein; his over-cautious pursuit of Rommel; his failure to exploit the breakthrough at Wadi Akarit; and his apparent willingness to allow the British First Army to shoulder the entire burden of the final drive to Tunis, while, characteristically, later claiming credit, nonetheless.

Eisenhower certainly remembered that, in the campaign in Sicily, Montgomery rationalized his lack of progress, because of his difficult and ferocious dog-fights against a determined enemy on the Plain of Catania. Yet, he operated over excellent tank country, while Patton fought his way around the perimeter of the island over extremely difficult terrain; he seemed to neglect to mention that it was he, himself, who selected the beaches for his invasion of the island, and then selected for himself the shortest and most direct route to Messina; he urged for Patton merely a supporting role, an assignment that would place Patton in support of his own operation. Despite all that, Patton reached Messina before he did.

It was not that long ago, so Eisenhower was well aware that Montgomery failed for days on end to gain his D-Day objectives; that he "pivoted" around Caen for weeks; that GOODWOOD, his loudly proclaimed break-out operation, failed so miserably; that his own senior British as well as American officers urged his removal; that operation TOTALIZE was similarly unsuccessful; that he badly miscalculated the Canadian advance to Falaise; that much of the blame for the Allied failure to close the Falaise/Argentan gap fell squarely upon his shoulders; that in late August his forces were still endeavoring to negotiate the lower Seine northwest of Paris. It seems that Monty's "touch" was the extreme opposite of the Midas touch. Yet, this was Eisenhower's chosen knight on the great white charger.

Interestingly and ironically, the members of my Eighth Tank Battalion had developed a mental picture of Montgomery that was not too far from being accurate. Of course they were not privy to the highest of counsels. Their vantage point was extremely remote, and their information was acquired by rumor, soldier scuttle-butt, and reading – hardly reliable sources.

Yet to them Monty was no stranger, and they believed that they "knew" the British General. They were convinced that he was cautious, plodding – the absolute opposite of their audacious, bold, successful Army Commander. They were completely familiar with the box in which he had placed himself at Caen. They cackled because the information that had been passed along led them to believe that he hesitated to move until every gallon of gasoline and every shell was accounted for. This was the image of Montgomery at the ground level. Consequently, my tankers remained dumbfounded, shocked, disillusioned and aghast that Eisenhower would choose Montgomery over their own Patton for priority of supplies.

When Ike gave the mission to Montgomery, he committed himself virtually to the full logistical support to the British 21st Army Group. That meant that Montgomery would be given priority for gasoline and all other supplies at the expense of the U. S. Forces. Montgomery, for all intents and purposes, would have it all. Yet, this infuriating subordinate was always reaching out for more – was never satisfied. He urgently reminded Eisenhower that he had pledged to provide all the resources to his main effort. By all resources he meant ALL resources. He wanted Patton stopped at the Meuse, and kept tucked away at that location, while he swept on to Berlin. If this had a familiar note, one has merely to look back and recall Montgomery's insistence during the Sicilian campaign that Patton and his forces sit and hold in defensive positions, while he alone would advance on and take Messina all by himself. (Eisenhower certainly remembered that. One can only imagine, and cringe at the thought, how very different the Sicilian campaign would have been if Ike had accepted his recommendation).

Now Monty was being given another "swipe" at the ball, but in a greatly enhanced operation. Eisenhower had placed himself on the horns of a difficult and frustrating dilemma. Montgomery had been told by Ike that he had priority of gasoline and all other supplies. To him, of course, that meant everything. But Eisenhower could not give him everything. He had to consider American Public Opinion, and he had to answer to General Marshall. The ratio of American troops in Europe versus the British heavily favored the Americans, and was increasing every day, and American achievements had completely overshadowed those of the British. Ike knew that the American public and Marshall would have difficulty absorbing and accepting the knowledge that virtually all resources were sitting squarely in Monty's lap. Moreover, it would be unsettling to learn that the bulk of the American First Army was being placed under Monty's control, and that he could deal directly with the

Army Commander, Gen. Hodges. But his greatest challenge would be to explain why the fast-moving Patton, whose operations had not yet crested, was stopped dead in his tracks, and stranded because of lack of supplies.

So Eisenhower was forced to hold out from Montgomery some supplies for American forces. For the bulk of these very limited resources, First Army, in support of Montgomery, would have priority. Patton would get the "leavings," a meager consolation prize. With these, he would go as far as he could, in his continuing attack to the east, before he ran out.

When the gluttonous Montgomery became aware of this development, he was absolutely furious. For him *all* still meant *everything*. Because Patton was not completely stopped, and he was not getting everything, he announced that Allied planning seemed to have slipped into total disarray. How can you ever satisfy such a guy?

Before making THE DECISION, Eisenhower and his SHAEF staff surely studied in great detail what have been enumerated as the convincing, compelling reasons for the Northern thrust. Conversely, it is safe to assume that during those studies, they also decided on the convincing, compelling reasons why Patton, if given the main mission, would have failed. We can only guess on what adversarial factors were considered during their deliberations, but it can safely be assumed that among others the ones listed below were certainly included.

Simply advancing *blindly* into Germany would not have fulfilled any strategic purpose.

Third Army would have been out on a limb, and liable to have communications cut.

Every mile advanced in September would have increased Patton's lines of communication, requiring more and more trucks to keep up the flow of supplies.

Divisions would have had to be immobilized in order to provide their trucks.

Close air support and aerial supply beyond Lorraine would have been extremely limited. Establishing advance airfields would consume scarce supplies and trucks.

The reality was that the conditions for a breakout and pursuit no longer existed in Lorraine.

Among the problems which Patton faced but failed to acknowledge, was the physical exhaustion of the Third Army, which would have faced furious resistance from a German Army defending its homeland for the first time.

A force amounting to twelve divisions would have had to be transported.

There will be no attempt here to address, debate, and refute in detail each of the assertions presented. However, some brief comments about a couple of them may serve to cast doubt about the credibility of the rest of them.

First, the comment about the furious resistance from a German Army defending its homeland for the first time. The place for that to occur was just inside the border behind the strong defensive positions of the Siegfried Line. As has been pointed out repeatedly, it would have been impossible for the Germans to do so. If Patton had continued to move, he would have swept through an *unmanned* Siegfried Line. A German opportunity lost! So, where would the enemy forces come from that would provide the furious resistance, that would hit Patton's open flanks, cut his lines of communications? They did not *then* exist. Had not the German Army just a short time before been badly mauled at Argentan/Falaise? The fleeing troops at that point had been more interested in saving their own skins than in flying off to try to intercept the speeding Patton.

Listed, also, was reference to the "physical exhaustion of the Third Army." No one in Third Army had been more challenged and active than we tankers of the 4th Armored Division. We were the ones who had fought the longest and hardest. I was one of those. Yes, I was tired. A steel worker after a day's work is tired, but is back up on the girders the next day. So it was with us. We were tired, but we were "charged up." We readily recognized what we had accomplished; there was a sense of euphoria; the adrenalin was flowing. We just could not wait to continue "accomplishing." So on September 2 we were rarin' to go – ready and eager to charge on toward Germany, which now appeared so close.

When the SHAEF staff had, obviously, decided what Patton could not do, it would have been appropriate to pose one question for them. "If you had been told, on August 1, what Patton would have accomplished during the course of that one month, would you have believed it?" The answer, of course, would have been a resounding, "No."

As already suggested, with the mission that he had assigned to Montgomery, Eisenhower, supported by his SHAEF staff, must have been convinced that it was possible for the Allies to end the war in Europe by the end of the year.

However, as we are well aware and history records, the Ruhr was *not* captured and the Rhine was *not* crossed in 1944.

But the war in Europe *could* very well have been won by the end of 1944 if Eisenhower had decided to go with the other option open to him, and that was to assign the main effort to Gen. Patton, and to provide him with the same priority of gasoline, ammunition, and supplies, and all other resources which he had designated for General Montgomery.

As reported, it was as early as June 27, over a month before Patton would lead his Third Army in combat, and as the offense in Normandy was badly bogging down, causing concern and even alarm among the leaders, that Eisenhower somewhat wistfully opined, "Sometimes I wish that I had George Patton here." Tragically, at a critical time in late August, Eisenhower had Patton "here," and instead of opening his arms to him, turned his back. To me, and I support my Eighth Tankers, it was incredible – defied all reason and logic. How could Eisenhower not have thrown his all behind Patton but "gone" instead with Montgomery? I was there, on the ground, in the "arena" – in a tank driving to the east, making things happen. I was completely convinced that if we had continued our push and persisted in doing what we had been doing – that the future great battles of Germany, which had earlier been forecast, would never have taken place and the war, indeed, would have been over before the end of the year.

I was far from alone. There were others who agreed with those contentions. On August 23, the day Eisenhower reportedly made his decision to go with Monty, Bradley was heard from. He proposed that his 12th Army Group could drive through the Saar all the way to Frankfurt. Although Bradley had had doubts about Patton, before the Third Army became operational, its exploits during August now made him a true believer. Compounding his confidence in Patton's abilities was his great anger at being forced to use his 12th Army Group in support of Montgomery's effort. It was no secret that Bradley loathed working with Montgomery. If Patton had received the nod, which Bradley heartily wished, his 12th Army Group and not Montgomery's 21st would have had the dominant role.

Another voice, a surprising and unexpected one, was heard from on this same day. Eisenhower's G2, Major General Kenneth W. D. Strong, said of the situation, "The August battles have done it and the enemy in the west has had it. Two and a half months of bitter fighting have brought the end of the war in Europe within sight, almost within reach."

There was also corroboration from a totally unlikely source that Patton's thrust was not only feasible, but also almost certain of success. That source, of all things, was a very senior German officer. He was General Siegfried Westphal, General von Rundstedt's Chief of Staff. He contended that, "The overall situation in the West, [for the Germans], was serious in the extreme. The Allies could have punched through at any point 'with ease' until mid-October, and would have been able to cross the Rhine and thrust deep into Germany unhindered."

According to historian and author Cornelius Ryan, Westphal's boss, von Rundstedt himself, considered Patton "a far more danger-ous opponent than the overly cautious, habit-ridden and systematic, Montgomery."

Patton had yet another staunch supporter. It was the highly respected British military analyst and critic, B. H. Liddell Hart, who has been previously quoted. He considered that the American Armored Divisions generally, and Wood's 4th Armored Division in particular, had performed remarkably. He claimed that if the American tankers had been allowed to continue their advance, and to slice through Germany by way of the southern "indirect" route, the war against Hitler could well have ended in the fall of 1944. Instead, he pointed out, the Germans were able to put together a tenacious defense, and another two seasons of brutal fighting was ensured.

And now from Patton himself. When he heard that supplies — gasoline, ammunition, and all others, – were to be thrown to the north, leaving his Third Army with no gas with which to move, he was heart-broken, because he, better than anyone, knew the consequences. He instantly declared that Eisenhower's decision to halt the Third Army at the end of August was a "fateful blunder."

As early as August 21, Patton recognized the German weaknesses. He strongly believed that if constant and consistent pressure were placed on the retreating columns, they would crack, and the war would be swiftly concluded. His tanks continued doing just that – applying constant and consistent pressure, and by the end of August Patton believed that he had the Germans right where he wanted them.

He had earlier declared that, if he were provided with the necessary gasoline, he could be at the Rhine in ten days. My private calculations supported his contention and indicated that if he was exaggerating, it was not by much.

However, it was on the twenty-ninth of August, two days before ele-ments of the 4th Armored reached the Meuse, that Patton clearly came face to face with reality. His tanks were speedily advancing, crushing what little resistance the enemy was able to produce. He should have been on a real "high." Instead, he was well aware that this situation would not last, for at any moment he was expecting Eisenhower to hook on, give him a yank, and bring him to a halt.

That date, he would later write, was, in his opinion, the critical one in the war. He said, "and hereafter many pages will be written on it, or rather the events which produced it. It was evident that at time there was no real threat against us as long as we did not stop ourselves or allow us to be stopped by imaginary enemies. Everything seemed rosy when suddenly it was reported to me that 140,000 gallons of gasoline, which we were supposed to get for that day, did not arrive. I presented my case for a rapid advance to the East for the purpose of cutting the Siegfried Line before it could be manned. It is my opinion that this was the momentous error of the war." *(Unfortunately, this was the rare occasion when Patton's assessment proved inaccurate. As has been pointed out, there have NOT been "many pages" written on it. Historians seem to have "by-passed" this most intriguing and most significant episode in the history of WW II in Europe. The words between these covers represent my attempt at this very late date in my life to produce some of the "extensive" pages which Patton had hoped would be produced, but never were.)*

In his book, *War As Knew It*, Patton, after learning of the loss of the 140,000 gallons of gasoline, said, "at first I thought, [Patton was wary and not completely trusting – there was basis for this – of Eisenhower and Montgomery and even to a lesser degree – Bradley], it was a back-handed way of slowing up the Third Army. I later found that this was not the case, but that the delay was due to a change of plan by the High Command, implemented, in my opinion, by General Montgomery. "

But Patton had not quite given up on what was appearing more and more like the inevitable. He stated, "I saw Bradley, Gen. H. R. Bull [Eisenhower's G3], and Allen, Bradley's Chief of Staff, at Chartres on the thirtieth. I presented my case for a rapid advance to the east for the purpose of cutting the Siegfried Line, before it could be manned. Bradley was very sympathetic, but Bull, and, I gather, the rest of SHAEF's staff did not concur."

The realization that he was being cut off from supplies – and thus in essence stopped – frustrated and angered Patton greatly. He never wavered in his deep belief that if he had made a final push along his axis of advance, it would surely have led to the collapse of the German Army in Western Europe.

On September 1, as my battalion was nearing the Meuse, and on the day when Ike finally and in practice became the Allied Ground Commander, Patton wrote to Frederick Ayer, his brother-in-law, "I am impatient with my friends [Eisenhower and Bradley] for not letting me go faster, as I am sure....that the Boche [Germans] has no power to resist."

Recognizing that Montgomery would be receiving supplies at his expense, Patton noted, "Monty does what he pleases, and Ike says, 'Yes, sir.'" Patton believed at that point, as he had before, that Eisenhower was either incapable, or unable (political, Churchill?) to command Montgomery.

As will soon be covered in detail, there were many instances during the course of their long relationship that made Patton believe that Eisenhower was biased, and leaned too often toward the British. Now this latest decision of Ike's served to reinforce those beliefs. More than once, Patton mentioned to his staff, "they now have two enemies to fight: the Germans and SHAEF, whose boss was the best General the British had."

Patton unquestionably was "flip of lip;" he often "sounded off;" his frequent quips could be very funny, but could also cut and hurt; some of his statements were downright outlandish; there were many cases when he should have bitten his lip. However, when it came to military assessments, he bored in seriously, and was usually deadly accurate.

Thus, it was not emotion or bravado, or careless boast, but considered, rational, professional, experienced judgment, that led him to his absolutely firm belief that he could have been through the Siegfried Line before it could be manned, and, like Bradley, he believed that his push to the Rhine would deprive Germany of its critically important and valuable Saar Basin.

He was completely objective in assessing his capabilities and limitations – as a Combat Commander he recognized them in his military actions, he was not impetuous as many believed; he carefully weighed his chances. He did not "shove off half-cocked." Yes, he was certainly audacious (one of his favorite words), but never foolhardy. Yes, he was aggressive. He stated that, "If I have a 50/50 chance I'll take it, because the fighting qualities of the American soldier led by me will give me the 1% necessary."

He was a realist, and not guilty of wishful thinking. He saw that the roads ahead were clear. He just knew that the Moselle could not possibly be defended, that the road to Germany was wide open and waiting. His axis of advance would carry him through Lorraine. Then it was on to Frankfurt. He never wavered in his strong belief that it could have happened.

Earlier it was stated that Eisenhower needed a knight on a great white charger who was battle-tested, aggressive, masterful, indomitable, and inspiring to get him to the Rhine and the German heartland. He had that knight in Patton, for there was hardly anyone who was more comfortable on the back of a horse than Georgie. Patton, as viewed from any vantage point, stood in stark and marked contrast to Montgomery – had an absolutely superb and unparalleled combat history dating back to WW I, and continuing through North Africa and Sicily – all of which was which was completely familiar to Gen. Eisenhower. Patton was already a known successful battlefield commodity. He had constantly and graphically demonstrated that regardless of what the situation required, he was able to get the job done.

From his first day in combat on August 1, he was charged up and rolling, and took to the nature and circumstances of the European battle and its environment like a duck to water. He did not require a "break-in" period; he began achieving merely hours after assuming command. His exploits in August were well nigh unbelievable. He was, without question, the big Allied "star" during that month.

Yet, Patton was not the "chosen one." Eisenhower had decided against him – had permitted "his man" to slip through his fingers.

Because of Patton, the last week in August for the Allies was momentous. His sweep across France was sensational. Historians agreed then, and still do, that it was one of the very great military achievements. Because of it, Patton would receive universal acclaim, and his fame would move into legendary proportions.

Eisenhower and his SHAEF staff must not only have been impressed with this unexpected sweep to the East, but must have gloried in the rapid closure being made toward German soil. They must have been glued to their situation map, whose symbols undoubtedly changed almost by the minute, and had their ears cocked toward the crackling radios, which continued to bring them more and more good news.

Thus, they were well aware that Patton had the momentum; was engaged in a highly successful pursuit; was aided by almost perfect tank conditions which would continue for his superb armor forces; that his advancing elements were much like the Cavalry – moving swiftly, audaciously – a daring, fast-shooting style that would also continue.

From their maps they must have found it difficult to comprehend the most impressive daily output in miles of Patton's tanks; that they would advance as much as 328 miles in twelve days.

The SHAEF staff must have been not only excited but euphoric to realize the nearness of the German border and the Rhine River when Patton's forces were across the Meuse. At that point they were not much more than 180 miles from the Rhine with merely another 20 miles or so to that second great symbol and objective – Frankfurt. During the last part of their sweep to the Meuse, Patton's tanks had averaged nearly 30 miles a day. If they had continued on at even half that speed, they would have been at the Rhine in not much more than the ten days which Patton had earlier predicted, and they would have been on the river well before the days shortened and the Autumn rains became deluges.

On September 2, our first day of "sitting along the Meuse," and the day after Eisenhower assumed full Allied Ground Command, Ike began his efforts to create appropriate contact with the front by meeting with his 12th Army Group Commander, and the leaders of his Armies and the Ninth Air Force at Bradley's Headquarters in Chartres.

This was the perfect and undoubtedly final opportunity for Bradley, Hodges, and Patton to make their last gasp pitch and plea for Eisenhower to go with Patton instead of Montgomery.

But Eisenhower could have surprisingly trumped them by making his own pitch. *A great Field Commander is flexible, can adjust rapidly to changing situations. Above all, he has the courage and is quick to make a correction, a change, if a more dramatic situation presents itself.*

Eisenhower had a rare second chance.

He could have declared, "Georgie, I have watched your spectacular advance in total amazement. Because of it, I have changed my mind. I am going with you instead of Monty. I want you to move out in the morning, and continue moving east, as you have been doing. We'll immediately begin to 'tip the table' in your direction, and 'soup' you up and help every way we can, as you advance across the remainder of France and into Germany. Good luck. Keep up the great work."

That, of course, did not happen. Instead, the senior Commanders, to their great and total dismay, were told that the Americans would support Montgomery. The only concession made was the confirmation that Third Army was not completely dead, as Monty wanted, but would be hanging by a thread. As previously expected, for Patton it would be a day-by-day advance, depending, apparently, on what his beggar's tin cup would collect each day. As an immediate concession, Eisenhower temporarily raised Patton's gasoline allowance enough so that he might be able to advance. Upon hearing later about that decision on Patton, Montgomery, as could be expected, complained bitterly. So the "tentative" decision made on August 23 had not been tentative at all. Although remarkable events later followed they had no bearing whatsoever on the decision. The die had been cast.

Gen. Patton and Gen. Wood *together* have been prominently mentioned within these pages. No pair of individuals could have been more astonished, disillusioned, dumbfounded, and heartsickened than those two by Eisenhower's decision.

An especially poignant quote attributed to Brig Gen. Hobart "Hap" Gay, frequently Patton's very loyal Chief of Staff, best describes how totally crushed those great warriors must have been. Gay recalled, "Patton and Wood were often together, particularly so when the shortage of gasoline grew critical. One evening at dusk, I saw them standing alone, facing to the East, with tears in their eyes, as they foresaw the awful waste of lives – lives of our boys being sacrificed, unnecessarily so, by lack of fuel for their armor."

Incomprehensible as it seemed to me (and others) Eisenhower made an unfortunate decision and stuck with it. On the following pages the merits of that decision will be examined by answering the questions, "How did Montgomery do with his major, (single) thrust and "everything?" "How did Patton do in his very secondary role with the 'leavings'?"

However, before answering those questions, this appears to be an appropriate time to pause and study the relationship between Eisenhower and Montgomery, and between Eisenhower and Patton.

CHAPTER 15

GENERAL DWIGHT D. EISENHOWER – FIELD MARSHAL BERNARD LAW MONTGOMERY: THE RELATIONSHIP

In sharp contrast to his first meeting with George Patton, Gen. Eisenhower's initial encounter with Gen. Montgomery was anything but auspicious; in fact, it was a total bust. It proved to be a precursor of a relationship that would exist under the most difficult and trying of circumstances.

In the late spring of 1942, Gen. Marshall sent Eisenhower, a recently promoted Major General, to visit London and to report back on the military situation then existing. After an intensely crowded schedule during which he conferred with anyone and everyone of military consequence, he, accompanied by an also-new Maj. Gen. Mark Clark, found himself on the south coast of England. This was an area where British and Canadian troops were engaged in extremely intensified training. Upon arrival, Eisenhower and Clark were ushered into a small farmhouse, which featured a large map fastened to a wall. As they stared at the map, they awaited the arrival of the Commanding General, Lt. Gen. Bernard Law Montgomery.

When he arrived, he appeared very much out of sorts. It was obvious that he was extremely annoyed, for he mentioned at the outset that he had been directed to take time from his very busy schedule to brief the two visitors (of lesser rank).

The briefing had barely begun when Eisenhower lit a cigarette. Instantly, Montgomery stopped his presentation, and asked who was smoking. Anyone who knew Montgomery was well aware of his great aversion to cigarettes. Eisenhower, of course, had no such knowledge and readily admitted that it was he. At that Montgomery in brusque, strong, and pointed terms informed Eisenhower that he did not permit smoking in his presence. Ike quickly extinguished his cigarette, and the briefing continued. After Montgomery had completed his briefing and departed, Eisenhower was left burning, furious, and angry, for he believed that he had been humiliated. It was well known that Ike had great difficulty overlooking slights, and that one must have lingered a long time.

The cigarette incident appears very minor in nature, for subsequently they had endless, critical meetings together. However, those two men, one a heavy smoker and the other with a strong dislike of smoking, would have had great difficulty working closely together on a regular basis in close proximity to one another. During the high-pressure, crucial days of the war in Europe, Eisenhower was up to four packs a day, and there was hardly a moment when a cigarette was not between his fingers. At that point, however, Monty was hardly in a position to tell Eisenhower to stop. On this relatively minor matter (and there would be others of much greater import) Monty and Ike were like oil and water, they just did not mix.

During the weeks and months which followed, the relationship between Eisenhower and Montgomery would be a puzzle, an enigma – difficult to explain, to rationalize – even today. There would throughout their relationship be suspicion, distrust, disrespect, disloyalty, and acrimony. It would be difficult, testy, contentious, and at times strained almost to the breaking point.

General Montgomery was basically a strange individual – not a likeable person, in contrast to the more personable Eisenhower (except on the frequent occasions when he lost his temper). Many have enjoyed disparaging Montgomery's looks. He was described variously as a small guy, 5' 7", thin, wiry, bony, with a sharp nose, eyes that darted about quickly, hawk-like. He was smug, boastful with an arrogant, abrasive demeanor, a loner with few friends among contemporaries or individuals in high places.

Yet, the sight of this slight British officer with his baggy, unpressed corduroy trousers, head sticking out of an unmilitary turtle-neck sweater with strong, unblinking eyes, black beret with the two traditional patches, would cause tremendous excitement, and would attract waves of admiration, adulation, and affection. Ironically, this unattractive, unimpressive individual had a magnetism, a tremendous "hold" on the British people, and particularly upon the British soldier.

There is a "chemistry" that brings unlikely individuals together to become fast friends, and two completely different personalities to become a devoted husband and wife. There was a rare "chemistry" between

Montgomery and the British people that was difficult to explain. But **it was there!** He was virtually worshipped as an icon. That bonding undoubtedly owes its genesis to El Alamein.

As is well known, the British had suffered over a considerable period of time a long run of evacuations and defeats; they were wearied and demoralized by what some called valorous setbacks. They were thirsty and hungry for some sort of victory. Montgomery provided that at El Alamein. Though it was somewhat tainted – the details of the battle did not matter – it was a victory.

Montgomery became an instant hero; in a little over a year he became England's symbol of victory; many called him England's savior. No matter what he did or did not do after that battle, the mantle of heroism rested comfortably upon his shoulders, and was never close to being dislodged. Among his men, he was a legend which – no matter what – was imperishable.

His relationship with Prime Minister Churchill was unique, and had a direct bearing on his relationship with Eisenhower. Going back to North Africa, it is well to remember that Montgomery was not considered a natural choice for Army Command, despite his many qualifications. When Churchill decided to make a change in command of the Eighth Army, he selected for that assignment Lt. Gen. William ("Strafer") Gott. Unfortunately Gott was killed in an airplane crash, being shot down just before he was to assume command. Montgomery was handy and "available," and was assigned to command that Army. The Eighth Army would be the vehicle that provided Montgomery with his "name" and fame.

Much later, once again, Montgomery was not a first choice of Churchill. The prime minister apparently wanted General Alexander to be the Ground Commander for Operation Overlord, the Normandy Invasion. For some reason difficult to understand, Alexander was not extracted from his command in Italy. Once again Churchill reached out to a "handy" Montgomery, and he was given that super-important and powerful assignment. Churchill was well aware of Monty's "hold" on the British public and military. He was a politician. Whether he liked it or not his career would be intertwined with that of Montgomery. Consequently, it would be in his best interests to protect and, where possible, advance Monty's career, and along with others to "suffer" him. Churchill never had any illusions about Montgomery, as evidenced by the oft-quoted, "In defeat unbeatable, in victory unbearable."

It is certainly no secret that there were powerful differences between Eisenhower and Montgomery over strategy, and their disagreements have generated many debates about the conduct of the war in Europe.

Montgomery always felt superior to Eisenhower. Thus, he had difficulty being a loyal subordinate, and was openly and consistently critical of Ike. Monty early on said of Eisenhower, "He has but to smile at you, and you trust him at once." Beyond that, one has great difficulty finding any other uttered words of approbation.

There were many contentious issues between Monty and Ike, but the two most significant were Monty's views on command and control, and his insistence on the single (pencil) thrust.

On D-Day, with Eisenhower in England, Montgomery was the Ground Commander. He commanded his 21st Army Group, and Bradley's First Army was under his control. That command structure remained until August 1, when Bradley's 12th Army Group was activated. It would include his First Army and Patton's newly activated Third Army. Monty would remain in nominal control of the Allied Armies, until September 1, when Eisenhower assumed command. For all practical purposes Monty's tenure actually ended on August 1, when Bradley became Commander of the 12th Army Group. Montgomery did exercise the power of his broad command at Argentan, but he erred badly with unfortunate results. He over-estimated the rate of advance to the south of the Canadian forces, and stopped Bradley from advancing to the north. The result: the Falaise/Argentan gap was never closed. Eisenhower was well aware that Montgomery was in error, but compounded the error by doing nothing. Ike believed that although he was the Supreme Commander he should abstain from intervening, because Montgomery was the nominal Allied Ground Commander, and he hesitated to send operational or tactical instructions to Monty. He acted as an interested but "hands-off" by-stander. Significantly, he had done that before, during operation Husky in Sicily. At such times Eisenhower was not an actual battle leader, but more of a super military director.

After the breakout in Normandy, Montgomery had constantly *pestered* Eisenhower, was actually insufferable in his demands, for broader and greater control. He strongly believed that if he had total control of ground operations he could shorten the war. He was convinced that Eisenhower's Headquarters (SHAEF) in London was too far removed from front-line operations to be able to direct those day-to-day operations. He favored correcting the situation by creating a super Ground Command, which he, of course, would head, as an additional element between Eisenhower and the Army Groups. He would, thus, "relieve" SHAEF of its "labors." By his actions he left no doubt that he firmly believed Eisenhower was primarily a political Commander, unfamiliar with the day-to-day operations of fighting the war.

Yet, on other occasions Monty indicated that he did not want to surrender command of his Army Group to become Eisenhower's Deputy Ground Commander. As a graphic example of his constantly "reaching out," he finally decided that he wanted to keep command of his 21st Army Group, **AND** take on the second "hat," that of super Ground Commander. Monty's aspirations became abundantly clear to an astonished Eisenhower, who finally with great exasperation said, "Monty wants to have his cake and eat it, too."

Montgomery was an insufferable subordinate. He was always "on" Eisenhower, demanding more. Many wondered how Eisenhower could "stand" him. Those individuals credited Ike with "forbearance of heroic if not saintly proportions." Monty was supercilious in his treatment of most Americans, but in particular – Eisenhower. There was universal agreement that if Monty had been an American, he would have been "long gone."

It appears that Montgomery's two greatest failings were, first, his inability to "get on" with his contemporaries, which included British as well as Americans, and, second, which was most difficult for his associates to "take," his insistence that he was always right, and that all had gone according to (his) plan – when it had not.

Montgomery was not always forthright with Eisenhower. For example, during planning for Operation GOODWOOD, General Dempsey, commanding the British Second Army, explained, "to get air support for a tank thrust against the Germans, Monty felt it necessary to overstate the aims of the operation. In doing so he did not take Eisenhower into his confidence. Such reticence was a habit of his – 'There's no need to tell Ike.'"

It had been reported that on July 21, three days after Monty had kicked off the most disappointing GOODWOOD, Eisenhower pleaded with Montgomery to renew his offensive. Apparently he did not "get through" to Monty, so he enlisted the aid of Churchill and asked him to persuade Monty "to get on his bicycle and start moving." This is a good example of the great patience and restraint showed by Eisenhower in his relations with Montgomery.

Patton would state that Eisenhower handled Montgomery with kid gloves. He had a good point, for the admonishments, which Monty received from Eisenhower, were few and far between, and when administered were remarkably gentle. On one occasion Ike opened up and admitted that, "Montgomery's the only man in either Army that I can't get along with."

Some time after the Normandy invasion, Monty wrote to Field Marshal Sir Alan Brooke, Chief of the Imperial General Staff (CIGS) and Churchill's Chief military advisor, as he would do more than once, "As a Commander of land operations, Eisenhower is quite useless. There must be no misconception on this matter; he is completely and utterly useless."

Monty wrote to Brooke again after, Ike visited him on August 13, "Eisenhower's ignorance as to how to run a war is absolute and complete." Monty's comments were received by receptive ears, for this is the same Brooke who after the war told of his first meeting with Eisenhower: "He certainly made no great impression on me . . . and if I had been told of the future that lay in front of him I should have refused to believe it."

Eisenhower and Montgomery had disagreements concerning Operation Dragoon. Because Eisenhower continued to push for the landings in Southern France, with which Montgomery strongly disagreed, he believed that this was another example of Eisenhower's lacking in the proper sense of strategic priorities.

There were other instances when Montgomery not only disagreed with Eisenhower, but also showed his disdain for his Commander. On more than one occasion he "stood up" Ike by not attending a critical and important meeting, declaring that he was "too busy" and sent, instead, a "stand-in." Such was the case shortly after Eisenhower moved his Headquarters to Versailles, when he had a conference with all his major Commanders, some of whom had flown in from considerable distances. Conspicuous by his absence was Montgomery, who sent in his stead his Chief of Staff, Major General Sir Francis de Guingand. Bradley reported that although Eisenhower appeared unperturbed, Monty's absence was viewed by the other Commanders as an affront to the Allied Chief. Monty's failure to take part in that particular conference was significant, as it restricted the effectiveness of the important gathering.

Montgomery was particularly and constantly critical of Eisenhower's choice of the location and layout, and thus effectiveness, of his Headquarters. He was absolutely correct in his contention that SHAEF remained in London much too long after D-Day, and as the war progressed on the European mainland.

On September 1, with my 4th Armored Division situated east of the Meuse River, SHAEF finally made the "bold" move from England to France. The Headquarters was set up in, of all places, Granville, which was located on the western coast of the Cherbourg Peninsula. There, Monty would point out, Eisenhower was three to four hundred miles from the battle area, farther than he had been in London. Montgomery complained, "He had no communications, no telephone, not even radiophone – it took 24 hours for information to reach him from the front, and another 24 hours to get back." This meant a 48-hour delay, and no modern battle can be run in those circumstances.

Monty also believed that Eisenhower's role, as Supreme Commander was an all-consuming one. Because of that, he contended, "It would be altogether too much for one man to leave his 'lofty perch' so far from the front at Cherbourg to exert direct control over such a 'massive ag-glomeration' of land forces as the Allies had."

SHAEF's next move did nothing much to improve matters. On September 20, the day after the Arracourt tank battles began for the 4th Armored Division in Lorraine, SHAEF moved to – of all places – Versailles. The Headquarters would be located in the Trianon Palace Hotel. There Eisenhower and his staff worked and lived in majestic splendor. At that location they were almost the width of a country away from us of the 4th Armored Division, who were living and fighting in the rain, cold, muck and misery of a sodden Lorraine.

In early December, General John Wood left his 4th Armored Division and flew to Versailles to call upon Eisenhower. He later said to his friend, newspaper writer, and later biographer, Hanson Baldwin, "You wrote of Eisenhower 'trudging in the snow.' What snow? His butler at the Trianon Palace must have been remiss that day – not to have the walks cleared off. I came out of the snow and slime and mud and blood of the Saar at that time, and the sight of the luxury of Eisenhower's Versailles Court was a nauseating experience for a soldier." On this Montgomery would have been in wholehearted agreement with General Wood.

During the Normandy invasion, the breakout from Normandy, and the sweep across France, Montgomery was the overall Ground Commander. However, he knew full well that he was really the nominal Commander, a kind of Ground Deputy to Eisenhower. He was well aware that his role as Ground Commander was a temporary one, that it was inevitable, "in the books," for Eisenhower at some point to take over full command of the ground operations. Nevertheless, as the weeks passed he just could not reconcile himself to the thought of having to give up his ground role, and he fully believed that at some appropriate time the "temporary" would be dropped, and he would be the full-fledged, permanent Ground Commander.

But on August 23rd his bubble burst. Ike paid a visit to Monty's Field Headquarters in Normandy, and informed him that he intended to take command of the land battle at the end of the month, and that his policy would continue to be an advance to the Rhine on a broad front. He also said that he would give the British Second Army priority in supplies, and declared that he would see to it that Monty retained "operational coordination" over the northern flank of the Allied advance.

Even though Monty was now aware that the inevitable was about to happen, he kept thinking and hoping against hope that he could somehow push it away.

It happened! On September 1, a most significant milestone in the war, General Eisenhower became Allied Ground Commander, and assumed full control of all ground operations. This was not an impetuous, hasty development, but had been planned for quite some time. On this day Montgomery lost one of his two "hats," that of nominal Ground Commander, or "Deputy" to Eisenhower. He now became merely the Commander of the British 21st Army Group. Because Bradley also commanded an Army Group (the American 12th) they were now battlefield equals. Word had been out that this would happen; a hue and cry was immediately raised, and the British public were furious at what they perceived to be a demotion for their beloved Monty. Earlier it had been mentioned that it was in Churchill's long-range interest to protect and advance Monty's career. What occurred was a vivid example. On that day, incredibly, to assuage the British people and as a sop to Monty himself, he was promoted to Field Marshal. In effect the British people said, "So there!" As is well known, a Field Marshal is the highest British military rank. It carries with it more prestige than plain ol' General. So now Monty was a Field Marshal and Ike merely a General. As could be expected, Eisenhower was upset, but Bradley and Patton were absolutely disbelieving, furious, and "sick."

That day would have profound and endless ramifications. Despite his promotion, Montgomery was greatly agitated, angered and overwrought. From the moment when Eisenhower assumed command of the Ground Forces their relationship took an abrupt, sharp, downward turn. That relationship almost instantly began to unravel and would continue to do so precipitously during the weeks and months ahead. As has already been described, Monty had been constantly critical of Eisenhower. But from this date forward that criticism would have far greater dimensions – would be deeper, more bitter, more cutting.

Montgomery would never be able to accept why he, the successful Commander of the 3rd Infantry Division in 1940, of the Eighth Army in North Africa, Sicily, Italy, and the Allied actions in Normandy and after, would be forced to turn "the saber" over to an individual who had not commanded above the battalion level. Critics on Monty's staff derided Eisenhower and claimed that his experience did not extend much beyond his role as Chief of the Operations Division of the U. S. War Department.

For Montgomery, commanding the Allied Ground Forces was a constant, unrelenting obsession. He believed that it was his destiny, that he was rightfully the anointed, chosen one. He was convinced that he was the one with all the qualifications – the command experience, the battlefield knowledge, the record of accomplishment. Because he had such an exalted opinion of himself and his capabilities, he would be constantly damning and slamming Eisenhower. He would never let go of this obsession. He pushed hard, persisted until the very end of the war to obtain for himself command of all the Allied ground elements.

Conversely, he firmly believed that Eisenhower was ill-prepared for the task of running the ground war; was out of his depth.

He was of the firm opinion that SHAEF could not run the war from Granville or Versailles – that the campaign needed a full-time Ground Commander who could devote all his time and energies to matters of immediate tactical importance. That man, he contended, was not Ike, who had distracting priorities, and who had to devote much of himself to overall broad strategy, political problems, and the relationship of allies.

A constant, contentious issue between Montgomery and Eisenhower was the "single thrust." Monty deeply believed that Eisenhower's "bulling ahead" on all fronts was categorically wrong-headed. He had told Eisenhower repeatedly, never letting up to the point where a lesser man than Eisenhower would have exploded (and Ike nearly did), that the only way to finish off the war was with one powerful and full-blooded thrust (under his command, of course).

Monty hit this point hard after September 1, in a discussion with Chester Wilmot, a British newspaperman and historian. Monty related, "When Ike came to see me in Normandy, he said first that he intended to take over command of the battle itself at the end of the month, and second that his policy was to advance to the Rhine on a broad front. I told him it couldn't be done. We couldn't win that way. I said administratively we haven't got the stuff to maintain both Army Groups at full pressure. The only policy is to halt the left and strike with the right, or halt the right and strike with the left. We must decide on one thrust, and put all the maintenance to support that. If we split the maintenance and advance on a broad front, it will mean that we are so weak everywhere that we will have no chance of success. He did not agree. He said 21st Army Group should go for the Saar-Frankfurt area. The root of the trouble was that politically he did not dare stop Patton. Patton was the most public hero of the moment. If he grounded Patton, as he should have done, there would have been a tremendous outcry in America. He wasn't big enough to face it." (If politics were involved in Eisenhower's ultimate decision, Monty was not hindered by it, but greatly benefited from it. Ike must have listened to him that day, for subsequently he chose to "strike with the left and halt the right [Patton]."

As the discussion with Wilmot continued, Monty "unloaded" on Ike as never before, and obviously "got off his chest" some deep-seated, festering resentments. Some of his statements were:

•Ike's decision to take over command was a disaster; he had neither the experience nor the organization.

•He had never directed any battle himself; he did not know the technique of command, and had no firm principles of strategy and no strategic policy.

•Because he had no ideas of his own, he used to go 'round from one Commander to another getting their ideas, and then he would try to rationalize a plan which was essentially a compromise between the demands and suggestions of his junior Commanders.

•A Supreme Commander must have strong principles and a clear plan, and must issue his orders to his Commanders on the basis of these.

•It is hopeless if he tries to work the other way round, and evolve a compromise plan from the various suggestions of his subordinates.

•In Ike's case it was particularly unfortunate, because he was extremely susceptible to the personality of the last Commander he saw before making his decision.

• In modern war the Supreme Commander must have a firm, consistent, and continuous control over the battle.

• Modern war moves so fast that the battle can go off the rails in 12 hours. "The Supreme Commander must be in such a position that he always has firm control. Otherwise some headstrong Commander like Patton will muck up your battle plan before you know it."

It is perfectly obvious from these assertions that Monty had anything but a high regard for his Commander, and never bothered to hide that fact from anyone, including Ike himself. Ten days after that momentous first day of September, Monty would continue with his "lessons" to Eisenhower.

On. September 10, Ike flew to Montgomery's 21st Army Group. This was a case of the overall Ground Commander stopping by to look in on a major subordinate command. No sooner had his feet hit the ground than he was hit with a barrage of words. Montgomery launched a lecture on strategy that was so basic that it was brazen, contemptuous, and downright insulting. It was as though Eisenhower was a brand new second lieutenant, and was being given his first instructions on tactics. As the words gushed forth, Monty had difficulty containing himself. He scorched Eisenhower with a damning critique of the way the war had thus far been run. He stayed in character and was abrasive, but this time was abusive and belittling, as well. Finally even the ever-patient (with Monty) Eisenhower had had enough. It has been reported that Ike placed his hand on Monty's knee and said, "Steady, Monty, you can't speak to me like that, I'm your boss."

Eisenhower, during the many difficult weeks in Europe, did an absolutely masterful job of keeping Allied relations on an even keel. To this day he is universally admired, applauded, and praised for his great accomplishments in that regard. There are many who believe that he was unique, that he was absolutely the right man for the job, and that there are few who could have done nearly as well.

However, a point was reached when British and American relations not only became strained and extremely difficult, but they were completely shattered, and like Humpty-Dumpty could never be put back together again.

Unfortunately and regrettably, this resulted primarily because of another faulty and ill-conceived Eisenhower decision, and it occurred during the "Battle of the Bulge." On December 20, during the early days of the battle, Ike divided command between Field Marshal Bernard Law Montgomery, commanding the British 21st Army Group, and General Omar Bradley, who commanded the American 12th Army Group. His reasoning was that the German advance had split the American First and Third Armies, and cut Bradley's communications with Gen. Hodges, his 1st Army Commander. Because Bradley's Headquarters was on the south flank, Eisenhower decided to put Montgomery in command of all forces north of the Bulge, and Bradley in command of those in the south. With that line-up Montgomery would be commanding Bradley's American First Army. As can be imagined, Bradley was angered, furious, so much so that he went to the limit and threatened to resign. As it turned out, Eisenhower's decision was a huge mistake. Once again, whatever Monty touched seemed to turn sour.

Ike wanted a counterattack at the base of the Bulge, with Montgomery pushing from the north and Patton from the south. By the 27th. Eisenhower was leaning hard to get the counterattack started. Patton was ready to go in the south.

•But Montgomery declared that the Germans would be making one last assault; therefore, he wanted to wait, stop it, and *then* counterattack.

• He had a contrary plan. He wanted to hit the Germans on the nose of the Bulge, and to drive them back to the starting point, instead of along the base where the Germans could be cut off and destroyed.

• Typically, Montgomery again delayed, causing Eisenhower frustration and near panic. Relief came with word that Montgomery had a new plan, and would launch it by New Year's Eve.

• But Montgomery never meant it. On December 30, he told Ike that he could not attack until January 3 or later, and once again demanded (is this August, September?) that Eisenhower give him sole command of the Allied Land Armies.

• Then again, the same old refrain. Monty claimed that Eisenhower's policies had failed; that he must now give way to a more experienced Commander; that with him in command he would attack with a single thrust by his 21st Army Group toward Berlin, leaving Patton where he was, something that should have been done months ago.

• He did not start his counterattack until January 3, and concentrated on pushing the Germans back from the Meuse River rather than cutting them off along the base, along the Our river line.

• After Eisenhower put him in command of the northern flank, Montgomery later claimed that he brought the British into the fight, and, thus, saved the Americans. (Bogus claim. How could he have tried to "sell" that one – 81, 000 American casualties, 1400 British; 19,000 Americans killed, 200 British.)

• Montgomery declared that it had been a "most interesting" battle for him, "I think possibly one of the most interesting and tricky battles I have ever handled." Then he had the unmitigated gall, the unspeakable effrontery, to declare that GIs made great fighting men, when given proper leadership — him of course.

All that was very bad, but the very worst was yet to come. On January 7, Montgomery held what most charitably could be termed an "ill-advised" press conference. But it was more than that, it was abysmal: the ostensible purpose of the press conference was for Montgomery to describe how he had won the Battle of the Bulge. He related, "On the first day as soon as I saw what was happening, I took certain steps to ensure that if the Germans got to the Meuse, they would certainly not get over the river. And I carried out certain movements, so as to provide balanced dispositions to meet the threatened danger. I was thinking ahead." (But he made no such dispositions, took no such steps.) He continued in a demeaning and patronizing manner, to belittle the American effort. It was a typical account of the battle.

Consequently, Montgomery was quickly pictured in the newspapers as having been responsible for the Bulge victory and for single-handedly rescuing our shattered American Armies. Monty was depicted as St. George to the rescue, and the one who had arrived in time to save and bail out the American command from disaster. As could be expected, the British "ate" the news in big bites, and with great relish. Once more they were aroused enough to insist again that Monty be named as Deputy to Eisenhower for super command of all Ground Forces, (another promotion?) All this, despite the fact that ever since Normandy, the Americans had proved to be far more competent fighters than the British. On top of that, there were at that time in the E. T. O. 50 U.S. divisions in contrast to the 15 of Great Britain.

The press conference had tremendous repercussions. American leaders just could not believe what they had heard, and were stunned and infuriated, as were the American troops who had fought in the battle *(of whom I was one)*. The American public was angered, greatly perplexed and wondered, "What's up? That is not the way it was reported to us."

Bradley and Patton by now had only total contempt for Montgomery. Bradley made it perfectly clear by announcing that if he were placed under Monty's command, he would ask for relief, and Patton declared he would join him.

The sky was dark with venom. Finally, that great leader and orator, Churchill, practiced damage control in a speech in the House of Commons. In an effort to clear the air and smooth the violently troubled waters, he extended a much-needed apology to the Americans for Montgomery's words and actions. Churchill pointed out some graphic, telling statistics – for every British soldier engaged, there were 30/40 Americans; for every British soldier lost there were 60/80 Americans. He credited the United States for the Allied victory, and continued by calling the "Battle of the Bulge" the greatest battle of the war, and one that he believed would always be regarded as an ever-famous American victory.

It was during the battle and after all those frustrating weeks that Ike, finally, had enough of Monty. He rebuffed him at every turn. If Monty kept insisting on a single thrust, Ike told him that he would ask the Combined Chiefs of Staff to choose between them.

And so the war ended with little attempt to repair the breach. Each side went its own way. There was no longer any evidence or semblance of unity, amity – those were irretrievably lost.

Monty had never changed his spots. He continued to be Monty. Patton could not contain himself, and blurted, "Monty is a tired little fart. War requires taking risks, and he won't take them. "

In 1946, not long after the war in Europe had ended, Montgomery was appointed to the highest position in the British military, Chief of the Imperial General Staff (CIGS). Even with the war behind him, it was quickly apparent that Montgomery's personality had not changed for the better. He was still an abrasive individual, supercilious, haughty. His megalomania persisted, which apparently even the royal family found difficult to tolerate. For whatever reason, his tenure was brief, and he gave up his office in 1948.

Those two aging soldiers who had had such a contentious relationship during the war would have a tension-packed visit together a dozen years after the war had ended in Europe. It was in the spring of 1957 that Montgomery, then serving as Deputy Commander of the North Atlantic Treaty Organization, (NATO), came to this country on an American speaking tour. He arranged for a visit with the Eisenhowers at Gettysburg, something that he had long wanted to do. Prior to the visit, he spoke in Baltimore to the English-Speaking Union – during which he made some very unfavorable comments about the foreign policy, particularly in the Middle East, of the Eisenhower administration. This, of course, did not set well with the President. As if that were not bad enough, Monty told reporters that he would visit Eisenhower at Gettysburg. He added that he had read all about the battle, and that as a military man, he would have "sacked" both General Robert E. Lee and General George Gordon Meade, the Union Commander. When he heard of this, Eisenhower, needless to say, was more than agitated, he was livid.

As could be expected, the initial meeting was extremely strained, and the situation progressively deteriorated, during the hours and days that followed. As the two toured the Gettysburg battlefield, they were followed closely by hordes of newspaper people who strained to hear every word uttered by these famous generals. Montgomery continued to insist loudly for all to hear that the top two Civil War generals should have been sacked, and strongly intimated that Eisenhower agreed with him. (How could Montgomery of all people, so blatantly, vociferously, and categorically talk about sacking generals? He surely must have been well aware that after the GOODWOOD disaster "they" were after HIS scalp. During that episode, questions had quickly risen concerning his competence. Eisenhower, for once, had been angered and dismayed by his conduct of the operation. Criticism raged almost uncontrolled between both his British and American staff members. They wanted him sent packing. Speculation was rife about who his successor would be. Once again, he was saved "by the bell." So the very nerve of the guy to be talking about the sacking of generals....)

Newspapers were immediately filled with headlines announcing that the two generals agreed that the Civil War generals should have been "sacked." One headline read, "Eisenhower Joins Montgomery in Criticizing Meade and Lee." Another reported, "Lee, Meade Deserve 'Sacking,' Ike and Monty Say at Gettysburg."

As was expected, there was a tremendous outcry throughout the land, but especially in the south, where the ladies were particularly shocked, distressed, and resentful. *Newsweek* declared that of all the British generals, there was none who managed to irritate the Americans more, (and more often), than Montgomery. This despite Viscount Alanbrooke having been quoted in a recent publication as saying that Eisenhower had lacked combat experience during the war, and that his leadership had suffered as a result.

By the end of the Gettysburg visit the relationship, which had always been difficult, was strained to the absolute limit.

In late 1958, more than a year after the Gettysburg visit, Montgomery's memoirs were published. In the book he said uncomplimentary things about Ike, and made statements that were cruel and inappropriate, as well. He stated that the war could have been won, and thousands of lives saved, by December 1944, if only Eisenhower had allowed him to make his pencil-line strike across the Rhine. As could be expected, President Eisenhower was infuriated.

What hurt Eisenhower deeply was the later realization that the book, so critical of him, had probably already been finished, when Monty visited Gettysburg the year before. But for unmitigated gall and *chutzpah* Montgomery won the Kewpie Doll. In 1958 he willingly accepted Eisenhower's hospitality, and stayed in the White House for three days, knowing what he had said of his host in a book soon to be out.

Monty's memoirs finally "did it." After its publication, Eisenhower refused to have anything more to do with his former subordinate. The contentious and tempestuous relationship, which spanned some years and included many circumstances and life-and-death situations, was completely and irrevocably broken.

CHAPTER 16

GENERAL DWIGHT D. EISENHOWER –
GENERAL GEORGE S. PATTON, JR.:
THE RELATIONSHIP.

Surprisingly, there is a general lack of awareness of the early relationship between Dwight Eisenhower and George Patton. If one recognizes and understands that early relationship, it makes their last days truly remarkable, stunning, not entirely unpredictable.

George Patton was older and militarily more senior than Eisenhower. Patton graduated from West Point in the class of 1909, while Eisenhower's class was 1915. Thus, at the very outset, Patton had a seniority of six years. That would have been seven, if Patton had graduated with his entering Class of 1908. But George had to repeat his plebe year, and thus, graduated a year after his original Class.

Patton was five years older than Ike; George was born in 1885, Eisenhower in 1890. So, initially, in two important categories, Patton had a substantial lead over Eisenhower – age and military seniority.

That lead increased substantially after the devastating World War I broke out in Europe. Patton, who all his life would seek combat, had plenty of it in France. He became the top American Tank Commander. He commanded the largest American tank formations in action in France. He was severely wounded in combat, and ultimately received a decoration which he had fervently coveted, the Distinguished Service Cross, for extraordinary heroism. He ended the war as a temporary colonel.

Eisenhower, on the other hand, did not serve in France, was not in combat during World War I. While the war raged, Ike commanded a tank-training center at Camp Colt in Gettysburg. He did so well that he was promoted from Capt. to temporary Lt. Col. However, he lamented missing the war, and feared that he would be forced over and over to explain why.

These two officers met after the war in the autumn of 1919 at the home of the Tank Corps, Camp Meade (now Fort Meade), Maryland. Patton was senior in rank, had a distinguished combat record, had been wounded and highly decorated. He was a war hero, and was already beginning to be someone "known." Eisenhower was well behind in all categories. Thus, it was natural that on tank matters Patton would serve as a kind of mentor to his younger and less experienced *protégé*.

Many have the misconception that George and Ike were peers. As has been pointed out, they were nowhere equal in age, length of service, experience or rank. Their personalities differed greatly, as well. Patton was brash, egotistical, impatient, and self-confident. Eisenhower was quieter, self-effacing, with an easy-going manner, a disarming smile, and fun-loving. Patton was rich, moved in the highest social circles, and knew people in high places. Eisenhower's background was modest and mid-western.

At that time everyone seemed to think that, because of his head start and colorful personality, there would be no limits to the goals Patton would seize. Conversely, for a long period of time, people did not believe that Eisenhower would achieve much at all. However, although they had different personalities, both were passionate in their efforts to advance their careers.

Despite these considerable differences, they became very good friends and would remain so for many years. One of the factors that drew them together and helped them to bond was their firm belief that the tanks of the future should have an independent role, and not be a subordinate part of the infantry and controlled by the infantry. Both recognized the great battlefield potential of tanks, and were in agreement that it definitely was the weapon of the future.

Both were so sold on tanks that they wrote articles for their respective branch journals – Eisenhower in the *Infantry Journal* and Patton in the *Cavalry Journal*. These articles highlighted the mobility and firepower of armor, and predicted a crucially important exploitation role in battles of the future. They believed that well-designed tanks could maneuver in mass, and either outflank the enemy or tear gaping holes in the enemy lines, and cause the collapse of an entire front.

Their writings challenged solid existing infantry doctrine, and were considered almost heresy by the infantry. The Chief of Infantry was so irate that he clamped down hard on both officers, and they were ordered to desist. These factors served to cement their friendship. They rode, studied, and played cards together. The last straw for George and Ike was the passage of the National Defense Act of 1920, which placed the Tank Corps under the Chief of Infantry. The message was loud and clear for both. Eisenhower returned for assignment to the traditional duties of that period.

Patton wrestled long and hard. After his deep involvement with tanks during the war, he had great reluctance and difficulty leaving them. He now recognized that there was no future for him by staying with tanks. He recognized that he would be serving in small units subservient to the infantry. That was not for him. So, he returned to his first love – the Cavalry at Fort Myer, Virginia, which was still glamorous and exciting duty.

Subsequently, Patton was selected to attend the Command and General Staff School at Fort Leavenworth, Kansas. He graduated in the top ten per cent of the class of 1924. Ike attended the school two years later. George, in his eagerness to help his friend, sent him a hundred pages of notes, which he had compiled during his student days. Ike graduated first in the class of 1926. Patton wrote Ike a glowing congratulatory letter for graduating and being the big No. 1. Patton believed that his notes may have assisted Ike in his laudable achievement, but there was no indication from Ike that such was the case.

As it has been for centuries, the inter-war years were bleak for true warriors, and were so for both Ike and George. Patton continued his self-promotion and self-study, which enhanced his reputation. In July of 1940 Patton again left the Cavalry and returned to tanks. He was transferred from the Third United States Cavalry Regiment *(where I was a brand new second lieutenant)* and became Commander of the 2nd Armored Brigade of the 2nd Armored Division at Fort Benning, Georgia, with a subsequent promotion to Brigadier General.

Although they would not serve together during the inter-war years, the two friends remained in contact by correspondence. In that same year Eisenhower was a Lt. Col., still considerably far behind the advancing Patton, and concerned and worried about his future, fearing that he would not soon receive a significant and important assignment.

In late summer of that year they again picked up their correspondence. Patton, now a Brigade Commander and a Brigadier General, had indications that it might not be too long before he became Division Commander of the 2nd Armored Division, with a subsequent promotion to major general. He still seemed to be looking out for his friend, for he made a most generous overture. Patton asked Ike if he would be willing to serve as Division Chief of Staff, or a Regimental Commander, if he did, indeed, assume command of the division. Either job would assure Ike of a promotion to colonel. Eisenhower was gaining a reputation as an excellent staff officer, but was concerned that because of that, he might miss commanding a combat unit. So he jumped at Patton's offer, and agreed that he very much wanted to be back with tanks, and once again associated with Patton. However, Ike was concerned that he was almost three years away from his Colonelcy. The War Department must have agreed, for they denied Eisenhower's transfer request, stating that he was too junior in rank to serve in those capacities.

Circumstances brought the two together during the Texas-Louisiana maneuvers of September-October 1941. Both excelled on those maneuvers – Patton as Commander of the 2nd Armored Division, and Eisenhower as a key maneuver planner. Ike was credited with devising the strategy by which General Kreuger's Third Army defeated General Lear's Second Army. Each in his own way cemented his reputation as a potential senior leader. General Marshall, the Army Chief of Staff, was greatly pleased with the performance of each in his particular role.

It was clearly evident that Marshall was particularly "taken" by Eisenhower, and after the maneuvers directed his transfer to the War Department General Staff. Shortly after, a most unlikely event occurred. Ike was promoted to Brigadier General, a huge jump. This was the first step and first star in his sensational, unprecedented, meteoric rise which would gain for him overall command of operations in North Africa, Sicily, and Europe.

George visited Ike in Washington in February 1942. During their talks, Patton repeated that he considered Ike "about his oldest friend." In turn Ike bemoaned the fact that he was still desk-bound, and reminded his friend that he still yearned for a field command. But it was too late for Eisenhower. He would never return to tanks. His star was already zooming to the outer reaches of the heavens.

Early in 1942 the War Department decided that it was necessary to train American troops in desert warfare. Patton was selected to create the first Desert Training Center near the town of Indio, 200 miles east of Los Angeles. After a four-day reconnaissance of southeastern California and western Arizona by Piper Cub, he selected a vast 20,000 square mile area of rock, cactus, mesquite, dry salt beds, and huge jack-rabbits. It turned out to be an absolutely splendid training area. *(I can readily attest to that, for I spent seven months training and maneuvering in that environment.)* More than 60,000 troops would train at that vast complex. Patton's performance and success in the desert was so good that it enhanced his already glowing reputation. He received considerable publicity, and became even better known to the American public.

But the **big** story was Eisenhower. He started off in 1941 as Lt. Col., "paused" for a few months as a "bird, eagle" Colonel, and by year's end was a Brigadier General. Shortly after, in March of 1942 he was a Major General. Then less than a year later, on February 11th, 1943 he added to his uniform a fourth star – from Lt. Col. to four-star General in two years. This was stunning, sensational, and unbelievable. Such a remarkable advance was totally, absolutely unheard of. It would be difficult to find in the annals of the United States Army a situation that would come even close to this one. Remarkably, Eisenhower not only "jumped" his own very distinguished class of 1915, upon which the "stars fell," but every class before that going back to Patton's class of 1909 and beyond, which totaled hundreds of West Point graduates.

In one fell swoop the substantial head start that Patton had had, the broad gap that had separated George and Ike, had been dramatically and irrevocably eclipsed. The coin had flipped. Eisenhower was now senior in position and superior in rank to his tank mentor of some months back. During the moments when their early friendship was cementing, they speculated that George might well become the Black Jack Pershing of World War II, and that Eisenhower would be his Stonewall Jackson type lieutenant. Now the roles would be reversed. Ike would become the Black Jack of World War II and then some, while Patton would serve as an important combat lieutenant.

That such a development would be happening soon became dramatically evident. Churchill and Roosevelt had agreed on an operation that would take place in late 1942. It would be called "Torch." The initial concept would be to have the Allies neutralize the Vichy French regime in Morocco and Algiers, and then seize Tunisia, thereby trapping Rommel's German – Italian Army between the Torch forces and Montgomery's Eighth Army, which was to break out of defensive positions near El Alamein, and drive Rommel westward into Tunisia.

The individual selected to command the Allied Forces in the Mediterranean was none other than Patton's one-time tank *protégé*, General Dwight D. Eisenhower, a soldier who had never before commanded above battalion level. His new command was designated as Allied Force Headquarters (AFHQ).

Ike was sent to London in April 1942 to coordinate planning for the operation. At the end of July Patton was told that he would command the Western Task Force, the invasion of Casablanca. So Eisenhower and Patton would serve together in North Africa, with Patton now a subordinate of Ike's. Eisenhower was delighted when he learned that Patton was to be part of his new command. On August 5, George flew to London, and attended two conferences conducted by Eisenhower. While there, George was asked his opinion of the Torch plan. He concluded that it was much too complicated and required revision.

It was during that visit to London that two very significant elements seemed to take root. Patton began to be disdainful of the British. As time passed, that dislike would seem to grow into almost an obsession, and would make him a virtual Anglophobe. The second was that it was here the impending difficulties of their relationship seemed to begin.

While he moved about London, Patton observed that most American officers seemed too British.

As for Eisenhower, it was there that Patton exhibited the first signs of displeasure and distrust of his old friend. He began to see him in a new light. He watched Ike extremely critically, picking up what he sensed to be flaws of which he had hitherto been unaware. Perhaps Patton was looking at Eisenhower with different eyes, which unknowingly or perhaps without admitting it held some resentment and jealousy. Patton noted that Ike did not seem as "rugged mentally" as he once thought, "he vacillates and is not realistic."

In mid-November of 1942 Patton flew to Gibraltar, and met with Eisenhower inside the "Rock." He found the Headquarters depressing – his feelings were undoubtedly nudged by the disdainful attitude of the British staff officers on the AFHQ staff. He also noted that some of Eisenhower's words were already becoming British, such as "tiffin" for lunch and "petrol" for gasoline. At that point, he observed, "I truly fear that London has conquered Abilene." Patton was disappointed, as well, by the amount of time Eisenhower spent on what Patton termed "trivial things."

As time passed, it was inevitable that Patton would begin to draw comparisons between Black Jack Pershing, the Supreme Commander of the AEF during WW I, and Eisenhower, the Supreme Commander of Torch. Patton had served under Pershing, had observed him closely, had tremendous respect for him, and considered him a family friend. George, in this regard, tried to be objective, but as time passed he considered Eisenhower to be pale by comparison, and found him wanting.

Operation Torch proved successful despite some awkward political bungling by Ike. Initially, there was considerable tactical bungling, as well. Kasserine was Eisenhower's first real battle, and some believe that to some extent he almost "blew it." His actions and failings may have allowed Rommel to get away. American firepower and German shortages saved him. Overall his performance was considered well below par.

Conversely, Patton's star was on the rise, because he performed impressively in Morocco. Eisenhower was effusive in his praise, and in early February 1943 he selected Patton to command the assault force in the invasion of Sicily.

As has been earlier described, Patton took a "time out" from the planning to turn around the II Corps, to give the U.S. Army its first major victory against German troops, and to emerge as the Army's unquestioned best Combat Commander.

Patton stayed in character and continued to be "flip of lip," and to make inappropriate, off-hand remarks. In a cable on February 3rd, 1943, Ike instructed George "to assume a Sphinx-like quality," so that he would not appear to be acting on impulse, but rather upon study and reflection. He also tersely warned Patton to curb his "ready and facile tongue." Patton's criticism of Eisenhower continued to fester, and one big reason was nationalism. George did not believe that the U.S. Army at Eisenhower's hands was being given a fair share. Patton, in an entry in his diary, which was excerpted by a New York newspaper, condemned Eisenhower as "an ass for his pro-British bias by telling British General Alexander "he did not consider himself an American, but an Ally." Bradley agreed completely, and chimed in with the words, "Ike was too weak, much too prone to knuckle under to the British, often . . . at our expense."

On May 20, an Allied victory parade was held in Tunis. A number of senior British officers were included in the official reviewing party with Eisenhower. Patton and Bradley shared a minor reviewing stand with French officials and lesser military officers. Patton was not only distressed but extremely angry. Patton and Bradley agreed that it seemed to give the British overwhelming credit for the victory in Tunisia, and to slight the American troops who had fought and died there.

Patton recognized that the bonds of his twenty-four year friendship with Eisenhower were now showing considerable "slippage." Little did he know that at the conclusion of the operation for which he was preparing, and in which he would play a decisive role, those bonds would begin to become unraveled.

During the final presentations for that operation, the invasion of Sicily, Patton was, again, critical of Eisenhower, and believed that he had failed to exert his authority as Commander in Chief.

At his final meeting with Eisenhower five days before the invasion, Patton was deeply hurt that Eisenhower did not even wish him luck.

In Sicily, Patton followed up his North African successes with a brilliant, extraordinary operational campaign. Ike cited him for exemplary performance in battle. At the end of the campaign, Eisenhower reported to Gen. Marshall, and attributed the Allied victory to Patton's "energy, determination, and unflagging aggressiveness." He went further and declared that "the operations of Seventh Army are . . . going to be classed as a model of swift conquest by future classes at the War College."

Although Eisenhower praised Patton privately in correspondence, he was extremely chary about giving Patton a pat on the back publicly. Patton desperately sought the praise that he considered he had earned and deserved from Eisenhower. Perhaps Ike believed that this was the way to get the best out of Patton. He freely admitted that he could treat Patton "more roughly than he could any other senior Commander."

But in Sicily Patton's long and illustrious military career took its sharpest, most dramatic, most unfortunate turn, directly attributable to the impulsive acts of slapping two soldiers. He was at the zenith of his career. He was universally recognized as the hero and conqueror of Sicily. He was the odds-on favorite, virtually a lock-on, to be selected to command the American invasion force in Normandy, and to command the Army Group all across Europe. Instead he was for five months without a command; in limbo; in exile in a flea-ridden, antiquated palace in Palermo; in Eisenhower's dog-house. For weeks he was melancholic. He was as depressed as his environment, and he wondered if he would ever command again. When he was, finally, told that he would command Third Army, he would be doing so under Bradley, an officer who had been his subordinate. (Many still insist that we would have fought a better war if Patton had been the Army Group Commander).

Bad as that was, it could have been far, far worse. Patton, by the skin of his teeth, came within a hair of losing it all – a complete and catastrophic end to his military career. Back home the great combat hero was suddenly forgotten, replaced by a vilified senior officer. There was a great outcry – how could he have done such a horrible, terrible thing; it was beyond comprehension, reprehensible. He should be severely punished. A multitude of voices, egged on by correspondents, wanted his scalp, demanded his relief. One of them even claimed that Patton had gone temporarily crazy.

With widespread and extremely heavy pressure, Eisenhower agonized over whether he might have to send George home in disgrace. But he questioned whether Patton's conduct justified his relieving one of the finest Ground Commanders in the United States Army.

Eisenhower did not forsake Patton. He could have walked away from the tremendous heat that he was receiving by dumping George, but he chose, instead, to stand by him. Had Eisenhower succumbed to pressure, Patton's career would have ended, never to be resuscitated. There would have been no European war for him – no magnificent sweep across France; no relief of the 101st Airborne at Bastogne; no legend, forever; no military immortality.

Fortunately for Eisenhower, for the U.S. Army, for our nation, Eisenhower found the notion of sending Patton home in disgrace – appalling. Eisenhower would declare that the slapping incident could not be the end of his service, for "Patton is indispensable to the war effort, one of the guarantors of our victory, and Patton should be saved for service in the new battles facing us in Europe . . ." He must have agreed with the officer who mentioned that "Patton pays off in ground gains as well as occasional headaches."

As a result of Sicily, the word "friendship" to describe the Eisenhower/

Patton relationship became a misnomer. Eisenhower deeply resented Patton's irresponsible actions because it placed upon him additional burdens. As Theater Commander, he was the one who had to hold off the public and official wrath.

Patton's erratic behavior endangered and badly rattled the confidence that Ike had in Patton's emotional stability. As he had before, he recognized flaws in Patton's character, which more than once would serve to embarrass him. Patton, in Eisenhower's eyes, would from then on wear a pronounced stigma.

And a great irony – Patton never really understood or acknowledged that, throughout the slapping incident, Eisenhower stood firmly behind him, refused to accept the loss of a great leader, and "saved his bacon."

The slapping of two soldiers by a very senior officer is virtually unheard of, an extreme aberration, an act totally and completely unforgivable. Yet, one can rationalize without condoning. (During my military service, I visited wounded soldiers in battalion aid stations. I visited wards in hospitals populated solely by recently wounded soldiers. To walk among them; to talk to them; to pin decorations on their pajamas; to marvel at their cheerfulness, at their compassion for others who "were worse off than me," and their eagerness to get back to their units and buddies – is an intense emotional experience without equal. It really shakes you. Yes, I cannot condone, but I can empathize.)

Patton's exile ended with a summons from Eisenhower to join him in England. Patton landed in Prestwick, Scotland, on the morning of January 26, 1944. No band or honor guard were on hand to greet him – only a small group of less than senior officers. This was a graphic statement that he was still somewhat of an outcast in his own Army. During his first meeting with Eisenhower, he was informed that he would be given command of the Third Army still forming, with most elements still due to arrive from the United States.

That day also produced his first meeting with Kay Summersby, the Irish woman first assigned to chauffeur Eisenhower, who became a permanent member of the SHAEF staff, and part of Eisenhower's "inner circle."

Col. (M.D.) Charles B. Odom has written a small book entitled, *General George S. Patton and Eisenhower*. In it he states, "I had tried to portray the true feelings of General Patton as I had come to know him from intimate contact as his personal physician throughout the war. In that capacity I was privileged to spend many long evenings as a friend and confidant, listening and watching as he displayed his innermost feelings, and bared his soul."

Based upon his relationship with Patton, Col. Odom's words about the Churchill, Eisenhower, and Summersby connection are revealing. He states, "When General Patton was sent to England to assist in the planning of America's entry into the war, he found that Churchill had surrounded Ike with a marked preponderance of British officers. He also met Kay Summersby, an attractive thirty-year-old model, whom Patton considered to be a British agent planted in Eisenhower's inner circle to keep Churchill informed of all the activities that transpired in Ike's 'household.' She was a shrewd and knowledgeable woman. Patton remarked that 'through Kay, Churchill knew when Eisenhower talked in his sleep.' The excuse for her being planted in Ike's staff was that she could find her way around London, where all the signs had been removed because of a fear of a German invasion. She became very close to Eisenhower, had access to all his mail, and served as hostess at the numerous dinner parties given by Ike. She was his bridge partner throughout the war, and lived with him at a secluded cottage outside London known as 'Telegraph Cottage.' When Eisenhower moved his Headquarters to Algiers in North Africa, she followed and occupied a second rendezvous spot called 'Sailor's Delight,' an elaborate, well-guarded hide-away thirty miles outside Algiers . . . Patton did not begrudge Ike the company of Miss Summersby, but he always felt she was part of the reason for Eisenhower's undue allegiance to the British. He felt that she and Churchill had Ike's ear on what should have been strictly military decisions."

Dr. Odom declared that, "many of the reports written regarding the relationship of Patton and Eisenhower have portrayed them as having a lasting friendship. This could not be further from the truth." Dr. Odom made other significant comments about that relationship:

• "He respected Eisenhower as his Commanding Officer, but you can believe that there was no love lost for him. Patton resented the vindictive manner in which he was treated by Eisenhower and was always uncomfortable with him."

• "General Patton felt that publicly he was obliged to fawn and bow to Eisenhower as his military Commander, but privately he detested him and his Chief of Staff, Bedell Smith. Once when he was trying to persuade them to agree to having at least part of his Headquarters staff transferred from Sicily to England to assist in his command of the Third Army, he developed a sore on his lip. His reaction was, 'It is no wonder that I have a sore lip with all the ass kissing I have to do'."

• "Patton knew that Eisenhower had no tactical or strategic ability as a military leader and he (Patton) was convinced that he (Eisenhower) was surrounded by those who gave him poor advice. He felt that Eisenhower was prejudiced in favor of the British, and was strictly a politician."

George was out of the spotlight, and leading a largely imposed quiet life in England. Both Eisenhower and Patton had asked the press to conceal his presence in England. Then innocently and completely without realization, Patton once again put his head in the noose.

It happened in a small English town called Knutsford (what occurred would always be known as "The Knutsford Incident"). A group of English ladies were opening in the town the Welcome Club for American soldiers. It was to be a local, very low-key affair. Patton was invited, and the "good guy" accepted. Patton was at his most gallant self, and completely charmed the ladies in attendance. But as could be expected, some newspaper correspondents got wind of the affair, and were on hand. Patton was called upon for a few remarks. His perfunctory remarks have been completely forgotten, except for one statement, which almost hung him. In his short speech Patton expressed his belief that it was "the evident destiny of the British and Americans, and, of course, the Russians to rule the postwar world." Seemingly, very innocent words, but not so. The newspaper reporters hopped on those words, and in strident voices claimed that Patton's reference to the Russians was merely an afterthought. Once again there was a great uproar in the United States. Patton's words created a sensation. They soon became political as anti- Roosevelt politicians and editors poured gasoline on the fire. Eisenhower was absolutely irate, because he had directed Patton to avoid making statements and having press conferences.

As he did in Sicily, Eisenhower once again resisted the howling wolves. But he did say, "I'm just about fed up. If I have to apologize publicly for George one more time, I'm going to have to let him go, valuable as he is. I'm getting sick and tired of having to protect him. Life's much too short to put up with any more of it."

However, Eisenhower still needed Patton, who was commanding the fictitious Army Group preparing to invade Calais. On May 2, Ike finally rebuked Patton, and reminded him that he was "once more taking the responsibility of retaining you in command of the Third Army in spite of damaging repercussions resulting from a personal indiscretion. I do this solely because of my faith in you as a battle leader and for no other reason."

As could readily be expected, there would continue to be an uneasy relationship, and a constant "rubbing" between Eisenhower and Patton, as the war progressed across Europe.

On July 12, 1944, about two weeks before operation Cobra and the breakout in Normandy, and before his Third Army was activated, Patton would write in his diary, "Ike is bound hand and foot by the British and does not know it. Poor fool. We actually have no Supreme Commander, no one who can take hold and say that this shall be done and that shall not be done. There was a general uneasy feeling around SHAEF that

Eisenhower would never take hold of Montgomery."

Patton was greatly upset, and his regard for Eisenhower was not enhanced by SHAEF's refusal to acknowledge publicly (not even in the *Stars and Stripes*) the presence and electrifying achievements of Third Army and its Commander, until the end of August.

Later, as his supply of gasoline began to diminish markedly as he sped toward the Meuse, Patton pleaded to Eisenhower, "If you let me retain my regular allotment of tonnage, Ike, we could push on to the German frontier and rupture that Goddamn Siegfried Line. I'm willing to stake my reputation on that."

The constant grinding and grating between the two was clearly evident as Eisenhower with a sharp dig said, "Careful, George, that reputation of yours hasn't been worth very much." Patton was even quicker on the trigger, and shot back, "That reputation is pretty good now."

Eisenhower, as has been mentioned, almost never took operational control of his Armies, but acted more like the chairman of the board. True, he had given the "go" order for the Normandy invasion, despite concerns about the weather, but more often he was indecisive. He was certainly no military genius. So he was bound to have resented and envied the headline-grabbing ground-gainer, the achiever.

Not long after the German breakthrough in the Ardennes, the 101st Airborne Division (the bloody, battered bastards of Bastogne) were surrounded in that city. In what amounted to an emergency session, Patton met at Verdun with Eisenhower and the other top Commanders, who seemed stricken by recent events. Patton quickly took hold of the meeting by telling the group that he could attack the German "under-belly" with three divisions in 48 hours to relieve the 101st They were incredulous and snickered at his audacity. Eisenhower, clutching at straws, immediately gave him the green light. Eisenhower had just been promoted to General of the Army (after all, Monty was a field marshal), and as Patton was departing Ike jabbed him, "Funny thing, George, every time I get a new star, I get attacked." Patton, as ever nimble with the quip, retorted, less than half jokingly, "And every time you get attacked, I pull you out."

At the end of the Battle of the Bulge, Patton had a social meeting with Eisenhower and Bradley. Patton was not surprised when Eisenhower failed to make any remark about Third Army's remarkable achievement in the relief of the troops in Bastogne. In fact, Eisenhower made no reference whatsoever to Patton's contribution to the Allied victory. The tribute, which Patton so desperately desired, was once again denied. Throughout their relationship, all Patton had hoped for was some confirmation of his battle skills from Eisenhower, but Ike for some reason refused to recognize those achievements.

However, in March 1945, Eisenhower relented briefly, and extended, like water to a parched throat, what surely must have been most welcome words to Patton. He wrote to his Third Army Commander, who had just breached the Rhine defenses and crossed that river (triumphantly – before Monty), "You have made your Army a fighting force that is not excelled in effectiveness by any other of equal size in the world."

Immediately after VE Day on May 10, Eisenhower was unquestionably feeling his vulnerability and called a session that might best be termed, "The keep-the-lid-on-it meeting." He summoned his senior Commanders – his four Army Commanding Generals, Hodges, Simpson, Patch and Patton, and their Air Officers. He attempted to promote solidarity, and asked that they promise not to criticize publicly the way the campaigns in Europe had been fought. The meeting confirmed Patton's worst fears. He was dead certain that Ike was determined to cover up the strategic blunders which, Patton was convinced, he had committed during the war. *(Without question, Patton always considered that one of those grave errors was Ike's decision that is the subject of this book.)*

During that meeting, to Patton the words of Eisenhower had the symptoms of political aspirations. Afterwards, to his staff, Patton merely said, "Eisenhower is running for president." Many weeks later, he would have occasion to repeat those words.

Not long after VE Day and the meeting just described, my 4th Armored Division departed from the relatively untouched portion of Czechoslovakia, where we ended the war, to a chaotic Germany. That was a defeated, demoralized, devastated, desperate country. The need for law and order was paramount, as there remained no border police, no national, state or municipal police. Similarly, it was without government – no Burgomeisters (mayors), Kreis (county Commanders), Lander leaders. There were progressively increasing numbers of refugees and displaced persons, who would soon number in the thousands. Those desperate people were roaming the country seeking food and shelter.

That is the situation found by the 4th Armored Division as it moved into Bavaria, and to its assigned zone of occupation. My Eighth Tank Battalion was assigned the Kreis (county) of Vilsbiburg, which was east of Munich. We were still part of the Third Army, and our Commander remained General George S. Patton, Jr., who would be Military Governor of Bavaria.

Because I was the Battalion Commander, I became Commandant of the Kreis of Vilsbiburg. My office and bed were in the county Headquarters. My four tank companies, Service Company, and Headquarters company were spread in cities and towns throughout the county. Our job was to bring order and security to our area of responsibility, to start to pick the German populace off its knees and out of shock, and to "jump start" them on the road to some form of normalcy.

We were soldiers, warriors – not politicians or civil administrators; not any type of governor. We had not been trained for, and never expected to be placed in, a situation such as we were facing. However, we had fought a long, hard and successful war. We had faced great challenges, shouldered broad responsibilities. We had operated with mission-type orders. We won battles because of our aggressiveness, determination, flexibility, and good old American ingenuity. We often "threw away the book." We were mission-oriented, wanted to get the job done – and did. We would approach our new tasks in the same manner.

The problems which we now faced were completely different, and we were entirely without experience and expertise to solve them. We found that in our communities very little was working properly. We faced such problems as getting the water supply working again, straightening out the sewage system, getting power plants running again so that there was electricity. Bridges had to be repaired and built. Roads were in terrible shape, and needed much work. And a never-ending priority was getting food to the inhabitants of our county. We continued to approach our tasks with the same zeal we applied in combat.

To get things working we had to search for, seek out, locate individuals with experience, know-how, initiative, and leadership. These were very much in short supply. When we found the individuals whom we were looking for, we put them right to work.

We asked few questions. Our criterion was simply, "Could they get the job done?"

We had things underway; there was momentum, when Military Government officials began arriving to take over. They and we were two different "breeds of cat." We were combat, they were not. They had worked in government, apparently successfully, back in the States. They had experience, expertise. But they, too, were facing a situation which they had never faced before.

We had made the contacts, problems were being solved, and projects were being completed. So it was difficult for us to disengage, step back, and watch a different type of operation. It was particularly aggravating for us to observe individuals whom we had selected for leadership and supervisory roles being replaced by patently less experienced and less efficient individuals. Conversely, it must have been aggravating to the Military Government officials who were taking hold to watch the numbers of Germans who bypassed them and still came to us with their problems. Under such circumstances, as could be expected, there was considerable rubbing. Initially, lines of responsibility were blurred. But as time passed we learned to work together. We provided them with the support and security which they required, as they passed government back into the hands of the Germans. Ultimately, Military Government would justifiably take credit for establishing a fine track record for their work in Germany.

Little did we know, as we worked in our little community, that our situation and problems were not unique. We quickly learned that our Army Commander was, likewise, facing great and similar frustrations and discouragements, but in a higher, more complex environment.

After the war in Europe ended, Patton, probably the purest warrior our nation has ever had, wanted desperately to go to the Pacific, and to continue fighting the war until it came to a complete conclusion. That was his great hope. He quickly learned in no uncertain terms that he would not be going to the Pacific. He was greatly disappointed, but ruefully said, "There is already a star [MacArthur] in that Theater, and you can only have one star in a show."

Functioning effectively in peace in any capacity would have been difficult for Patton. However, since he had to be assigned somewhere, he would have liked to have headed the Army War College. Another job that had some attraction for him was command of the Army Ground Forces. He soon learned that those two jobs had been assigned to other individuals.

There was nothing left for him but to remain in Germany as Military Governor of Bavaria. It would seem that Generals Marshall and Eisenhower, who knew full well Patton's personality and temperament, and recognized that there was no "right" peacetime job for him, should have made a greater effort to find a job better suited for him than the one in Bavaria. But apparently Patton received no special consideration.

Patton had no wish for and was completely unprepared to become Military Governor of Bavaria. With the war over he was stale, burned-out, and had a monumental let-down. He was as ill prepared for peace in 1945 as he had been in 1919. He was forced to play a role that he did not want, and he had difficulty putting forth his best effort.

Jimmy Doolittle was a great friend of Patton, and he tellingly described his view of the Eisenhower/Patton relationship, "To Ike Patton was one of those rare, indispensable leaders who won wars; unfortunately, men like Georgie were too often unfit for peacetime assignments. I have thought Ike used Georgie as one would use a pit bull dog. When there was a fight, he would tell Georgie to 'sic 'em.' But when the fight was won, he would have to put him in isolation somewhere until the next scrap."

Early in his service in Bavaria, Patton would make "noises" about the Russians. Patton disliked them, was suspicious of them, distrusted them, and believed that they would cause us trouble. He made no bones about how he felt. At that early stage he had analyzed them accurately.

He firmly believed that we would be greatly concerned with the Russians for some time to come. He would periodically continue to offer his opinions on this subject. As always, it seemed, he differed markedly with Ike, and his views would cause continued rubbing. At one point Patton said, "Today we should be telling the Russians to go to hell, instead of hearing them tell us to pull back." Eisenhower had a different point of view. He advocated, instead, making every effort to cooperate with the Russians "to build a better world."

Although Patton continued from time to time to air his views about the Russians, it was his method of governing Bavaria that most alarmed Eisenhower. Once again, Eisenhower and Patton had completely different philosophies about how the job should be done.

A May 21, 1945, Joint Chiefs of Staff Directive called for the removal from government positions of all members of the Nazi Party. It is interesting to note that after the directive came out Eisenhower's Deputy Military Governor for Germany considered strongly that the directive was too broad, rigid, lacked flexibility, and hoped that it would be modified. It never was. Eisenhower made no such protestations. He declared, "The policy 'laid down' for us by the Joint Chiefs of Staff must be obeyed." Henceforth that would be the "party line."

In Bavaria, unfortunately, Patton would "fight the problem." He believed that it was time to forget Hitler, and embark on a fresh effort to restore Germany. He further saw a need "to compromise with the devil a little."

Patton complained to Ike, tried to reason with him. George mentioned that, as in other countries, civilian officials had to join the ruling party. He said, "It is no more possible for a man to be a civil servant in Germany and not have paid lip service to Nazism, than it is possible for a man to be postmaster in America and not have paid at least lip service to the Democratic Party or the Republican Party, when it is in power."

Patton also declared "by throwing out too many of what you might call middle class civil servants in our so-called de-nazification program... we are getting a great many inexperienced, inefficient people in their place." He added, "more than half of the German people are Nazis, and you would be in a hell of a fix if you tried to remove all Party members."

Of course, Eisenhower was troubled by those views, and disagreed completely with Patton. He stated bluntly, " The German government could be run as efficiently without Nazis, as with them. " His views were completely consistent with the policy laid out by the JCS. Ike never questioned it or deviated from it, and ruled that it had to be obeyed.

As time went on, Patton with his "loose" administration deviated from established policy. Eisenhower knew it and did not like it. There would then occur a rapid series of events which would lead to Patton's downfall.

On September 12, Patton received a letter from Eisenhower that was extremely direct and uncompromising. He said, "I know that certain Field Commanders [surely Patton] have felt some modification of the policy should be made. This question has long been decided. We will not compromise with Nazism in any way. I wish to make particularly sure that all your individual Commanders realize that the discussion stage of this question is long past, and any expressed opposition to the faithful execution of the order cannot be regarded leniently by me."

From the very outset Patton had given a relatively free hand to the individual he "inherited" who had been appointed as the first Minister President of the province, despite a spotty, checkered, inconsistent background. Patton's own government section permitted the Minister to "run his show" with little direction or supervision. As time passed he made a considerable number of Nazi appointees. When alarmed members of U.S. Military Government discovered this, they ordered the removal of those officials. Later, there was great consternation and frustration when it was discovered that numerous officials were still at their desks weeks after they should have been removed. That certainly exacerbated the situation. Those failures in de-nazification, of course, were reported to Eisenhower.

There were other aggravations and accusations. For example, a personal representative of President Truman, sent to Germany to investigate the conditions of displaced persons, stressed Patton's disdain for Jews.

Eisenhower, vacationing on the Riviera, became greatly concerned about those developments, and decided to fly in to examine the situation, but was delayed by bad weather. George and Ike finally met on the evening of September 16, and stayed up late discussing, not conditions in Bavaria, but their own futures. With all acceptable jobs apparently closed to him, Patton was to conclude, "At present writing it would seem the only thing I can do is go home and retire."

As the days passed after the 16th meeting, it was evident that Patton was still "fighting the problem," and not getting the job done to the satisfaction of his higher Headquarters. Eisenhower was losing what little patience he still had on the Nazi issue. It began to appear that Patton's days as Military Governor were numbered. And sure enough there would be a provocation that leaked gasoline on an already smoldering fire.

It was suggested to Patton that, of all things, he hold a press conference to clarify and explain the actions for which he was being criticized by the media. The press conference was scheduled for September 22. That day he appeared "out of sorts," edgy, impatient. Rather than holding a full-scale press conference, he permitted reporters to attend his staff meeting. Because of the rapid demobilization of the American Army, Patton had lost all his intimates, including his favorite press officer. They were the ones who protected him, and had endeavored to keep him out of trouble. They would have strongly urged him not to handle the reporters in this manner.

However, he went ahead, had his staff meeting, and it went well, but as Patton tried to leave, the reporters "buttonholed" him. They began aggressively to ask pointed, leading questions. In answer to a question, as he was often wont to do, he off-handedly mentioned "this Nazi thing. It's just like a Democratic-Republican election fight." He also said some disparaging things about the Russians. A reporter from the *New York Times* grasped Patton's comments, and almost immediately there appeared a headline back home that insisted that Patton had equated Nazis and non-Nazis with Democrats and Republicans in the United States.

As in Sicily and Knutsford, Patton was once again the center of controversy. And as before, they were after his scalp. Newspapers implied that he was unfit for occupation command. Others baldly proclaimed that he must "go." There was a suspicion (and a basis for it) that a small cabal of newspapermen were out to destroy Patton. Some later admitted that they had, indeed, tried to entrap him into saying things that would cause him further trouble.

On the evening of the 25th, Patton received a telegram from Eisenhower asking him to fly to Frankfurt to discuss de-nazification in Bavaria. The next day, the 26th., he was prevented from flying to Frankfurt because of bad weather.

That same day at a press conference Chief of Staff, Gen. Smith, when heavily pressed by reporters, declared, "We will not compromise with Nazism in any way." The same reporters who had been at Patton's Saturday press conference asked, "Could American policies be carried out by people [obviously Patton] who are temperamentally and emotionally in disagreement with it?" Smith exploded with scathing, vituperative words about Patton: "His mouth does not always carry out the functions of his brain. George acts on the theory that it is better to be damned than to say nothing." (As far back as North Africa and Sicily, Patton had disliked and distrusted Smith, who, he believed, gave Eisenhower bad advice. During the fight across Europe, that dislike bordered on hatred. The feeling was undoubtedly mutual, for Smith had Eisenhower's ear, and never failed to be critical of and to "cut" Patton.)

On the morning of September 28, the weather was still too bad for flying, so Patton took off in his sedan. George was emotionally drained. The press conference and its aftermath had taken a toll. So by the time the $7^1/_2$ hour trip in heavy rain to Frankfurt was finished, Patton was exhausted. During the trip, he had plenty of time to think, and had bad "vibes" about his forthcoming meeting. Being a realist, he predicted what was about to happen, and he steeled himself for it. His meeting with Eisenhower took place in Ike's spacious office in the I.G. Farben building in Frankfurt. The two were soon joined by two others – Eisenhower's Assistant Chief of Staff for Military Government and an advisor on de-nazification, an individual who had previously spent his career in academia.

That afternoon Patton was the corpse upon whom an autopsy was performed. Eisenhower's guests proceeded skillfully and surgically to slice Patton to bits. The situation was reminiscent, as well, of a prosecutor armed with all the cards and pounding and pounding at the witness. To say the least, it was cruel. Patton offered no defense – he sat there and "took it."

When the meeting was over, there was no doubt in Patton's mind, but that his "goose was cooked." They had destroyed him. He later said that he was "done to death by slanderous tongues."

It was perfectly obvious that Eisenhower had made up his mind even before the meeting. This time, he would not stand in support of his greatly troubled and beleaguered subordinate, as he had in Sicily and at Knutsford. After all, the war was over, and he was tired of standing between Patton and the constantly baying wolves.

After they were alone, Eisenhower resorted to the real reason for the meeting. He carefully and gingerly informed George that he would be "transferred," and would assume command of the Fifteenth Army, a paper organization devoted to studying the lessons of the war that had recently ended.

As they left the room, the press, of course, was almost in a frenzy waiting to learn the details of what had transpired at the meeting. Eisenhower offered no information. There was also no friendly dinner, no chit-chat, as was customary when the two had met together. Patton was immediately, summarily dispatched back to his Headquarters at Bad Tolz. Patton was now challenged by a serious, sticky dilemma – immediate resignation or a "kick" sideways to a demeaning paper command. Eisenhower wanted no public announcement until the Change of Command on October 8; however, with the press constantly hovering like buzzards, a leak was bound to happen and did. Ike was forced to make an announcement on October 2. The story, as could be expected, made headlines everywhere, and especially in the Army's *Stars and Stripes*.

The Change of Command actually took place on October 7. Because of heavy rain, the ceremony was held in a gymnasium. There was absolutely no sign of the anticipation or excitement normally associated with a Change of Command; no color or pageantry. This one was not only very simple, but was dreary and most depressing. Gen. Lucian K.

Truscott succeeded Patton, and he was definitely a "reluctant warrior" who seemed to be "dragging his heels," and was most perturbed about taking over the famed Third Army from its famed Commander. The Third Army flag was quickly passed from the old to the new Commander. Both made brief speeches. And to the obvious relief of everyone present, it was quickly over.

The friendship which began way back in 1919, started unraveling in Sicily, and continued to unravel during the weeks and months which followed, on this day imploded, was smashed to smithereens. Patton was reported to have described the disintegration of his friendship with Eisenhower by saying that he now believed the truth of Henry Adams' phrase that "a friend in power is a friend lost."

Patton was not only stunned, but was totally and profoundly humiliated. To a military man there is nothing more devastating, earth-shaking, disgraceful, than to be relieved of command. For Patton, the warrior who had performed so long, so successfully, so superbly, who had achieved so very much in combat, the toughest testing ground known to man, it was a shock which would leave him completely desolate.

Patton's Air Force friend, Otto Weyland, who had provided Third Army with absolutely superb fighter support all across Europe, later wrote and probably said it best, "I feel that the Third Army had died. To me, the Third Army meant Patton. When you left it, it ceased to be a thing alive."

Eisenhower, perhaps trying to "soften the blow," in a letter to Patton wrote, "My belief is that your particular talents will be better employed in the new job and that the planned arrangement visualizes the best possible utilization of available personnel." More from Ike; "the transfer in no way reflected upon his friend's loyalty, his administrative ability, nor his...soldierly qualifications." Pure pabulum, pure bunk. Such comments were so transparent, so demeaning, so much trash. Patton knew that he had been fired. It seemed that Eisenhower never truly grasped the terrible way he had hurt Patton by the manner in which he had relieved him of his beloved Third Army. On the day that he lost his Army, he again mentioned, as he had in May, his belief in Eisenhower's ultimate ambition, "Ike wants to be president so much you can taste it." It appears that the last time the two Commanders were together was on October 15, 1945, when they attended an intra-Army football game. The atmosphere was br-r-r cold.

Two months later, Patton was in Heidelberg, poised to return to the United States. He seemed edgy, depressed, restless, and impatient. On the morning of December 9 his always-faithful Chief of Staff, "Hap" Gay, suggested, as a diversion, that they go pheasant hunting. Patton eagerly jumped at the suggestion. Close to noon that day, after a short side trip to view an historical site, and just outside the industrial city of Mannheim, Patton's Cadillac and an Army $2\frac{1}{2}$ ton truck collided. Gay and the driver had minor injuries, but Patton's were mortal. He suffered, among other injuries, a broken neck. Ironically, this tragedy took place almost two months to the day after he had been relieved of his beloved Third Army.

He died on December 21, never to return to the United States. On December 24 he was buried in Hamm, Luxembourg, among men he had commanded. Again ironically, on that date a year before, his troops were knocking on the door to Bastogne, the relief of which would always be recognized as one of his greatest achievements.

Before he died, he told his wife emphatically that he did not want either Eisenhower, who was in the States, or Gen. Bedell Smith to attend his funeral. Smith was not listed among the pall-bearers, and neither Eisenhower nor Smith appeared on the final list of honorary pall-bearers.

One of Patton's final statements concerning Eisenhower: "I hope he makes a better president than general."

There has been considerable speculation about the futures and relationship of Eisenhower and Patton, if the latter had not died in Europe. One option, which Patton strongly considered, was resignation. He had informed an associate that he was planning to do just that by the first of the year. Once home he could then open up and criticize Eisenhower's conduct of the war, the significant errors and lapses in judgment that he had made, and his inept direction of the European campaign. Until the day he died, Patton contended (as I am doing) that had priority been given to him instead of Montgomery and Hodges, Third Army could have broken through the Saar to the Rhine.

Dr. Odom in his book said, "Had he lived I feel certain that General Patton would have written the book that he planned on his World War II experiences. Within that text he would have included the facts I am here reporting." In the same vein, he stated, "If Patton had lived to write his book, one wonders whether Eisenhower would even have been nominated, much less elected, President of the United States."

Gen. Geoffrey Keyes concluded, "The accident that killed Gen. Patton destroyed what could have been the greatest book to come out of World War II."

After the war was over, Eisenhower returned to the United States to succeed Gen. Marshall as Army Chief of Staff. The American public readily recognized him as the one who had launched the massive Normandy invasion, and as Supreme Commander of the great Allied victory in Europe. He was the General with the ever-present big smile – everyone "loved Ike."

Patton was known by the public for his audacity, and his great battlefield victories. He had color, was known for his flambuoyance and for getting himself into hot water. Whereas Eisenhower seemed to be the rock-solid, steady type, Patton was mercurial, the one who slapped soldiers, whose personal actions often seemed erratic, unpredictable.

If Patton had, indeed, written a book, one of two things would have happened. If that book was compelling, authoritative, well-crafted, open, telling, without hyperbole, with believable revelations, it might well have left Eisenhower with not much future after his stint as Chief of Staff, and might have thrown him off the track to the presidency.

On the other hand, the general public might have greeted Patton's contentions and his criticisms of Eisenhower as irrational, and those of an embittered old soldier who was "unloading" with "an axe to grind" and who was emotionally giving full vent to his feelings. If that were the case, Patton would have been left without a "voice," and shunted off to the ash heap of history.

Fate intervened, and neither of those two things happened. Eisenhower served two terms as president, and it was a period of relative quiet with little turbulence and controversy. The public, generally, has admiration for his record and accomplishments.

Patton has become a true American legend. People of all ages recognize his name. This is largely due to the movie about him, which has been shown repeatedly on TV. (Individuals who learn that I served under Patton ply me with questions about him).

Looking back, one can only conclude that Eisenhower and Patton served each other well – each "owed" the other; each paid a debt to the other. Eisenhower could have relieved Patton on more than one occasion, but saved him from what could have abruptly ended his military career. Patton, on the other hand, gave Eisenhower victories on the battlefields. Without Patton, Eisenhower undoubtedly would not have been able to defeat the German Army as rapidly and decisively as he did.

In a tribute to a 1909 graduate who became a great military hero, West Point some years after the war erected a statue, prominently placed upon its grounds, of General Patton in familiar combat uniform.

Eisenhower, who lived longer, would have the last embittered words. At a West Point reunion a reporter found Ike passing the statue of Patton, and remarked to Eisenhower, "General Patton was quite a legend." Ike replied, "Yes, mostly a legend." In 1946, a year after the war ended, Eisenhower would say, "It was Bradley, not Patton, who directed the campaigns in which Patton fought so brilliantly,"

In a tribute to a 1915 graduate who became a great military hero, West Point some years after his passing erected a statue, prominently placed upon its grounds, of General Eisenhower.

Now, the two long-time friends and later antagonists were together again, and only 50 feet apart. But the final, painful irony – the statues of these two wartime heroes with a lifelong relationship have their backs turned to each other.

CHAPTER 17

FIELD MARSHAL BERNARD LAW MONTGOMERY: HOW HE UTILIZED HIS PRIORITY IN GAS AND SUPPLIES

Now back to Montgomery. He was the one who had drawn the long straw, upon whom good fortune had smiled briefly, for Eisenhower had bequeathed to him the preponderance of the resources available in the Theater. How did Monty fare? How did he utilize the resources for which Patton had hungered, and the loss of which had left him totally frustrated and demoralized?

As has been described, Montgomery and his forces at the end of August, amazingly, had caught fire. They advanced east with uncharacteristic aggressiveness and speed. When the month ended, his advance forces were approaching the Belgian border. In September they continued moving at a (for them) meteoric pace. By September 4 they had seized, and were sitting astride, that critically important objective upon which they had long focused, the port city of Antwerp. Eisenhower had earlier ordered Montgomery, as he advanced along his channel route, to concentrate, first, on the capture of Antwerp, and then on to positions along the Scheldt Estuary which would enable the Allies to open and quickly use the port. Already, Montgomery had accomplished half of that mission.

However, at that point something absolutely unpredictable and sensational happened. Montgomery repaired alone to the solitude of his captured van. He must have been on a rare, unusual "high" because of his triumphant advance to Antwerp, for when he emerged he not only had "fire in his belly," but had in his "hip pocket" a grandiose, bold, imaginative, audacious, risky plan. When shown the plan (he had apparently lost all interest in the Scheldt Estuary), his associates were dumbfounded, amazed, and found it absolutely unbelievable, and completely out of character. How could Monty, always known for his cautious, deliberate, slow-moving, limited actions have come up with such a dramatic plan? One of his senior associates quickly declared it a "hair-brained" plan.

Bradley, although he and his units would be directly affected by the plan, was not made aware of it until some time after Monty had already sold it to Ike. When the plan was shared with him, Bradley stated, "Had the pious, teetotalling Montgomery wobbled into SHAEF with a hangover, I would not have been more astonished than I was by the daring adventure he proposed."

That "adventure" would be known as "Market Garden," or more aptly "Arnhem." "Market Garden" called for advancing a 60-mile salient pointed northeast of the initially planned direct line to the Ruhr. The drive would outflank the Siegfried defenses, advance through the presumed relatively weak German positions, and carry Montgomery across the lower Rhine on the shortest, most direct route to Berlin. (He was thinking big.)

From Antwerp to his objective at Arnhem, five major water obstacles crossed his path and stood directly in his way. The first two were canals north of Eindhoven. The third was the Maas (or Meuse). Eight miles beyond the Maas, the river Waal flowed under an arched bridge at Nijmegen. And at Arnhem the lower Rhine would be the last barrier. Only 20 miles beyond that was the German border.

What was termed a "carpet," over which armor could rapidly roll, was to be unrolled across the waterways. It would be three Airborne Divisions that would "roll out the carpet:" the U.S. 101st Airborne Division at Eindhoven, the U.S. 82nd Airborne Division at Nijmegen, and the British 1st Airborne Division at the forward point – Arnhem. And "rolling over" the carpet would be Montgomery's crack Guards Armoured Division.

Montgomery had argued persuasively that the Germans had a long front to defend and had few fixed defenses at the northern end of that front in Holland, and that a concentrated thrust on the left of the front would cause the relatively light defenses to crumble. Monty reasoned that he could quickly finish the war with a single quick strike from the Rhine all the way to Berlin across the North Sea lowlands, instead of battering ahead towards the Ruhr. He preferred to out-flank the German line of resistance with a bold dash to the north. It was a truly imaginative, audacious, exciting plan.

Eisenhower must have been intrigued and enthusiastic about the plan, for he, apparently, had quickly endorsed it. He must have thought it a fair gamble, and by approving the plan recognized that although it would take considerable "doing," he accepted the high risks that were involved.

Eisenhower and SHAEF must have believed that this was the best remaining opportunity for the Allies to win the war that autumn. They recognized that it was not the "full blooded thrust" that Monty had always demanded, but it came as close as the Allied logistical situation permitted.

Now Monty, the recipient of all available resources, with almost as full a priority as he had ever desired, had an enormous opportunity and responsibility. He was the Lone Ranger, the only one who could engineer a tremendous victory. It was upon his shoulders that SHAEF placed its entire future.

Bradley, although he conceded that it was a bold, imaginative plan, had reservations about it. He feared that Monty, in his eagerness to get around the German flank, might have under-estimated German capabilities on the lower Rhine. He believed the plan was too ambitious for the strength of the forces available to him. Bradley was also concerned that Monty was slipping off on a tangent that might leave him holding the bag.

If Monty swerved to the northeast, as he planned, he would uncover Hodges' left flank, and might force Bradley to take an Armored Division from Patton, turn it north, and give it to Hodges. But his fears and concerns apparently got to no one's ear, so the operation was definitely "on."

Montgomery's plan turned into action on Sunday, September 17, as "Market Garden" was launched. That day the skies over Holland were dark with aircraft as an Allied Airborne Army sent thousands of Airborne soldiers parachuting to the ground with the mission of securing bridges over assigned water obstacles. It was a rare daylight drop, which permitted better aiming at the drop zones. This worked out extremely well for all three Airborne Divisions, who enjoyed the most accurate drops they had ever experienced in training or combat. This was a most encouraging operational "kick off."

To make the operation successful it took 2800 aircraft and 1800 gliders to carry the Airborne forces to their landing zones. These were covered by 1200 Allied fighter aircraft.

For the operation, Montgomery had the 1st Airborne Army, commanded by U.S. Lt. Gen. Louis Hyde Brereton, while the backbone of the Airborne assault would be I Airborne Corps, commanded by British Lt. Gen. F.A.M. "Boy" Browning, which included the American 101st and 82nd and the British 1st Divisions.

It was the mission of the British 1st Airborne Division, commanded by Maj. Gen. Robert Urquhart, to take the bridges over the Neder Rijn at Arnhem, to establish a bridgehead around the town, and to be ready to be reinforced by the Polish 1st Parachute Brigade and the British 52nd (Airmobile) Division.

The objective of the 101st Airborne Division, commanded by Gen. Maxwell Taylor, was Eindhoven, where it was ordered to capture the bridges over the Wilhelmina Canal, as well as the Dommel and Willems canals. The U.S. 82nd, commanded by Gen. James M. Gavin, was assigned the job of seizing the Grave bridge over the Maas, and the bridge over the Waal at Nijmegen.

If, according to the plan, the three Airborne Divisions accomplished their missions, it would open up a corridor along which Lt. Gen. Sir Brian Horrocks' XXX Corps, led by the Guards Armoured Division, and including the 50th and 43rd Divisions, would drive rapidly to Arnhem, and then be ready to continue their advance deep into Germany.

The American landings achieved a great deal of surprise, and were, basically, successful. The 101st Airborne at Eindhoven seized its initial objectives with the exception of taking the Son bridge over the Wilhelmina canal, which was blown before they were able to reach it. The 82nd Airborne was successful in grabbing the Grave bridge, but the bridge at Nijmegen was another matter. Several hours after they had landed, their first attempt to seize the bridge was blocked by German troops, who quickly and professionally recovered from the surprise and shock of the American landings.

The British 1st Airborne Division at Arnhem had the most critical, important, and far-reaching mission. But it had a far less auspicious start than the Americans, and was immediately beset with difficulties. Almost at once, what could go wrong began to go wrong. This was not good news, and as the situation at Arnhem did not improve, an ominous feeling with a sense of foreboding began to creep in.

Because there had been strong opinions among the planners that there would surely be heavy anti-aircraft defenses around Arnhem, the decision was made to effect the landings in open scrub-land, which would require the parachutists to negotiate over seven miles of terrain before they reached the bridge that they were to capture.

Once on the ground and assembled, the troops began their advance on Arnhem. Almost immediately, they lost completely that vital, basic requirement for success in combat – communications. Consequently, the advance became confused, uncoordinated, disorganized. Unable to control his division, Gen. Urquhart, the Division Commander, himself moved up to the front. Instead of helping, this move exacerbated the problem.

However, his battalions continued their advance towards Arnhem.

One battalion was completely surprised and had the misfortune to meet the 9th SS Panzer "Hohenstaufen" Division unexpectedly. These German troops stopped the paratroopers about three kilometers northwest of Arnhem's western suburb of Oosterbeeck. Another battalion, advancing toward the bridge, met other elements of the 9th SS Panzer, and were also stopped at the western outskirts of Oosterbeeck.

The determined, aggressive, imaginative and resolute efforts of the 2nd Parachute Battalion, commanded by Lt. Col. J. D. Frost, enabled it to move toward the division's principal objective, the bridges. Frost by-passed resistance by utilizing a secondary road near the river bank. He gave his "C" Company the mission of seizing the railroad bridge, but as they approached the structure, it blew up in their faces. There were Germans tucked away in outlying houses about three kilometers from the highway bridge. Frost believed that those had to be neutralized, and he gave the mission to his "B" Company. Thus, it was with only his "A" Company and Battalion Headquarters that he drove onto the highway bridge, which he found intact. He seized the north end at 8:30 P.M. of D-Day. During the night, "C" Company and only remnants of a badly hurt "B" Company rejoined him. At its maximum, Col. Frost's strength at the divisional target and the ultimate objective of the whole "Market Garden" operation was 500 men. This would be the high-water mark. Everything after that was downhill: "Market Garden" was already in deep trouble.

The SS Panzer elements had reacted rapidly, and were effectively concentrating their forces. However, had Gen. Urquhart been able to gather up all he had at hand, and make one hard push on the night of September 17, he might have been able to break through to join Frost. That did not happen, and what might have been a golden opportunity was lost.

The next day, September 18, D-Day + 1, the 1st Airborne situation deteriorated, became a mess. Frost sent radio appeals to the two remaining battalions of the 1st Parachute Brigade. They responded by trying to slip around the south flank of the Germans who had stopped them on the previous day. The paratroopers were counterattacked by the Germans, who inflicted severe casualties, isolated several companies, and completely routed the two battalions. 140 men of one of the battalions survived, made one final charge toward the bridge, and failed.

Badly needed reinforcements for the 1st Airborne Division were delayed by fog in England, but by mid-afternoon the 4th Parachute Brigade and the remainder of the 1st Air Landing Brigade were able to land.

Once on the ground, elements of these units advanced into action at once, but to no avail. The situation became even messier. Gen. Urquhart had repeatedly been separated from his troops, and for a time was confined in a Dutch home. His Divisional Headquarters had lost contact with Col. Frost, and all elements of the 1st Parachute Brigade. The division was unable to inform its higher Headquarters, or any Headquarters, of its desperate and worsening situation. Regardless how desperate a situation is – there often is a glimmer of hope. In this situation that glimmer of hope was the 1st Polish Parachute Brigade. That highly respected, fearsome element was due to reinforce the 1st Airborne Division on D-Day + 2, and to land near the Arnhem bridge. If successful, that might somehow have saved the day. Again fate intervened, and this time more bad luck. Instead of landing on schedule, the Polish landings occurred four days after D-Day: terrible weather had delayed them. Even though the weather gradually improved, it still prevented planes from dropping half of their planned loads, and because of positions held by the Germans the Polish paratroopers were forced to land some distance from their original destinations. The Poles confronted other obstacles and difficulties, and were never a factor in the operation.

Back to D-Day. The XXX Corps with three divisions "hit the road" and began the armored push at 2:35 P.M. on the 17th. To ease and assist their kick-off, rocket-firing Typhoon fighter-bombers preceded the start of their thrust to the east. The goal of the tankers was to be in Arnhem in two days. They made good progress, and by the end of the day they reached Valkenswaard, slightly less than ten miles from Eindhoven. However, they would soon become greatly concerned and restricted by the very narrow corridor upon which they were advancing, and opposition from aggressive defenders far stiffer than they had been led to expect. The next day they had some tough fighting south of Eindhoven, and were not able to link up with elements of the 101st on the southern outskirts until about seven in the evening. They had been well aware that the Son bridge over the Wilhelmina Canal had been blown, so they rushed engineers forward to erect a Bailey Bridge, to enable the tanks to cross. The engineers labored all night, and did their job, for the first tank crossed the newly installed bridge at 6:45 A.M. It was now the 19th, D + 2. The British column was at this point already at least thirty-three hours behind schedule.

Once across the bridge they continued their advance, and by that evening the Guards Armoured Division had linked up with the American 82nd Airborne Division at Nijmegen. Before they could move out of the city, and attempt to get across the Waal, they hit fierce resistance by the Germans. After hours of fighting, they used their power, and the next day, the 20th, they thrust across the Nijmegen bridge, and moved to the east bank of the Waal. This action had cost them another day.

Now the end was almost in sight, the big objective was just up ahead. The Guards Armoured Division with the 43rd Division had only to advance ten miles from the Waal to Arnhem. They tried mightily to jump that narrow gap, but were stopped by the German 10th. SS Panzer Division. The British tankers could not overcome an extraordinarily severe handicap. As the tanks advanced to Arnhem, they were restricted, primarily, to the road, because the terrain on both sides was not conducive to cross-country maneuvering. Because the actions of the tanks were so limited, it was like the shooting gallery at Coney Island for the Germans. Instead of ducks one at a time, it was tanks.

Finally, the Allied units could advance no further. They were stopped cold. They would never reach Arnhem, the ultimate objective of "Market Garden." Even worse, it appeared highly possible that the armored column could be divided and encircled.

With that the ceiling came crashing down. "Market Garden" had imploded.

While this was unfolding, the British 1st Airborne Division, whose elements had gained the far bank of the lower Rhine River, found itself pinned down by fierce enemy counterattacks. On the 21st, Gen. Urquhart was forced to pull back his forces to Oosterbeeck, leaving Frost and his men still defending the bridge alone. That evening Col. Frost was seriously wounded. He had only 100 men left, and they were overrun and captured.

For five days those British Airborne troops with their red berets had fought furiously against continued ferocious onslaughts on their bridgehead. Whereas the "Market Garden" operation was replete with great disappointments, Col. Frost and his small battalion were, undoubtedly, the brightest light in an otherwise dismal operation. They shone brilliantly. They were the perfect example of a valiant, courageous, heroic stand that resulted in a valorous defeat.

The 9,000 officers and men of the British 1st Airborne Division and 1100 glider pilots had together fought the German II Panzer Corps, over a period of days, until they could fight no more. Of that number only 2,163 were able to survive the battles, and infiltrate back to friendly lines.

For the "Market Garden" operation as a whole, 3,700 American personnel and a total of about 11,000 men of all units were killed, wounded, or missing. A terrible, tragic loss.

What happened to "the most imaginative plan yet devised?" What went wrong? Montgomery had for the operation three Airborne Divisions, the largest and most ambitious employment of airborne troops in WW II. On the ground he had three divisions, plus air and ground support, and the logistical back-up required for such a massive operation. It was a tremendous force designed to advance initially only 60 miles to the east.

For the failure of this operation Montgomery placed much blame on the vagaries of the weather. He had a good point. Weather certainly handicapped his operation. It was the weather that delayed at a critical time the reinforcement of the British 1ˢᵗ Airborne Division by elements of its own division, as well as re-supply operations. It was the weather that severely delayed at a most critical time the reinforcement of the 1ˢᵗ Airborne Division by the Polish Parachute Brigade. Except for two days, weather restricted Allied fighter operations. Consequently, this permitted the enemy to launch their counterattacks without interference from the air.

However, the bad weather was typical of what might be expected in England and Holland at that time of year. A Commander in Monty's position with so very much at stake should have anticipated, expected bad weather and made provisions for it. Those should have been included in his battle assessments.

Another factor which was, undoubtedly, a great blow and markedly affected his operation was another stroke of bad luck – this time, something over which he had absolutely no control. An American officer made a tremendous, unforgivable blunder by having in his possession on an American troop-carrying glider a copy of the Allied operation order. His glider was shot down over German held territory, and the operational order was captured near General Kurt Student's Headquarters. Gen. Student was Germany's leading expert on airborne operations, and he was already conducting defense operations against the British. By the end of the day, with the captured operation order in his lap, he would from then on be able to conduct his operations based on exact knowledge of Allied intentions. Furthermore, the order was soon in the hands of Field Marshall Model, the German overall Commander, whose Headquarters, most fortuitously for him, was in Oosterbeeck, in the suburbs of Arnhem, and in close proximity to some of the 1ˢᵗ Airborne Division's drop zones. This was, indeed, a major set-back for Montgomery.

Undoubtedly, Montgomery's greatest blunder in this operation was his miscalculation of the strength of the enemy he would be facing. He, alone, was fully to blame. The problems that arose were largely of his own making. He had contended all along that the German defenses on their northern flank were weak, and that is why he pointed his advance to the northeast – to take advantage of their vulnerable situation. It was one of the critical factors which he, no doubt, hit hard when convincing Eisenhower to "go" with his operation. Bradley had warned that Monty, in his eagerness, might have underestimated the German capabilities.

It seems that during his planning, Montgomery was well aware that there were two Panzer Divisions north of Arnhem. He, somehow, was led to believe that they were resting and refitting. Thus, he must have assumed (to assume in battle is often fatal) that the two divisions would not be a factor in his operation, and he discounted them in his calculations, because they were "out of service." Amazingly and unbelievably, he had neglected to pass that vital information about those German units to his two key Commanders – Gen. Browning, Commander of the airborne troops, and Gen. Horrocks, the ground force Commander.

The two Panzer Divisions, the 9th SS Panzer "Hohenstaufen" Division and the 10th SS Panzer "Frundsberg" Division, were backed up by Division von Tettau, a collection of defense and training battalions of Armed Forces Command, Netherlands.

As soon as the Germans became aware of the Allied assault, the two Panzer Divisions reacted swiftly, and moved forward surprisingly quickly. Their defense was so tenacious and determined that they, as has been described, defeated the British 1st Airborne Division, and kept them from accomplishing their mission at Arnhem. Then in true armor style they applied shock action by taking head-on the advancing British armor. It was the two Panzer Divisions that Monty had discounted which stopped the British ground elements short of Arnhem, routed and defeated them. Thus, Montgomery's faulty assessment of the strength and composition of the enemy he would face contributed directly to his defeat.

Montgomery was responsible for another miscalculation. It has already been pointed out time and time again that Monty consistently demonstrated that he knew little about high-mobility armor warfare. In this situation it appears that he had not explored, was unaware of, or had disregarded the terrain which his tanks would have to traverse to reach Arnhem. As they advanced on the road, which was narrow and vulnerable, the terrain off the road prevented them from fully utilizing their mobility. Because they were largely restricted to the road, the front was not more than two tanks wide. Armor, if it cannot maneuver, is severely handicapped. Conversely, the Germans had a great advantage, for they were very familiar with the area in which they were operating, were able to pick their spots, and swooped in upon the British with telling effect. British armor versus German armor – it was no contest.

There was still another major mistake. The British 1st Airborne Division should have dropped its troopers near the highway bridge at Arnhem. It was a fundamental error to select drop zones $9^{1}/_{2}$ to 13 kilometers from the vital bridge which they were to capture. They had much too far to walk over bad terrain from their drop zone to their objective. The error was compounded by not moving forward the drop zones for the reinforcements who would arrive the next day. The new drop zones could have been on terrain that had been cleared, and much closer to the city.

Another point worthy of conjecture was Montgomery's selection of

Arnhem as the location for his crossing of the Rhine River. It was not a good choice, as it was too far north from the main line of advance. (What had happened to the direct thrust to, and seizure of, the Ruhr?) Wesel, some 50 miles upstream from Arnhem, would have been a far better choice. It was, indeed, at Wesel that Montgomery finally crossed the Rhine, but it was in late March *six months later* .

That crossing of the Rhine was done in typical Montgomery style. He had been engrossed for many days in – what seemed to many – endless planning and preparation. His decision, when finally made, evidently was to cross with great force. First, he had ferried along the canals of Belgium, Holland and Germany 45 landing craft and a formation of Buffalo amphibious tanks. Between March 20 and 22, British and American aircraft flew 16,000 sorties over the assault area and beyond, dropping nearly 50,000 tons of bombs. Huge quantities of ammunition and fuel had been stockpiled. Thousands of tons of bridge-building material and many thousands of engineers had been moved up to the assault areas. A smoke screen was laid and maintained along 75 miles of the Rhine. 80,000 men would make the first crossing, to be followed by many thousands more.

During the night of 23/24 March, 3,000 artillery pieces pounded away. By dawn of the 24th., bridgeheads had been established across the river and quickly expanded. Under the watchful eye of Prime Minister Winston Churchill, airborne troops landed across the river, and hundreds of gliders were engaged. It was certainly a big, big show.

Conntrast all of that with the simplicity and great effectiveness of Gen. Patton's operations. His Third Army, still spearheaded by the 4th Armored Division, made an electrifying leap. In breath-taking fashion they swept eastward, covering 65 miles in three days through and over the extensive, treacherous Schnee Eiffel Range to the Rhine River at Urmitz. They quickly charged to the south, hoping to capture a bridge intact. By March 21 they occupied Worms, and shortly after the 4th Armored Division reached an area on the Rhine near Oppenheim. The 4th was quickly ordered to pull back and let the 5th Infantry Division pass through. That division, during the night 22/23, crossed the Rhine River in assault boats, and established a firm bridgehead. By daybreak on the 23rd., 5000 men were on the east bank of the Rhine, with a loss of but eight men killed. The installation of a pontoon bridge quickly began, and before daybreak the next morning tanks of the Eighth Tank Battalion of the 4th Armored were crossing the Rhine, and would be well to the east by nightfall.

Another great personal triumph for Patton, which he often chortled about and enjoyed immensely. *He had beaten Monty across the Rhine.*

Now back to "Market Garden." It has already been reported, more than once, that Eisenhower declared that the Port of Antwerp was *"an indispensable prerequisite for the final drive into Germany."* The opening of the port had been one of the very important factors considered by Eisenhower in deciding to give priority to Montgomery's northern thrust. Yet, on September 10, when Eisenhower approved Montgomery's "Market Garden," the Port of Antwerp was completely disregarded. The headstrong Montgomery in his great haste and apparent frenzy to press east had "taken his eyes off the ball." He "passed" on clearing the Scheldt Estuary, an absolute requirement for a working Antwerp Port. So Eisenhower, too, "took his eyes off the ball," and by concurring with Montgomery's plan was every bit as guilty as Montgomery for the debacle. This was an astonishing, colossal, unforgivable mistake. It just had to be one of the gravest errors of the European campaign.

What is staggering and beyond belief is that the Port's vital passage, which was vitally needed NOW on September 10, would not be open to shipping until *over two and a half months later.* It was not until November 9 that the Scheldt was cleared and 17 days later, on November 26, that the first Allied convoy was able to unload at the "indispensable Port." Again, it was Bradley who had earlier warned that the priority for Montgomery was to utilize his resources to clear the Scheldt.

During the "Market Garden" disaster, the vast stores of gasoline and all other supplies which had been provided to Montgomery, at the expense of others, were squandered. There was no pay-off for those tremendous losses. They were just gone. Allied forces, in the weeks that followed, would suffer tremendously from a logistical void. A functioning Port would have helped greatly to assuage the logistical vacuum that developed. Without it there occurred, instead, a supply famine.

Patton, that "great offensive weapon," began "sitting" about October 8th, and Bradley soon joined him. As they "sat," the last good autumn days vanished, and the rains and floods arrived, followed by sleet, wind, and snow. By the time the offensive resumed in early November the weather was atrocious, and the fields so sodden, muddy, and sticky that tanks lost their mobility, as they could rarely leave the roads. The defeat at Arnhem and the delay at Antwerp together resulted in an irrevocable logistical loss to the Allies. With supplies available there could have been a much earlier autumn offensive.

Some final "Market Garden" observations:

...The "daring adventure" had failed.

...At the very outset it was a risky gamble, so out of character with Montgomery's cautious nature.

...The most precious commodity on the battlefield – time – was lost.

...Did the operation have something to do with Montgomery's single-minded determination to prove that his constantly announced strategy of the narrow, northern thrust into Germany was the right one?

...A bold plan requires a bold imaginative leader, and, importantly, the execution at the tactical level must be every bit as bold as the strategic concept.

...The last opportunity to end the war in 1944 vanished.

The Germans took maximum advantage of the unexpected "breather" that was provided to them. Between September and mid-December, it was reported that they tripled their forces to 70 divisions, and of the 15 Panzer Divisions eight were refitted with Panther and Tiger tanks.

With the "Market Garden" disaster, the still unopened Antwerp Port, the famine of supplies which kept most of the Allies "sitting," and the very tough fighting still ahead, the Germans were well aware of the predicament in which the Allies had placed themselves. If there was ever an opportunity for the Germans to "go for broke" this was the time. Apparently their plans to do so must have crystallized, and the time and place selected, for it was not long before they launched their massive Ardennes Offensive, which became the "Battle of the Bulge."

CHAPTER 18

GENERAL GEORGE S. PATTON, JR.:

HOW HE UTILIZED THE "LEAVINGS."

The last report of my Eighth Tank Battalion, Combat Command "B," 4th Armored Division, had us in a bivouac, south of Crantenoy, and a mere 5 km. from that major obstacle, the Moselle River. Just hours before, on September 10, it had been a warm, sunny, lazy Sunday afternoon, when, with absolutely no warning, we had been rudely uprooted from our enforced and unwelcome sojourn on the east bank of the Meuse River. In a minimum amount of time we had "mounted up," and during the last hours of daylight and into the early evening, we had "rolled" to our present location.

We were still in a severe case of shock and disappointment that the five-day window of opportunity had closed irretrievably upon us, and forfeited the final chance for Third Army to make it possible to end the war in Europe before the end of the year.

As we had sat along the Meuse, we were unaware that Third Army had received enough gasoline to enable it to resume its advance, and that other elements of our Third Army had been engaged since September 5. There were other unfolding developments, as well, that would directly affect us.

To our north, between the 5th and the 7th., Gen. Walker's XXth Corps of Third Army, operating opposite the fortified city of Metz, had hoped that they could secure a Moselle bridgehead with a rapid, armored thrust. That had worked well for them on the Marne and Meuse, but it had failed near Metz. The 5th Infantry Division of XX Corps made a shallow bridgehead over the Moselle River on the 8th of September, but it had to be withdrawn on the 11th., because of enemy pressure. Later, an attack by the 7th Armored Division of XX Corps stalled near Ft. Driant, because of stiff German resistance and other factors. Walker's Corps was now bogged down in its efforts to secure useable bridgeheads near Metz.

Maj. Gen. Wade Haislip's XV Corps, which had been shifted to 1st Army along the lower Seine many days before, was returned to reinforce Patton's Third Army. However, it was a skeleton corps, anything but a heavy-weight, and included only the 79th Infantry Division and the French 2nd Armored Division. They would be operating to protect Patton's right flank, which during our sweep across France had been unprotected except by air.

Bradley had warned Patton that Montgomery was pressing for higher priority of resources for his 21st Army Group, and that Patton should be prepared for a decrease in his already limited allotments. Then on the 12th. Bradley informed Patton that the supply situation had reached a critical point, and that he would give Patton two more days, until the 14th., to cross the Moselle in force between Nancy and Metz. If he were not able to do that, Third Army would go on the defensive from Nancy to the Luxembourg border.

Reports strongly indicated that Hitler was greatly concerned and had his eye, as well, on the Moselle River. He was genuinely alarmed by the threat that Patton posed, and wanted him contained before he could cross the river in strength. He gave high priority to reactivation of the Fifth Panzer Army, and even appointed a rising star, Gen. Hasso von Manteuffel, an armor expert, who was imported from the Russian front, to take command of that Army on September 11th. He would be the principal German Commander who would duel with Patton in Lorraine.

The Fifth Panzer Army, when Manteuffel took command, would initially have a few bones, but very little flesh – it was virtually a "nothing" – a Headquarters with no troops. However, that would rapidly change. What we had greatly feared and expected, while we sat alongside the Meuse, was now unfolding at an alarming pace. The Germans, with no hesitation, had used the delay in our offensive operations to gather their disorganized and routed elements, and reorganize them into viable combat units. Forces flowed into Lorraine from all directions. They came from the northern sector of the front, and from Southern France. Reinforcements even came from Italy. That Theater produced two Panzer Grenadier Divisions – the 3rd and 15th It was not long before Manteuffel picked up a couple of Panzer Corps, but more importantly a Panzer Division and two Panzer Brigades. Newly minted Panther tanks would come spewing directly from factories to Lorraine.

Unfortunately for Patton, Walker's XX Corps would never be a factor. He held a front of 40 miles with the 5th and 90th Infantry Divisions, and the 7th Armored Division. Metz, unlike its Lorraine sister city, was heavily and thoroughly fortified. It had as many as 43 intercommunicating forts on both sides of the Moselle, manned by 14,000 troops. So it would be an under-statement to say that Walker had his hands full.

Well to the south, the limited XVth Corps, with its limited mission, would also not be heard from.

Once again, Patton would place his hopes and the big load upon the XIIth Corps. And as it had been all across France, thus far, the great burden would be upon the hard-charging 4th Armored Division. Backing up the 4th would be the 35th and 80th Infantry Divisions. However, it was once again up to the 4th to set the pace and gain the ground.

Gen. Eddy, XII Corps Commander, as soon as he had some gas, put the 80th Division to work on September 5. Their mission, north of Nancy, was to get across the Moselle River. Elements of a Regimental Combat team near Pont-a-Mousson seized a bridgehead, but lost it to a German counterattack. The enemy still held the west bank at many points, and the 80th Infantry Division made continued attempts to push the Germans back over to the east bank in preparation for river-crossing operations, but were not successful.

The difficulties of the 80th north of Nancy caused Gen. Eddy to pause and consider his next move. He had earlier decided that even though Nancy was not fortified, as Metz was, he would not, because of surrounding terrain, make a direct attack upon that provincial capital. He would instead attempt an envelopment that would cut off the city from the east, and would, consequently, make the conquest of the city by the infantry much easier.

But now that the 80th had been strongly rebuffed, Eddy was concerned that the strengthening German defenses there would cause him trouble, if he attempted further crossings. So he decided to make the area south of Nancy the corps' main effort, and to envelope Nancy from that direction. He believed that German resistance would be weaker in the south than in the north.

Gen. Wood of the 4th once again differed with his Corps Commander, and objected to the Corps plan. He pointed out to Eddy that in the north there was but one natural obstacle to contend with, and it was the Moselle River. In the south, after crossing the Moselle, the advancing forces would have to cross as many as seven tributaries and canals to gain the rear of Nancy. The bridges over each of these would have to be seized and held; if they had been blown, supporting engineers would have to install the necessary bridging. Fording would be a difficult option, and the advance at best would be time-consuming.

Apparently nodding to Wood's objections, Eddy modified the Corps plan once again, which, in effect, resulted in a compromise. Combat Command "B" of the 4th together with the 35th Infantry Division, would have the mission of securing crossings over the Moselle in the south, and then swinging northeast.

Accordingly, Eddy would once again order the 80th to seize a bridgehead over the Moselle north of Nancy, where CC "A" of the 4th was located, desperately endeavoring in some manner to find a way to get across the Moselle.

By first light, early on the morning of September 11, my Eighth Tank Battalion, the forward element of CC "B," was already "rolling." In no time we covered the last few kilometers to the Moselle River at Bayon, and suddenly there it was staring at us. We had heard much about this imposing obstacle, so it was a long-awaited moment. However, our enthusiasm for, finally, reaching this goal was instantly smothered. Other than the river, the first thing we noted, much to our great disappointment and dismay, was the Bayon Bridge, which had been severely damaged. The spans were gone, with only the abutments remaining. Now our tanks would be at the mercy of the infantry and engineers, who would have to install new spans on the damaged bridge, or erect one from scratch.

As battalion operations officer and advance guard Commander, it was my job to assess the situation quickly. In no time I learned that elements of the 35th Infantry Division had by some hours preceded us to the river. They had the mission of establishing and securing a bridgehead, and then enlarging it, so that the engineers could do their work with a minimum of harassment.

More disappointing and dismaying news. The infantry had successfully established a small bridgehead, but aggressive enemy actions had not only prevented them from enlarging it, but had pushed them back. That small bridgehead was now dangling by a thread. The enemy had locations around the bridge zeroed in, and were regularly pouring fire upon them.

The first requirement was for our tanks to move immediately away from the incoming fire. What faced us was a discouraging, immediate future. Tanks cannot cross a major river without a bridge. As the situation now stood, it would take many hours for the Infantry, which had already been stymied, to establish an effective bridgehead. After that, for the engineers to install a tank bridge would require many more. We tankers considered that to be a totally unacceptable delay. For us, sitting and waiting and providing some supporting fire, for that scenario to unfold, just did not seem like a viable option. Something just had to be done, and done quickly. So we moved further north until we were out of range of enemy fire. Now we paused to get a good look at the river. The first look brought immediate excitement. Our fortuitous decision, some stroke of fate had brought us to the Moselle at this particular location.

It appeared from our vantage point that somewhere to the south the river had separated into three channels. The Moselle that we were analyzing at some distance appeared to have three fingers of sandy, gravelly spurs of ground from which short, wild underbrush grew. These fingers did, indeed, force the river into three channels. So in front of us was not one mighty, wide river, but three smaller, narrower rivers. We now believed and hoped that because the river had divided itself, each part should be shallower and narrower than the whole. So virtually in unison the word *ford* flashed through our minds. That such was more than an outside possibility again brought great excitement. But once more that excitement was quickly dampened. In our eagerness to examine the river, we had overlooked a problem, before the main problem. Virtually at our feet was the Canal de l'Est, a most formidable obstacle. Under normal circumstances, full-sized barges trafficked this canal, but apparently the locks had been damaged, for the visible barges were high and dry. The water was very low and the bottom extremely muddy.

What followed was a prime example of what a group of dedicated, relentless, ingenious, and irrepressible tankers can accomplish. With virtually no hesitation, tanks began blasting both sides of the canal with high explosive shells to create gaps. As the banks crumbled, the resulting debris rolled back to the bottom, creating a very rough bed. Again, with very little hesitation the first tank skidded down the side of the canal, crossed over the debris, and in low gear chugged and churned up the far bank. At first the tracks spun futilely in the mud, but they finally took hold, and the first tank laboriously made it up the bank and on to level terrain. One tank followed another. If one bogged down, out came the tow chain from the preceding tank. Finally, enough tanks were across to make the quick dash over open terrain to the river. The remaining tanks of the battalion were on "hold" so that not too many would be trapped on the open ground between the canal and river, in the event that the river could not be forded.

Once the river was reached, a similar but different challenge faced the tankers. If successful, this would be a very wet crossing. The lead tank upon reaching the first channel slowly and gingerly eased down the bank. We all virtually stopped breathing, not knowing how deep the swift-flowing water was. If it was deep enough to engulf and drown out the tank, our high hopes would be dashed, and back to the infantry bridgehead it would have to be. As the first tank moved down the bank, the water rose higher and higher, alongside it. When the tank leveled off at the bottom, the water was just above the broad fenders over the tracks, and a little over half way up the sides of the tank. The driver, well knowing that the slightest hesitation would flood out the engine, had it in first gear, and gunned the engine, kept it roaring, and slowly but steadily climbed the far bank, and reached level ground. Applying what had already worked, the remaining two channels were quickly crossed. *A tank had forded the Moselle River.* If one could do it, so could the others. And they did! Tanks fanned out and created multiple crossing sites over the canal and the river. Those that were flooded out were hauled out. It was still daylight when all the tanks of the Eighth Tank Battalion were on the east bank of the Moselle River – an unprecedented, absolutely remarkable achievement. Tanks just do not cross major rivers without a bridge – these just did. The classic crossing of a river has the infantry gaining a bridgehead, the engineers erecting a bridge, and the tanks crossing over it. In this situation none of that happened, so the accomplishment of the Eighth Tank Battalion of CC "B," 4th Armored Division just had to be labeled as an UNCLASSIC crossing of a major river.

Once across the river, the tankers did not stop to rest on their laurels. They spread out, seized the dominating terrain, knowing that there would be a quick and unquestionably astonished reaction from the enemy, who had paid most of their attention to the established bridge site. As they were enlarging the bridgehead, the tanks became engaged with the enemy, and were quickly involved in small battles. The first tanks across had immediately moved south to envelope Bayon. Among the enemy forces, they spotted five new moving tanks, and quickly destroyed three of them. By clearing and securing the east bank they made it possible for the engineers to move up and begin working on a bridge.

But the enemy was anything but finished. During the night, the Germans moved forces around and into position, and early in the morning all companies of the Eighth were busy repulsing repeated and determined enemy counterattacks. German artillery, during the night and increasingly in the morning, directed concentrations at the bridgehead, bridge sites, and the areas around them. The Eighth successfully repulsed the enemy's aggressive efforts, and once the situation was somewhat stabilized, it left the bridgehead in the hands of elements of the 35th Infantry Division, and began its difficult and arduous advance to the northeast. It faced the daunting challenge of making its way across the numerous water obstacles that stood directly across its path. It was still operating as the "Lone Ranger," for it was still the only unit of the 4th Armored Division on the east side of the Moselle.

Up ahead were the Montagne River, the Meurthe River, the Sanon River, and the Marne au Rhein Canal, not to mention various small but impeding tributaries. All in all, these represented treacherous, demanding challenges – not an appetizing fare to anticipate.

As we advanced, it was not long before elements of the battalion began hitting resistance. By this time we readily recognized that the Army that now faced us was not a beaten force. We were now reconciled that the great pursuit was over. Instead of sweeping over and around the fleeing fragments of shattered German units, we were now encountering enemy soldiers who fought hard for every foot of ground, and who counterattacked viciously to recover lost positions.

We knew that behind us the bridge at Bayon would be a very busy place. As soon as the engineers completed the bridge, the miscellany of military vehicles which had assembled in close proximity to the river would begin the slow and painstaking job of crossing the river over the temporary bridge. It would be single file, one by one. The first to cross would be the armored infantry half-tracks and the artillery self-propelled howitzers, and engineer vehicles which would endeavor to close up to the Eighth as quickly as possible so as to be in position to provide assistance and supporting fire to the tankers. Then it would be the jeeps, half-tracks, trucks and other vehicles of the remainder of CC "B." Since only CC "A" of the 4th was north of the river, the huge "tail" of the remainder of the 4th Armored Division would follow, and after that the 35th Infantry Division. There would be vehicles crossing incessantly for many hours yet to come.

For the remainder of that day, the 12th., and all day on the 13th. and 14th., the elements of CC "B" had bitter fights against fanatical and resourceful resistance. The tankers teamed up with the armored Infantry, fought tenaciously, and were assisted greatly by close artillery support. Bridges were blown, and sites were defended heavily and vigorously. Heavy rains fell, and conditions became absolutely miserable. It required vicious fighting to seize control of bridge sites, so that the engineers could install the required bridging in a minimum of time. Further delays resulted when the division's bridging was completely exhausted, and the engineers had to call for immediate help from the rear.

Finally, CC "B's" battle-weary and exhausted elements reached their final water obstacle, but by far the most onerous one. It was the Sanon River and almost directly behind it the even more formidable and dangerous La Marne Au Rhein, a broad, steep, deep major European canal. What further complicated this horrendous water complex and hazard were the bodies of water which ran perpendicular to and intersected the canal and river.

Starting very early the next morning, and lasting all day and well into the evening, barrage after barrage of artillery, together with tank and other fire, was laid down on the opposite bank, hoping to soften the enemy, but to no avail. The enemy responded by tenaciously and vigorously defending from the opposite bank with heavy machine-gun, mortar, and artillery fire, together with telling rounds from skilled snipers. So on the 15th it was "no gain." For the first time since our initial engagement in July, the Eighth's bivouac area had not moved from that of the previous night.

But enough was enough. Early the next morning our forces side-stepped to the left, found a spot for crossing that was lightly defended, crossed over an engineer-installed bridge, seized the high ground on the north bank, cleared it to Crevic, where we had been held up the day before, and continued the advance to the north. Although we hit heavy resistance along every foot of the way, our gain was eleven miles. This was a very modest advance when compared to the heady days of August, but under the circumstances a full and busy day, and a significant and substantial achievement.

As has been described, CC "B" was heavily involved on September 12 as it advanced to the northeast. On that same day there was, as well, considerable activity north of Nancy. That most important and eagerly awaited achievement occurred at a place called Dieulouard, where the 80th finally secured a bridgehead over the Moselle, and bridged the river. That was the day after CC "B's" crossing. Gen. Wood, without hesitation, ordered CC "A" to use the infantry crossing and to move over the river the next day. During the very early hours of September 13, the Dieulouard bridgehead was hit with a strong counterattack, which brought Germans almost within rifle range of the bridge. CC "A" countered by sending a troop from the Cavalry reconnaissance squadron across the river. They successfully broke up the counterattack, and pushed forward until they were stopped by German assault guns.

When daylight came on the 13th., the Dieulouard bridgehead was still threatened. After some delays, confusion, and consultation by senior Commanders, CC "A" decided to gamble and to "go for it." This they did successfully as a tank-heavy task force pushed across the river, shoved aside the German attempts to stop the thrust, picked up speed, and with no water compartments in their path to delay them, headed straight down the highway toward that large town, Château-Salins. German opposition was now disorganized and scattered, and the tanks advanced much the way they did in France during August. They roared through roadblocks and ground fire of all types. They reached the high ground west of Château-Salins late in the afternoon, after a penetration of 20 miles. As expected, it took some hours for the remainder of CC "A" to get across the river in a classic armor river crossing.

At this point, it is well to recall that Bradley had earlier warned Patton that if he were not able to cross the Moselle "in force" by the

14th., he would have to move to the defensive. By late afternoon of the 13th., the entire 4th Armored Division "in force" was on the east side of the Moselle, and they had made significant penetrations to the east "to boot." Thus, the 4th beat Bradley's deadline by one day, and again "saved the day" for Patton. Significantly, it would enable George to continue his advance awhile longer, until his threatened gasoline spigot was turned completely off.

On the morning of the 14th. it appeared that Château-Salins would be CC "A's" next objective. It was a large town, a road center, and from the volume of incoming fire it appeared that the town would be strongly defended. Instead, Gen. Wood decided once again, as he had done during the previous weeks, to exploit weakness rather than attacking strength. He ordered CC "A" to by-pass Château-Salins, turn south, and advance aggressively toward a town called Arracourt, about which much more would soon be written.

As in August, conditions for tanks were still almost perfect – firm ground; open rolling terrain; good road net: and only scattered resistance. By early evening CC "A" was establishing its defenses around Arracourt.

Elements of CC "A" used the 15th to make wide sweeps from their base around and outside their positions, and conducted surprising and extremely profitable raids and ambushes.

The 16th proved to be for the 4th Armored Division and Third Army a most unusual and momentous day. As has just been described, it was on the 16th that the Eighth Tank Battalion with its accompanying infantry crossed Le Marne au Rhein, cleared part of the north bank, and advanced 11 miles. It was much earlier that CC "B," spearheaded by the Eighth, had forced a crossing over the Moselle by fording, had aggressively overcome numerous water hazards, and forged the southern portion of the vise that now sealed off, and isolated from the east, the city of Nancy. Further, by advancing between Nancy and CC "A" that day, the forces of CC "B" had helped reopen CC "A's" supply lines, which had been isolated in the Arracourt area.

Also on the 16th CC "A" sent a battalion-sized task force from Arracourt to assist CC "B" across the Marne-Rhein Canal. With most of the tactical elements of CC "B" already across, CC "A's" task force finished clearing the north bank, thus easing the crossing of the remainder of CC "B." In the process, they had forged the northern portion of the vise that gripped Nancy from the east.

CC "A," spearheaded by the 37th Tank Battalion, had swept ruthlessly from Dieulouard to Château-Salins, and then on to Arracourt, overcoming and destroying the disorganized resistance in the path of their advance. Their raids around Arracourt resulted in the capture of hundreds of Germans and the destruction of many guns and vehicles.

So, after several weeks of operating on widely separated axes, CC "A" and CC "B" physically and symbolically came together on this day at the Marne-Rhein Canal. There were no ceremonies, no fanfare, no shaking of hands to mark this achievement. It was business as usual. It was a job that had to be done and was. An added bonus: because of the 4th's exploits on the east side of the Moselle, the 35th Infantry Division was able to occupy Nancy on the 15th with little opposition and virtually no destruction.

Now, what next? The hard chargers in the division were ready to do just that – to charge ahead, once again. It appeared to us that we should immediately exploit our advantageous situation, and pursue the enemy as we had done so effectively in August. Once again the road to Germany was open, and if we moved now, the enemy did not have the necessary reserves to block an eastward armored advance. Why not move out immediately on two separate axes, with CC "B" setting its sights on Saarbrucken and CC "A" on Saarguemines? We well knew that we would have Patton's endorsement, for he was as eager as we were to resume the war of movement in which his Army had demonstrably excelled.

However, our Corps Commander had contrary views. He did not believe that XII Corps was ready to support an immediate armored advance. Among the considerations was the strong belief that the limited supplies that were reaching the 4th Armored Division could not sustain a full-scale armored thrust.

So he turned to other situations which he believed needed attention. At Dieulouard, the Germans had reorganized and been reinforced, and were still attacking the 80th Infantry Division, and had actually cut the route that CC "A" had taken to Château-Salins. Despite the 4th Armored's sweep east of Nancy, there were Germans still close in to the city. So the 35th Infantry Division, which would be in direct support of the 4th when they advanced, was given the mission of clearing the high ground northeast of Nancy.

On September 17, CC "B" was directed to move towards Château-Salins, passing behind CC "A," so as to relieve some of the pressure on the Dieulouard bridgehead. As we neared Château-Salins, it was quickly obvious that the enemy had, once again, used most profitably that gift which we had provided – time. They had concentrated reserves around Château-Salins, and these fully prepared forces now "owned" the very ground which CC "A" had occupied a few days before. They had positioned themselves to block one of the important routes to the east, and would surely be causing us some grief. It would soon be determined if Gen. Eddy's "tidying up the battlefield" (a strongly-held Montgomery principle) which might have effectively strengthened the XII Corps foothold across the Moselle, was a preferable choice to that of moving right out aggressively to the east and maintaining the momentum.

By the 19th., Gen. Eddy had the 4th Armored, backed up by the 35th Infantry Division, ready to resume the attack to the east. This was five days after CC "A" had reached Arracourt. But on that day there was a most surprising and totally unexpected development. Because of it, the attack was never launched, and the 4th Armored Division and Third Army lost the initiative in Lorraine, and for a long period in the war.

Hitler had been well aware of the situation and of CC "A's" exposed flank. He decided that this was the perfect opportunity to hit hard, and ordered Gen. Manteuffel to roll up Third Army's right flank, and block further advance. So under cover of the early morning fog, large numbers of Panther tanks from his Fifth Panzer Army pushed through CC "A's" outposts and kicked off what would become a massive tank battle. Tanks from CC "A's" 37th Tank Battalion, assisted by tank destroyers from the 704th T. D. Battalion, immediately engaged the advancing German tanks, and a running fight ensued. The Germans had the momentum because their attack had been so sudden, and was such a stunning surprise. Despite the countering fire of CC "A' s" elements, the aggressive advance of the enemy pushed almost to CC "A's" Headquarters. In desperation the armored artillery joined in the battle. They leveled their howitzers and fired point blank "right in the faces" of the advancing Panthers. This effective supporting fire helped stop the enemy advance, which was pushed back. The fog was an advantage and disadvantage to both sides. The fog enabled the German forces to gain tactical surprise, and most importantly protected them from attacks by U.S. fighter planes. The U.S. Shermans were out-gunned by the Panthers, but the fog enabled the Shermans to close in and cleverly out-maneuver the enemy. The furious tank battles raged for hours; it was back and forth, nip and tuck, all day. Although the Germans had new tanks, the performance of the German tankers did not quite measure up. Their tactics at times appeared timid when compared to those of the aggressive, ingenious, battle-tested and experienced tankers of the 37th Finally, late in the afternoon, after taking severe losses, the German attack stalled, and they broke off the engagement. When the results were totaled, the figures were amazing. The forces of CC "A," unbelievably, had destroyed 43 German tanks while losing only five of their own.

And far to the north on this same day, the 19th., Montgomery's forces were fighting desperately to "stay alive" in Operation "Market Garden," which already appeared doomed.

On the morning of the 20th CC "A" quickly learned that the tank attack that they had received the day before was not an isolated, one-day affair. In an attack very much like that of the previous day, the

Germans again hit CC "A," and again a furious battle ensued. And as the day before, the enemy lost tanks – this time, 25 to CC "A's" six. It was clearly evident that these engagements were anything but minor skirmishes, and the situation now confirmed that this was, indeed, a major tank battle.

For the next five days the tank battles at Arracourt continued. Each of the subsequent engagements mirrored the fight on the first day. The Panther tanks would attack under the cover of the morning fog, would be met, hit hard, and disorganized by CC "A's" counterattacks. More enemy tank losses would result, and they would break off the fight. The German tank losses were adding up at an alarming rate.

The enemy attention and attacks were not confined to the Arracourt area. The sizeable and well-organized forces in the vicinity of Fresnes en Saulnois and Château-Salins were also throwing their weight around, with constant probes and limited attacks along the CC "B" front. Here again, every time they hit and pulled back it was with losses.

They must have decided to shoot their wad, and now it was CC "B"s turn to be hit with a massive attack. It happened early on the morning of the 24th, a gray, cold day of dense fog and heavy rain. The Eighth Tank Battalion was occupying and defending the left flank of CC "B," and faced the Forêt de Château-Salins. Out of the cover of those woods and shielded by the horrible weather conditions, came a small armada of Panther and a few scattered Tiger tanks, supported by a sizeable force of Infantry, which began to advance slowly and carefully towards our positions. Thus began another hectic, vicious tank battle – this time a duel. They had the guns – we had the position. Because they were coming at us head on, we knew that we could not knock them out by trying to penetrate the thick steel sloped front plates of their tanks. Because of the horrible weather and our positions on the dominating terrain, their advance was methodical – stop and go. Our Tank Commanders and gunners well knew that to get the necessary "kills" to stop the attack, they had to resort to the best ingenuity they could muster, and to use all the weapons in their arsenal. Our gunners zeroed in on the enemy tank turrets, which had less armor than the tank sloped front plates. They used their armor-piercing rounds to damage turrets, the shrapnel from high explosive rounds to cause casualties to Tank Commanders and crewmen, and the white phosphorus rounds to set fire to the tanks. As the enemy tanks advanced, they had to stop to set themselves before they fired. Because of the heavy mist, it was difficult for them to see through their periscopes, and to aim and fire their shots.

Nevertheless, the enemy with their powerful guns kept up constant and well-distributed fire along the crest of the ridge, hoping to catch one of our tanks in the open.

Consequently, our tankers had to be elusive, to be exposed for a minimum amount of time. Our gunners would get off three, four or five quick rounds with their turrets exposed on the ridge, and then the tanks quickly pulled back into defilade, side-slipped to the right or left, so they would be a different target, and moved up again to aim and fire at another tank.

Despite immobilized and burning tanks around them, the enemy methodically and relentlessly moved closer to the ridge. It was still nip and tuck – it could go either way. It could even turn into a close-in slug-fest. And then the unexpected, the almost impossible happened. It came so gradually that the tankers, intent upon their battle, were late in noticing it. The sky, which had been ceiling zero, suddenly had a small, bright blue spot in it, and the spot soon became larger, and then a hole in the sky. What is even more remarkable and astonishing, and something of which we had been totally unaware, P-47 fighters, knowing of the struggle taking place below, had been circling and circling for just such an opportunity. The moment the hole opened up, they grasped that unexpected stroke of good luck, and down they swooped right on top of the battlefield. They brought devastating fire – strafing guns and exploding bombs. The tide of battle turned in an instant. Right after this totally unexpected blow, the enemy lost all interest in the fight, and withdrew at a pace far faster than their advance, leaving much destruction behind. Our fighter support was the trump card in that closely contested, see-saw struggle.

The Germans back in the cover of the Forêt immediately began sending harassing fire at long range – both direct fire from tanks and high explosive fire from their artillery – but there was no sign of a follow-up attack. It was "no gain" for them, for they were back where they started. Moreover, it was an unfortunate adventure for the Germans, for in addition to substantial personnel losses inflicted by elements of CC "B," 23 of their tanks had been destroyed and an unknown number damaged.

We had little chance to "lick our wounds" the next day, the 25th., for the pesky Germans would not let up, and continued pressing and poking with fire. But suddenly out of the blue our attention was directed elsewhere. We received unexpected and surprising instructions; we would be moving the next day. The 35th Infantry Division would move up to take over the positions that we would be vacating.

The early hours of the 26th. found us moving toward Arracourt, under cover of darkness. In a cold and continuous downpour we marched 25 miles, and linked up with CC "A." We took positions on their right flank – to their east and south. To our right was the town of Rechicourt, and just beyond it the much-discussed Le Marne au Rhein Canal, which would be good protection for our right flank.

The developments on the 26th., to us, were startling and momentous. We were ordered to assume a position of defense. This was a mission which we had never expected to receive; we were an offensive weapon. If we were tied to the ground, we would not be using the movement and mobility of our tanks, and, thus, would be just another division. It appears that some time after Eisenhower conducted a meeting at Versailles on the 22nd, Patton received orders which directed him to "hold present position until supply situation permits the resumption of the offensive." The word that we received from Third Army was phrased a bit differently, but meant the same. We were ordered to "suspend all offensive operations and to consolidate gains." For Patton to have to issue such instructions must have caused him great anguish and pain, for he who abhorred defensive warfare more than anyone was now placed on the defensive.

Upon arrival in our new area, the tank companies immediately moved to occupy and secure the ridges to our front, which were the dominating terrain. The remaining elements took up positions in a valley that ran alongside the Arracourt-Rechicourt road. *And there we would sit from the 26th. of September to the 8th. of October.*

The Germans, however, were far from finished. From our estimates they were down to about 25 tanks, but they just would not quit. Instead, they continued to try aggressively to break through our positions. Although theirs were not deep, sustained attacks, they were more than a nuisance, and continued to cause us casualties. Finally, the rain stopped, the weather briefly cleared, and the fighter aircraft reappeared. Between them and our tanks the Germans were forced, finally, to stop altogether what had become a progressively faltering counteroffensive. They had been determined, they put up a great, vicious fight over a period of many days, and they gave up only when they were down to virtually their last tank.

However, it was not yet over for us; they continued to hang in there. The enemy still had long-range artillery, and an abundance of ammunition. Day after day and night after night the enemy artillery stood off and fired indiscriminately. They knew generally where we were located, and would send unobserved fire aimlessly and haphazardly into our positions. They knew that they were bound to hit something, and they often did, causing us frequent and senseless casualties. We never knew when the rounds would come and where they would hit. Sitting and "taking it" was demoralizing, and it restricted the movements of our men, interfered with their rest, and put them on edge. The last days for us would be one of the most exasperating, frustrating, wasteful periods of the war.

All things must eventually come to an end. For the first time since we broke out at Normandy, we were completely out of action. We were relieved by the fresh, newly arrived 26th Infantry Division on October 8, and moved back to the rear, to pup tents in the muddy, sodden fields of Lorraine. From that day until November 9th., when the 4th Armored Division resumed the offensive, it was no longer Blitzkrieg but "Sitzkrieg."

Hitler had earlier ordered Manteuffel and his Fifth Panzer Army to stop Patton and his Third Army with its 4th Armored Division. He failed. Now we were stopped – *not by Manteuffel but by our own higher Headquarters.* Patton had earlier written to his wife, Beatrice, "Books will some day be written on 'that pause that did not *refresh* anyone but the Germans'." Until he died, Patton never stopped insisting that had the priority of supply been given to him, his Third Army could have broken through the Saar to the Rhine. Now he was forced to succumb to yet another devastating "pause."

The preceding chapter described what the "First Team" did with the preponderance of all resources. It "crashed" in Holland.

What did the "Second Team," which barely got into the fight, do with the "leavings?' It established a large and secure bridgehead over the Moselle, from which the November offensive would be launched; by its outflanking Nancy the capture of that city was made relatively easy; it drew into the area and destroyed elements of two Volksgrenadier Divisions, two Panzer Divisions, two Panzer Brigades, and a miscellaneous array of separate units. By its actions it completely blunted Hitler's urgent, vital mission to stop and destroy Patton's tanks, and to drive back across the Moselle and on to Nancy.

To be able to do that, Third Army had to win decisively the fiercest, greatest, bitterest tank battles fought on the western front during WW II, and perhaps ever. Yes, there may have been more tanks at Caen, but the armored engagements there did not nearly approach the intensity and magnitude of "The Arracourt Tank Battles."

Prior to the events in Lorraine, the 4th Armored Division had proved that it could range far and wide, envelope, exploit, and pursue. However, there may have been those who wondered how it would react in a completely different situation, if it were heavily attacked and had to defend. Any such doubts were quickly dispelled. The Arracourt tank battles showed that in a different circumstance the tankers were still tough and stubborn, and proved conclusively that in hard, difficult, defensive fighting they were every bit as good as they had been on offensive operations.

The "Tale of the Tape" is most graphic. During that defensive struggle over a period of nearly three weeks, the 4th Armored Division seized 2,727 P.W.s, and killed 4,639 of the enemy. Material losses were every bit as significant: 63 self-propelled guns, 743 miscellaneous vehicles, and 63 artillery pieces destroyed. But the most amazing, telling statistic is that after the battle ceased, 281 German tanks littered the fields of Lorraine.

That is what Patton, with his 4th Armored Division, did with his "leavings."

A final reminder: *What has been described in this chapter never would have happened if Patton had been permitted to continue his move to the east on September 2. There would have been no Fifth Panzer Army to stand in his way. Well before September 19, the date of the first enemy tank attack, Patton would have been sitting on the Rhine.*

CHAPTER 19

WHAT IF...?

Once the breakout in Normandy was effected, events moved much more swiftly than the most optimistic had ever anticipated. By the fourth day, the 4th Armored Division had seized Avranches, at the base of the Cotentin Peninsula. It was the all-important hinge that opened up Brittany to the south and the rest of France to the east. Patton in strength was soon deep in Brittany.

The Germans gathered themselves quickly. Only two days after Avranches was seized, they were already driving to the west and had dead aim at that city. If they were successful in recapturing that narrow neck, they would drive a wedge between the 1st and 3rd Armies, and split those forces. A battle of significant proportions between German and Allied forces ensued in the vicinity of Mortain. The determined push of the Germans came close to reaching Avranches, but it was blunted when they were just a few kilometers away. They were hit hard by American Infantry, and pounded heavily by artillery and air. The Germans were badly hurt, and pulled back.

Hitler, however, insisted that they continue to go for Avranches, although the generals on the ground recognized that it was pointless and futile. After discussions with Hitler that resulted in delays, the Germans began to withdraw to the east. The time wasted by the Germans proved extremely costly, for it enabled the Allies to fashion a narrow noose between Falaise and Argentan. The Germans realized that they were trapped, and in desperation they continued to retreat to the east, and in the process suffered horrendous losses. Had the noose been squeezed tight, the Germans would have suffered a mortal blow. As the survivors scrambled toward the Seine, they were anything but an organized force. Much farther to the south Patton had routed the forces that had tried to stand in his way, and as they, too, fled, he pursued them aggressively and relentlessly. After he crossed the lower Seine north of Paris, Montgomery caught fire, and by September 4 he was sitting at Antwerp. Earlier, on the 1st., Patton had established substantial forces on the east side of the Meuse River.

As the planners and senior Commanders now looked east, it must have been a glorious sight. The Allies had advanced much farther and far more rapidly than the planners in their most optimistic dreams had ever envisioned. Out there along the whole front all they saw was a beaten, disorganized, fleeing enemy. Excitement began to take root. All we had to do was to keep chasing them. Why, with the way things were progressing it had all the earmarks of a short war, surely over before the end of the year.

The euphoria, however, became tempered. An uneasiness had gradually been creeping up on the senior personnel, and a shadow had crossed that bright picture. It was not all wine and roses after all, and they now realized that there was a big fly in the ointment. The faster the Allies had advanced, the greater the burden they had placed on those who supplied them. The logistics timetable had also been radically altered, but this time adversely. Logistics now became a serious, glaring, and unsettling problem. It had become progressively more and more difficult, with limited port and beach facilities, to push forward the needed supplies. With Antwerp not operational the situation would become even worse.

To their great dismay, the leaders at higher Headquarters now realized that in order to force an early end to the war, they could not divide up the available resources evenly among all the Allied units occupying a very broad front, and expect an aggressive and rapid advance. What was required was a single, strong force with a preponderance of logistical support to drive a wedge deep into Germany. There were only two candidates for that job – General Bernard Law Montgomery and General George S. Patton, Jr. In this text there has been developed for both candidates an extremely comprehensive, detailed, revealing, "resume" for the job. The "Head Hunter" – Eisenhower – was keenly aware of the records and accomplishments of both candidates, and would certainly be expected to compare them objectively. Had he done that based on the revelations in this text, one would have expected that for him the blinking signs, ringing bells, and whistles would have indicated Patton, Patton. That, as we know, did not happen. The "Head Hunter" examined his own factors, and as we also know his choice for the job was Montgomery. The British Field Marshall then failed in his mission, and did not do the job for which he was selected; the war did not end in 1944, but continued until May of 1945.

Although this is being written 60 years after that decision was made, the assertions made here are anything but 20/20 hindsight. As has already been mentioned more than once, Patton at the time stated categorically that the decision was the wrong one, and bemoaned it until the day he died. I agreed wholeheartedly and independently with Patton. I was aware of and weighed the same factors as Patton, but at a far different vantage point, the grunt level. I was even more optimistic than he. As we neared the Meuse River, I was convinced that the war would be over by Thanksgiving. I was so convinced that, as I have already mentioned, I "put my money where my mouth was."

Accordingly, I made bets to that effect, some heavy, with my fellow officers and men. My belief and contentions were based on the premise that we would simply continue rolling, and doing the things we had already had been doing so successfully. After our ten day "rest" along the Meuse, there was no doubt, then, that I had lost my bet. When I paid off on Thanksgiving Day, we were heavily engaged, still in Lorraine – in the bitter cold, sleet, and deep and sticky muck, and where frequently ours was a front one tank wide.

As I paid my bets, I could not help but wonder. Because of the euphoria that we were experiencing in late August were my bets hasty, impetuous and reckless? Or could I have actually won my bet if Patton had been given the gas and supplies? Of course, I will never know, but I have always speculated, and been haunted by the possibilities.

So, WHAT IF ?

What follows will be one answer to that question. Because of several pertinent factors that will be discussed, this reply will have a high degree of authenticity. I believe that I am unusually qualified to be making these observations. All across France until Eisenhower made his decision, I, with my tanks, had been at the point of Patton's spearhead. I was there! I had a key role in making many of the good things happen. I was able to see, sense, hear the sounds, and have the "feel" of battle. By this time many of us strongly believed that Patton had a sixth sense, a special battle sense. To a lesser degree we had acquired some of that as well. I was not up in the sky boxes, the press boxes where the critics were – I was down on the playing field where the action was – or, as Teddy Roosevelt would put it, "in the arena." So, here goes my answer to that question.

Moving out on the second of September would have been no different than it had been when we moved out on the 1st. It was just a matter of continuing to turn the crank. The days would still be long, the nights short; the fields would still be dry and the creeks, streams, and rivers low; the enemy would still be disorganized and fleeing.

We would not have had to face what Monty did when he moved out in his operation, "Market Garden." There were not five major water obstacles with substantial bridges for us to cross. We would not have been moving on a single, vulnerable, restricted road which linked up the five water obstacles. We would not have been confined to the road because of uninviting terrain on either side, which would have hampered or prevented bold moves by tanks off the road. We would not have had lurking and ready to pounce upon us, two largely ignored but extremely capable, battle-ready Panzer Divisions, together with supporting forces.

No, what would have been up ahead for us was pretty much what we had left behind, and in some cases better. There would be virtually no water cross-compartments. The Nahe River would cross our path as we closed in on the Rhine: later in the war, we had no difficulty crossing it, so we can assume that it would not have been a problem. The towns, villages were small and spread out – not concentrated. There would have been no large cities in our path – those would be well off to our right, and we would be by-passing them. The road net was excellent and favored us, with the more prominent roads pointing in the direction that we were heading. Our flanks were relatively unprotected, but they had been all across France, so that was nothing new. We would still have air cover which would provide warning, and with the 7th Army closing in from the south our right flank would have been in better shape than when we drove through France.

The Rhine River would have easily been within our grasp. From the Moselle River to Saarbrucken, as the crow flies, was approximately 60 miles. From that city to Mainz on the Rhine was only another 80 miles, for a total of 140 miles. During our last days before reaching the Meuse, we had daily advances of 37, 51, 30, 17 and 27 miles by taking full advantage of the days with their long spells of daylight. What is truly amazing is that in our zeal to reach the Meuse, we had advanced 328 miles in 12 days. If we had moved on the 2nd, what would have prevented us from continuing at that pace? The 140 miles to the Rhine was less than half of those 328 miles.

Bradley, some days back, had finally been won over by Patton, and now was a believer. He was convinced that Patton was "the man." He had argued and pleaded with Eisenhower, before the decision was made, to "hand the ball" to Patton: point him toward the Saar and Rhine, and let him run. Bradley already had plans in mind if Ike concurred, and gave the mission and logistical priority to Patton.

The moment Patton received the green light Bradley would have tilted the whole American "table" in his direction. He would immediately have made available to Patton infantry and armored elements to follow, reinforce, and support him. Most importantly, the bulk of the trucks in the 12th Army Group that were carrying gasoline would also have been steered in Patton's direction. Trucks in units not geared for action would have been stripped, and would have become carriers of fuel and ammunition for Patton. The tonnage of gasoline hauled forward from the supply points would have increased quickly and dramatically.

For us at the point of the action, if the 4th Armored Division had moved out aggressively on the 2nd, it would have been "business as usual," no different from the day before. We had our job to do, and would have been unaware of all that was taking place behind us. However, we were acutely aware that it would not be long before we were closing in on the German border, and after that it was the "home stretch" to the Rhine. As he had before, Patton would have led with his XIIth Corps, spearheaded by the 4th Armored Division. The division would have continued to operate with two combat commands on separate but parallel axes, thus presenting the enemy with a wide front which they would have to defend. The 4th, as it had before, would personify mobility, not only with its tanks but also with its armored infantry mounted in half-tracks and its self-propelled artillery, as well. General Eddy would have concentrated the 35th and 80th divisions, and would also have made them mobile. The infantry would have been mounted in trucks, and their division artillery would be hooked up to trucks. He would have positioned these divisions with one behind each combat command, and they would have stayed closed up so as to be ready to "hop to it" at the earliest sign that the advance elements of the combat commands were hitting trouble.

For his eyes and close support, Patton would continue to utilize his tactical air. He could rely on the Air Force to come up with the resources necessary to enable the fighters to support him for the next 140 miles. As they roamed the skies, the skilled pilots would quickly spot trouble, would alert the forward advancing elements, or they, themselves, would eliminate the problem with fire from their very impressive aerial arsenal. The relationship between the troops on the ground and the pilots in the air had for long been absolutely superb, and would continue to be.

For close-in observation Patton's forces would use their "Maytag Messerschmitts," the tiny artillery spotter planes. Fully loaded gasoline and ammunition trucks would have been positioned well forward so as to ensure that the tanks, half-tracks, and self-propelled artillery were "full up" at first light each day.

Naysayers will continue to claim that Patton just could not do it, that he would have been "out on a limb," and would have been cut off and destroyed. Well, he had been "out on a limb" all across France, and who in Germany at that moment was capable of cutting him off, much less destroying him? The Germans were less prepared and less capable of resisting Patton in Germany than they had been in France. With the favorable conditions that would have continued to exist, Patton's forces could have reached the German border in 3-4 days. If it was four days, that would have meant that they had averaged 15 miles a day. They had already proved that they could advance nearly twice as fast. If they had continued to advance 15 miles a day from Saarbrucken, they would have reached the Rhine in about 6 days. Thus, it would not have been bravado or hyperbole when Patton had announced many days before, "I can be on the Rhine in ten days."

As soon as he crossed the border into Germany, and continued streaking toward the Rhine River, he most certainly would have requested the high command to place Airborne units and their aerial carriers on high alert, and ready for instant deployment. These were the same ones that Monty would use in the "Market Garden" operation. However, Patton would not have needed an Allied Airborne Army; one already proven American Airborne Division would do, and Patton would not have expected "the skies overhead dark with aircraft." As he looked ahead, bridges would be one of his very prime concerns. He absolutely had to have them. There was a good chance that he would seize some bridges intact and roll right over them. With his speed and the surprise of his advance, the likelihood was that the Germans were not yet orga-nized enough to have in place teams of demolition experts to blow the bridges. (Many months later, the Germans had known for weeks that the Americans were closing in, yet they badly botched the destruction of the Remagen Bridge). But Patton could not take that chance. It would do him no good to reach the Rhine, and not be able to cross it. If he had to stop, sit back and wait for engineers to bridge that exceptionally wide water obstacle, he would have completely lost his momentum, the shock and surprise would have been gone, and he would have become extremely vulnerable. Most importantly, he would once again deliver to the Germans that most precious combat commodity, "time," which they desperately needed and always used most productively. He had to cross the Rhine to gain the next critical objective, Frankfurt, which sat alongside another major water obstacle, the Main River.

Timing it so that the airborne troops would land just before his arrival, Patton would have radioed, "Now!" The airborne units would have quickly been on their way, and would have taken control of the important bridges over the Rhine and the Main. Oh, yes, these airborne units would have had to travel nearly half again as far as they did to Arnhem, but air-force ingenuity and determination surely would have propelled them to the Rhine. It is important to note that the bridges seized for Patton would be in Germany, not Holland, and Frankfurt was much more important, more critical, and far outshone Arnhem as an objective.

After crossing the Rhine, Patton would have shoved his tanks quickly across the short distance to Frankfurt. In no time there would have been piercing screams of anguish all across the land. The cry, "Patton is across the Rhine, Patton is across the Rhine, Patton is at Frankfurt" would have reverberated through every German city, town, village. It would have been frightening and demoralizing for the German people to comprehend that Allied boots were stomping around that national icon, the Rhine river; that their enemy was now in control of one of their country's most vital and crucial lifelines; that enemy forces had entered their heartland, and seized another important symbol, Frankfurt. The name Patton would have stricken fear into the hearts of all Germans. It would have caused great consternation, and broken the spirit of the German people. His reputation as a fierce warrior was not only well known, but had been embellished. He would have been at the peak of his performance, and his enemies knew it. The general populace, instead of testing his will, would have been ready and even eager to surrender to him. The shock waves and fear would have reached the military as well – every unit at every level would have been affected and infected with the growing hysteria – Regiment, Division, Corps, even Army Headquarters. Well before his string of successes across France had stunned the senior German officers, the high command, he was so feared and so respected by the German military that, without blinking an eye or moving a muscle, he had kept a whole German Army tied to the Pas de Calais.

The German military would have faced a monumental dilemma. Should they pull back the forces facing the elements of the 1st Army and the British 21st Army Group, turn them around, and as they panicked, push them helter-skelter toward Patton at the Rhine? If they did, they knew full well that the Allied forces which they were facing would immediately move forward, and push right behind. The Allies would have greatly relished being handed the tremendous advantage of fighting an adversary who had begun moving away from them with his back exposed. (These Allied forces would have had that capability, for Patton would not have insisted on being given "everything," as Monty had.)

Or, would the Germans have continued holding their line to the west, and tried to find, gather, and assemble a force sizeable enough and strong enough to hit Patton with a formidable counterattack? Here also they were at a disadvantage; it would take them time. In this situation time was not a German but a Patton ally. It would have been only a bit over two weeks since the German forces suffered a semi-massacre at Argentan/Falaise, and they were still "licking their wounds" and trying to regroup.

Under circumstances then existing, neither of those options was practicable or attainable for the Germans.

Patton would have been anything but idle. With the 4th Armored Division tanks across the river, he would have had Eddy push the 35th and 80th Infantry Divisions of XIIth Corps across, to hold the bridges and the areas around them. Then he would have sent off his armor to continue cutting a wide swath through the German countryside. The infantry and armored units, which Bradley had earmarked as reinforcements for Patton, would also be closing up on the Rhine. Among these would be the 6th Armored Division, which had returned from several wasted weeks in Brittany. Very soon a large and extremely potent American force would be controlling an extensive and critically important part of Germany.

The Germans were boxed in, were in a very serious "bind." I have previously reported that during our tactical operations (we were well aware of this right after our breakout in Normandy) once we were around and behind the enemy, they recognized the futility of further fighting, and invariably and often quickly they lost their will to fight. It is human nature to fight for survival. So it would have been with the German people, as they decided what was best for them. As Patton roamed the countryside, he would have found all over the land, in cities, towns and villages, white sheets hanging from windows.

That principle would have applied in a strategic sense, as well. By this time the military high command would surely have recognized, as so many of their soldiers had during the past weeks, that the "jig was up." They, too, were survivalists. They wanted to save themselves. More importantly, they wanted to save their nation. As military men who had been laying down their lives for their country, and now saw the futility of continuing to fight and watch the further destruction of their nation – they surely would have sought the best possible solution to the "fix" that they were in.

It would have been clearly evident to them that the quickest, best, and only solution was to get rid of Hitler. They certainly now knew him for what he was. As far back as the third week in July, some of their cohorts stuck their necks out, put their careers and lives on the line, and made a serious attempt to take Hitler's life, but unfortunately the plot had failed. Gen. Dietrich von Choltitz, who was summoned before Hitler after the July 20th assassination attempt, found him drooling, drugged and a raving lunatic. In the days that followed he, with his military decisions and directives, did nothing to enhance his reputation and regain the confidence of his military leaders. On the contrary, he aggravated, angered, and frustrated them. He, primarily, was the one who, kept a German Army anchored at the Pas de Calais, anticipating and fearing the main assault by Gen. Patton. Because of his obstinacy, the Germans still held their ground even after it was known that the decoy was already in France. Against the advice and protestations of his military Commanders, he insisted that they repeat in Normandy their futile attack to regain Avranches. Field Marshal Gunther von Kluge warned Hitler about the futility of further resistance in the Mortain area. It fell on deaf ears. Hitler sacked Kluge, and recalled him to Germany. Kluge committed suicide, instead. Gen. Josef Sepp Dietrich, one of Hitler's favorites, declared, "There was only one person to blame for this stupid, impossible operation, that madman Hitler." Before the end of August, the German Commanders who had to fight the battles believed the continuation of the war to be pointless, and accepted that the war had been lost. If Hitler, instead, had concurred in the withdrawal of his troops to the east in a timely manner, he would have saved much of his Army that was butchered while trying to flee to the Seine, and could have been available to him then. With Patton on the Rhine, Hitler's war had turned very "sour," and was beginning rapidly to curdle. He would by this time have exchanged bravado and confidence for panic and irrationality. Any credibility and relevance that he might once have possessed would have completely vanished. He was "ripe for the picking." By this time the military leaders would have grabbed him for "safe keeping," and taken control of the nation and its armed forces. Before "throwing in the towel," the senior members of the military would have put their heads together, devised an approach to the Allies for an early end to the war, and would have negotiated the best possible long–range terms for their country.

If this had happened, the ramifications would have been almost earth-shaking. It is sobering yet truly exciting to visualize and realize the extensive, monumental benefits that would have accrued to the world. The war would have been over well before the end of 1944; there would have been no "Market Garden;" the "Battle of the Bulge" would never have happened; many, many thousands of military and civilian lives would have been spared; much suffering would have been alleviated; German cities and towns would have been saved from destruction; the German nation would have rapidly been rebuilt; Russian political influence would have been blocked and ultimately greatly diminished.

Of course, no one will ever know the outcome, if Patton had, indeed, been given priority of gasoline and supplies, and told to "go." What is asserted here is pure speculation. It is just one possible scenario. However, it is written by one who was there – who saw it all, experienced it all, and who believes that it is a *believable* scenario.

Nevertheless, this scenario, surely, will be criticized as pure fantasy and as "pie in the sky" by the critics and naysayers, from their lofty perches. They will scoff gleefully at the picture that I have painted. I will be declared guilty, as well, of exaggerating the Patton *persona* into an unbelievable, super-duper hero, a bigger-than-life warrior.

But this I know and this is *irrefutable*, under no circumstance would Patton have failed as totally, completely, and miserably as Monty did with his "Market Garden" operation.

This I also know and claim with a great degree of certainty – based on his long record of accomplishment, achievement, success, Patton, as he had done so many times before, in this situation, at the very least, *would have performed something dramatic, dynamic, electrifying.*

As a reminder, although Patton did not get the gas, for the rest of the war he continued to perform superlatively, brilliantly. It was he who turned his Army 90 degrees from East to North, and relieved the surrounded 101st Airborne Division at Bastogne. It was he who electrified America by leaping 60 miles in two days across the difficult Schnee Eifel to reach the Rhine – the first offensive victory after weeks of winter stagnation. It was he who swept across Germany and into Czechoslovakia. *(I know what he did, for I was there and fully engaged in all of those actions.)*

Let us face it squarely and concede that Patton *"could have pulled it off."*

If he had, many of the pages in the history books covering WW II in Europe and its aftermath would read quite differently today.

WHAT IF?

APPENDIX

OTHER "MISTAKES"
BY
GENERAL DWIGHT D. EISENHOWER
AND
HIS SHAEF STAFF

1. Gen. Bradley's and Gen. Patton's roles should have been reversed. Patton was the better choice to be the U. S. Ground Force Commander for the Normandy invasion, and subsequently the American 12th Army Group Commander.

2. Failure to recognize, anticipate, and plan for the deadly terrain through which the Americans would have to fight once the bridgehead was secured and the land battle began in earnest. Fighting in the Bocage came as a complete shock.

3. Gen. Montgomery should have been relieved from *Field* Command after the GOODWOOD debacle.

4. A Corps with two Armored Divisions never should have been sent west to the Atlantic ports, when they were perfectly positioned in Brittany to attack to the east.

5. SHAEF Headquarters throughout the campaign in France (and later) was too far removed from the fighting front to be effective tactically or administratively.

6. Failure to close completely the Argentan/Falaise gap.

7. Failure to execute a deeper double envelopment to the Seine River that would have trapped the routed Germans.

8. Gen. Eisenhower waited too long, until September 1, to take Allied Ground Command.

9. Concurring in and approving Montgomery's "Market Garden" plan.

10. In conjunction with 9. – permitting Montgomery to advance

to the east, neglect clearing the Scheldt Estuary, and to leave the Port of Antwerp unusable.

11. Intelligence breakdown, which enabled the Germans to have complete surprise for their Ardennes offensive.

12. Splitting the forces during the Battle of the Bulge, which gave Montgomery command of the northern sector, including the American 1st Army.

Note:

Shortly after the war ended in Europe, as soon as May 10th, Gen. Eisenhower summoned his four Army Commanders and their Air Officers to a discussion meeting. He seemed intent on promoting solidarity, and strongly intimated that they should not criticize publicly the way the campaign in Europe bad been fought.

The meeting confirmed Gen. Patton's worst fears. He was now dead-certain that Ike considered himself vulnerable, and was determined to cover up the strategic blunders which Patton was convinced he had committed during the war.

Close friends of Patton like Dr. Charles Odom and Gen. Geoffrey Keyes were convinced that if Patton had lived and returned to the States, he would surely have quickly resigned from the Army. Once that occurred, he would have, been free to open up.

By written and spoken word. he, undoubtedly would have been critical of and criticized Eisenhower's conduct of the war, and would have pointed out the significant lapses of judgment which he believed Ike had made with his inept direction of the campaign in Europe.

I am completely convinced that among the significant aspects and events that the two generals would have focused on would have been the thrust of this book, as well as the "Mistakes" which are listed above. Eisenhower, on the one hand, would have tried to suppress them, while Patton, on the other, would have endeavored to expose them

BIBLIOGRAPHY

The authors and their publications below listed were of invaluable assistance in providing me with background information to supplement my personal knowledge of events discussed in this book. The assist gained from these sources was most significant and I am profoundly grateful for it.

"Bernard Law Montgomery," David Craig, ARMOR, May/June 1992.

"Casualty of War," Col. Cole C. Kingseed, ARMY, May 2000.

General George S. Patton and Eisenhower, Charles B. Odom, M.D., New Orleans, LA., 1985

"In Defense of Montgomery," Alistair Horne, MHQ, Autumn 1995.

"Monty And Ike At Gettysburg," Glenn La Fantasie MH9, Autumn 1995.

"Battle of the Bulge," Stephen E. Ambrose, "America's Great Battles, 1775-2002," Military History Magazine and MHQ.

World War II, Ivor Matanie, Zigzag Publishing, 1998, an imprint of Quadrillion Publishing Ltd., Godalming, Surrey, England.

Eisenhower's Lieutenants, Volumes I and II, Russell F. Weigley, Indiana University Press, 1981.

A Soldier's Story, Omar M. Bradley, Henry Holt and Company, 1951.

Patton: a Genius for War, Carlo d'Este, Harper Collins, 1995.

Eisenhower, A Soldier's Life, Carlo d'Este, Harper Collins, 2002.

General Patton, A Soldier's Life, Stanley P. Hirshson, Harper Collins, 2002.

War As I Knew It, George S. Patton, Jr., Houghton Mifflin, 1947.

ABOUT THE AUTHOR

Brigadier General Albin F. Irzyk USA (Ret.) fought WW II in Europe as a 27/28-year-old Tank Battalion Commander. Was twice wounded. Commanded the 14th Armored Cavalry Regiment along the "Iron Curtain" during the Berlin Crisis of 1961.

Served two years in Vietnam, one of which was as Assistant Division Commander of the 4th Infantry Division. Among his decorations for valor, he holds the Distinguished Service Cross for extraordinary heroism.

He and his wife, Evelyn, reside in West Palm Beach.

Printed in the United States
43437LVS00004B/232-249